BRAIN&
BEHAVIOR

BRAIN& BEHAVIOR

RESEARCH
IN CLINICAL
NEUROPSYCHOLOGY

edited by

Arthur L. Benton

ALDINETRANSACTION
A Division of Transaction Publishers
New Brunswick (U.S.A.) and London (U.K.)

Library of Congress Catalog Number: 2009018245
ISBN: 978-0-202-36318-9
Printed in the United States of America

Library of Congress Cataloging-in-Publication Data

Brain and behavior : research in clinical neuropsychology / Arthur L.
   Benton, editor.
      p. ; cm.
   Originally published as: Contributions to clinical neuropsychology.
      Chicago : Aldine, c1969.
   Includes bibliographical references and index.
   ISBN 978-0-202-36318-9 (alk. paper)
      1. Neuropsychiatry. 2. Clinical neuropsychology. I. Benton, Arthur
   Lester, 1909- II. Contributions to clinical neuropsychology.
      [DNLM: 1. Neuropsychology--methods. WL 103.5 B8134 2009]
   RC458.B64 2009
   616.8--dc22

                                                      2009018245

Contents

Preface

Clinical neuropsychology is a field that has developed with remarkable rapidity during the past two decades. Drawing on clinical study, animal experimentation, and developmental observation to accomplish its essential purpose of elucidating the nature of the relationships between brain function and human behavior, it covers an extraordinarily wide range of topics. The distinctive behavioral syndromes associated with focal cerebral lesions, the developmental and pathological aspects of the "body image," the concept of hemispheric cerebral dominance, the definitional problems posed by the aphasic, apractic, and agnosic disorders, and the neurological background of dyslexia and developmental language retardation in children are but a few of the diverse topics in the field and indicate its breadth.

The historical background and present status of the discipline are described by Poeck in his introductory chapter. His survey provides a framework for the subsequent chapters in which each author covers a particular problem area in which he has done important investigative work. Ettlinger and Blakemore analyze the present status of our understanding of interhemispheric relations as disclosed by studies of the behavioral effects of commissural section in animals and man. Weinstein discusses the puzzling phenomenon of the phantom and its implications for the concept of the body image. Geschwind, whose work has been so influential in reviving interest in the anatomical approach to the field of aphasia, poses the problems that need to be solved if a sound understanding of the anatomical background of the aphasic disorders is to be achieved. Benton outlines a number of questions concerning "constructional apraxia" that remain unanswered by investigative work to date. Semmes addresses herself to the formidable question of whether there are discrete basic types of somatosensory function and offers a new and fruitful formulation. Vignolo presents a truly masterful analysis of the concept of auditory agnosia and describes his own recent empirical research in this area.

Because they have been written by active investigators with an intense interest in their respective topics, these chapters possess a quality of immediacy and give a sense of work in progress, of "unfinished business." In addition to providing scholarly reviews of past work and assessments of present knowledge, they pose keen challenges to the researcher whose task it is to advance our understanding of the complicated relations between brain and behavior in man that are reflected by the topics discussed. Thus the reader with investigative interests will find them tremendously stimulating as well as informative.

The series of lectures that formed the nucleus of the contributions in this volume was supported by Training Grant MH–05062 from the National Institute of Mental Health to the Department of Psychology, University of Iowa. The lectures were given in the Spring of 1967 and the final versions of most of the manuscripts were submitted at the end of that year.

A.L.B.

Contributions to
Clinical Neuropsychology

1

Modern Trends in Neuropsychology

Klaus Poeck

Neuropsychology is a relatively young science. Originally, its objective was limited to the study of the psychological disturbances observed after circumscribed or diffuse brain lesions in man. Increasingly, however, the field covers also the examination of comparable behavioral disorders in animals, particularly in primates. This development corresponds to the general trend towards interdisciplinary, problem oriented research.

The most prominent among the neuropsychological syndromes are:

Aphasia, i.e., a particular receptive and expressive impairment in dealing with verbal symbols.

Disturbance of spatial orientation and *constructional dyspraxia*, i.e., difficulty in putting objects or parts of objects in proper spatial relationship.

Apraxia, i.e., impairment in performing gestures or in handling objects properly.

The group of *agnosias*, i.e., disturbances of recognition in one or other sensory modality that are not explained by perceptual deficit. Conventionally, visual agnosia, auditory agnosia, and tactile agnosia are distinguished.

These behavioral disturbances were described in detail by Continental authors mostly between 1870 and 1930. For a certain period of time, the clinical description of these symptoms enjoyed general acceptance and their interpretation remained basically undisputed. After World War II, however, the classical symptoms were studied anew, and it was recognized that many of the old observations were open to serious methodical objections.

The classical papers were based on the examination of single cases or of small groups of patients, which were selected because they presented with a striking symptom. Every examiner had his own way of testing, and it was held legitimate to adapt the method of examination to the particular conditions of the individual case.

The tests applied were never standardized. No norms existed for the performances of normal and brain damaged control subjects. The influence of unspecific variables—for instance, of age and education—was not taken into consideration. Performances were evaluated exclusively according to the personal experience and knowledge of the examiner and there was no quantification of data but instead a very crude classification, as pass or fail.

The aim of research had been the description of so-called pure cases, presenting an isolated psychological or sensory defect, not complicated by other behavioral disturbances. As a rule, however, the pure symptoms were nothing else than an artifact brought about by the method of examination; testing was limited to the performance the author was looking for, and further possibilities, particularly the dependance of a given symptom upon other specific and unspecific variables, were not even discussed.

The interpretation of the findings was centered on the recognition of *Grundstörungen*, that is, of basic disturbances which of necessity cause certain symptoms. The assumption of these *Grundstörungen* was likewise highly subjective.

It was inevitable that many of the results of this type of research were seriously biased according to the expectation and the subjective opinion of the author. In essence, this methodological approach led to a wealth of scattered data that were not really comparable with each other and that did not establish convincing concepts.

With regard to the anatomical basis of psychological deficit, two extremely opposed positions were held. Some authors, e.g., (1) Kleist (1934) and the Vienna school, maintained that it was possible to localize precisely the small lesion producing almost any given symptom. They did so even in the presence of diffuse overall brain disease or large space-occupying lesions with damage to a great area of brain tissue. Others, for the most part members of (2) the Gestalt school, defended a holistic view and some of them went so far as to deny any circumscribed localization of centers at all. Classical examples of these contrasting positions are statements such as the following: "We speak with the left hemisphere" (Broca, 1865) *vs.* "We do not speak with the left hemisphere, we speak with the whole brain" (Hoff, 1964).

It is apparent from the foregoing critical considerations "that the complexity of the psychological effects of brain lesions has been grossly underestimated by most clinically oriented investigators. A majority of investigations has been inadequate with regard to definition of the independent variables, the range and diversity of dependent variables and the theoretical framework in which psychological deficits resulting from brain lesions are presumed to be subject to identification" (Reitan, 1966, p. 128).

New progress in this field of research began when experimental psychologists, mostly in the Anglo-American countries, introduced their precise methods of experimental work and evaluation of data to the study of behavioral disorders in brain-damaged patients. The nature of these symptoms was no longer explained on the basis of single or selected cases. Although single cases can call attention to new phenomena, the significance of these phenomena can be demonstrated only by the examination of great series of unselected brain-damaged patients.

The classical "handmade" methods of testing were abandoned because their validity was not evaluated. Instead, the patients were examined by standardized and valid methods. At the present time, clinicoanatomical inferences are drawn with extreme caution.

This approach is not as new as it seems to be. In the second half of the last century, Hughlings Jackson had already demanded that the researcher "try to classify the facts in order to show their true relations to one another and consider them on the psychical side as defects of mind and on the physical side as defects of the nervous system." Jackson insisted on the necessity of studying and classifying the phenomena before any attempt was made to correlate them with morphological changes. What he was aiming at was the patient's *performance* and not so much some theoretical concept: "Put down what the patient does get at and avoid all such terms as amnesia" (cf. Head, 1926).

In this introductory chapter, I intend to indicate several lines of research that appear representative of present day neuro-psychological work. Particular emphasis is laid on those fields discussed in detail in this volume.

Disconnection Syndromes: A New Anatomical Aspect

A very important step toward a precise anatomical basis for certain neuropsychological symptoms is the concept of disconnection syndromes, developed by Geschwind (1965a). This concept is based on "split-brain" experiments in cats and monkeys as well as an investigation of patients with cerebral lesions. The background of these studies is illustrated by the following anatomical data.

In mammals, the cerebral cortex of each hemisphere sends out efferent—i.e., centrifugal—projection fibers to structures in the brain stem and spinal cord that subserve the coordination and execution of movements. Likewise, the cerebral cortex is reached by afferent—i.e., centripetal—projections, originating in the various somatosensory receptors. The great majority of these efferent projections cross the midline at the level of the brain stem. Consequently, each hemisphere sends out motor commands almost exclusively to the contralateral limbs and receives somatosensory informations mainly from the contralateral half of the body.

The visual pathways coming from both eyes cross at the base of the brain in the optic chiasma. From here, they travel upward and reach the primary visual projection area in the occipital lobe. The arrangement of fibers in the chiasma is not such as to connect the right eye with the visual cortex of the left hemisphere and vice versa. Rather, each of the hemispheres receives signals from the contralateral visual half-field of both eyes.

The motor and sensory signals carried along these crossed pathways, however, do not remain restricted to the contralateral hemisphere. It has been domonstrated, in particular by the method of conditioned reflexes, that the signals are also transmitted to the other hemisphere. For example, if an animal has learned to perform a conditioned task with his right forelimb (in other words, with the motor area of his left hemisphere), subsequent testing discloses some degree of learning also in the motor area of the right hemisphere. The pathways subserving this interhemispheric transfer are called the *commissures*. The neocortical commissures connect corresponding points on the cortical surface of both cerebral hemispheres. The most important of these is the corpus callosum.

In the split-brain experiments referred to above, all neocortical commissures as well as the optic chiasma were sectioned so that the transfer of signals from one hemisphere to the other was interrupted. Somatosensory afferences were practically limited to the contralateral hemisphere, and the visual input of the right or left eye, respectively, was projected only to the ipsilateral hemisphere. Consequently, each of the hemispheres "knew" everything it had learned before the operation by the direct crossed route as well as by the indirect transcallosal route via the other half of the brain. However, the ipsilateral hemisphere no longer participated in learning processes when the contralateral hemisphere was trained after the operation (cf. Ettlinger, 1965).

The application of these experimental results to human neuropsychology was studied first by Gazzaniga, Bogen, and Sperry (1962, 1963, 1965) and Gazzaniga and Sperry (1967) in four patients who underwent split-brain surgery for the treatment of intractable epilepsy. In man, the situation for examining the functions of the two independent hemispheres is particularly favorable because of a distinct functional asymmetry between the two halves of the brain. The best known (but not the only) example of this asymmetry is the lateralization of a circumscribed area for the organization of language performances.

The importance of interhemispheric transfer across the neocortical commissures was demonstrated in a series of tasks requiring the subjects to match sensory information with the appropriate verbal concept. The patients were able to identify objects verbally only when the stimulus was given to the right hand or to the left eye. In both instances, the signals were projected to the left hemisphere, where the language area is situated. When the signals were projected to the right hemisphere, the patients were not able to name an object they had palpated or seen or to select its name by way of multiple choice. Some patients were not even able to say whether they had perceived a stimulus.

In contrast to this impairment in the sensory-verbal association, the subjects could carry out rather complex tasks with their left hand, that is, with their right hemisphere, provided these tasks did not call for language performances.

These findings and many further consistent observations not reviewed here in detail were explained convincingly on an anatomical basis. It was obvious that a sensory stimulus arriving in the sensory area of the right hemisphere could reach the ipsilateral motor area over association pathways within the same half of the brain and thus elicit appropriate motor behavior. It was equally obvious that because of the split-brain operation the same stimulus could no longer travel across the neocortical commissures and reach the language area of the left hemisphere.

The split-brain experiments gave a new impetus to the study of subcortical connections and their functional significance. It was recognized that many neuropsychological symptoms do not indicate dysfunction or loss of function in a circumscribed, specialized area of cerebral cortex but do indicate the interruption of association fibers connecting two cortical areas of different functions within the same hemisphere and the interruption of commissural pathways connecting corresponding areas of the two hemispheres.

It is true that a similar hypothesis had been advanced earlier by some authors under the heading of the so-called *Leitungsstörungen*. The classical example is Liepmann's (1900, 1908a) theory that the neural basis of apraxia consists in the interruption of subcortical fibers linking the language area with the motor area. Another case is that particular impairment in the repetition of spoken language termed "conduction aphasia." By this is meant that the disturbance is due to the interruption of fibers associating the auditory receiving area with the language area (Isserlin, 1936).

Apart from these two instances, however, the concept of *Leitungsstörungen* had not gained broad acceptance. This was partly due to the impact of the holistic view of Gestalt psychology and partly to the difficulty in assessing reliable anatomical data in human disease processes that all too often bring about widespread damage to the brain.

It meant a renaissance of anatomical reasoning in neuro-psychology when Geschwind, after an extensive review of the literature and the description of pertinent personal cases, postulated a disconnection mechanism to be the basis of various types of aphasia, of the apraxias, and of the agnosias (Geschwind, 1965a). His ideas are most convincing where he assumes disconnection between sensory or motor areas and the language area. As a consequence of these lesions, afferent signals cannot be associated with verbal concepts and verbal concepts cannot be transformed into motor performances.

This view appears very promising for the understanding of the agnosias and apraxias. In the classical papers, testing for the presence of agnosia required the patient to match the perceived object with the proper name. If, in the absence of severe primary sensory deficit and of gross aphasia, the subject did not succeed, he was considered agnostic. Remarkably enough, the patients with visual agnosia described by Stauffenberg (1914) asked for permission to palpate the object, instead of looking at it, in order to be able to give the correct name. It is very likely that many cases of visual agnosia or tactile agnosia did in fact present with a modality-specific aphasia, that is, a disturbance in sensory-verbal association limited, by anatomical reasons, to a given sensory modality.

Testing for apraxia included observation of spontaneous motor behavior, execution of verbal commands, and imitation of movements. On the basis of the split-brain experiences and related observations in human pathology, it could well be that deficient performance in one or some of these situations does not correspond to a major or minor degree of apraxia but rather to a different locus of lesion and that at least certain types of apraxia must be considered as language dependent. Geschwind's views on apraxia have recently found an interesting confirmation in the case report of Smith (1966). This right-handed man had been subjected to a left hemispherectomy. On postoperative examination, he exhibited no sympathetic dyspraxia of the left hand when he was to carry out purposeful movements on oral command.

Sympathetic dyspraxia is frequently observed after a left-sided cerebral lesion involving the anterior part of the speech area. It is explained by the interruption of a pathway connecting the motor region of the right hemisphere with the left frontal region, where Broca's area is located. The fact that this patient was able to carry out verbal instructions at all proves that he was understanding them with his right hemisphere. In order to perform purposeful movements on oral command, he had to establish verbal-motor associations within one hemisphere, i.e., the remaining right half of the brain. Since the pathway needed for this association was intact, it is fully explained on an anatomical basis why this patient had no "sympathetic dyspraxia."

A New Formulation of Old Concepts

The main stream of recent neuropsychological research has been the re-examination of the classical syndromes. The necessity to test the old data once more was the logical consequence of the growing methodological dissatisfaction mentioned above. The aim of this work was to penetrate more deeply into the description and analysis of the aphasias, of constructional dyspraxia, and of finger agnosia, to name but a few.

Moreover, evidence is accumulating that would suggest that certain of these symptoms are not unitary in nature, so that their existence must be questioned and their dependence on other basic disturbances should be evaluated experimentally.

Research in the field of *aphasia* had long been centered on three problems: (1) the relationship between handedness and hemispheric dominance for language; (2) the description of various aphasic syndromes; and (3) the precise localization of lesions within one hemisphere producing these types of language disorder.

Only recently has a very important aspect been studied, the linguistic structure of aphasic language.

In this brief review of recent progress in this field, we exclude the problem of cerebral dominance for language and its relation to handedness since it is dealt with in another context below.

The *description of aphasic syndromes* depends, of course, upon the classification of various types of language disturbances that are observed clinically. Unfortunately, until now no classification has been accepted by the majority of researchers and every school has developed its own particular diagnostic scheme, which makes a comparison of the findings of different groups somewhat difficult. The spectrum extends from the Pavlovian concept, based on the assumption of specialized cortical organizations termed "analyzers" and "signalling systems," to the holistic view that there is only one "true aphasia" accompanied to a varying degree by additional symptoms that do not intrinsically belong to aphasia proper. For a discussion of relevant theories, old and current, see Brain (1965) and Tissot (1966).

In clinical practice, the behavioral distinction between motor, or expressive, and sensory, or receptive, aphasia, suggested by Weisenburg and McBride (1935) and others before them has proven useful, especially with the mental reservation that these are not "pure" and clearly distinguished forms but rather two variants of one basic disorder having certain characteristic properties of their own and other features in common.

Recently, however, even this gross distinction has been sharply criticized (Bay, 1967), and it has been suggested that for the time being any classification be abandoned and replaced by the detailed description of deficits present in a given patient. This standpoint reflects the above mentioned uncertainty with regard to an appropriate or "natural" order of subtypes of aphasia. On the other hand, agnosticism of this type can apply only to problems of research in the field of aphasia. Clinical practice requires some pragmatic subdivision of aphasic syndromes.

Comprehensive description of aphasic speech demands broad

testing of the patient's performances, and real progress could be expected only if there existed a battery of tests agreed upon by most researchers in the field. The performance of a patient on this battery, covering most aspects of language behavior and related functions, could then be charted on a profile sheet. The similarity of performance curves in certain groups of patients would suggest the "natural" occurrence of distinctive types of language disorder, provided the selection of tests had not introduced too much bias on the part of the examiner. At the same time, these curves would allow the recognition of certain characteristics observed in all aphasic patients if their performances are compared with those of nonaphasic brain damaged patients.

Pioneer work in this field has been done by Benton and Spreen (cf. Benton, 1967b) and it is anticipated that an international agreement on appropriate methods of examination will eventually be reached that will bring about a generally accepted classification of aphasic disorders.

It is evident that the precise demarcation of aphasic as opposed to nonaphasic language disturbances in brain-damaged patients is a serious problem that still awaits clarification, if it can be solved at all. Recently, Critchley (1962) pointed to the "conception of a spectrum of speech defect depending upon the intrinsic difficulty of the test situation, and ranging from the 'normal' subject at one extreme through the linguistic pattern of nondominant hemisphere defect, up to—at the other limit—a fully fledged aphasia from disease of the dominant half of the brain" (p. 213). A very interesting study on the linguistic structure of language disturbances in right brain damaged patients has been published by Marcie, Hécaen, DuBois, and Angelergues (1965).

The problems of *localization* have recently made some progress. The first observation in the second half of the last century were made mostly on patients with vascular lesions of the brain. In many cases there was in addition widespread cerebral disease so that a precise localization was not possible, although authors used to draw very liberal conclusions in this respect. Moreover, vascular

lesions depend upon the anatomical distribution of blood vessels
and on the larger or smaller area of the brain tissue suffering from a reduced or blocked oxygen supply after the stenosis or
occlusion of a cerebral or extracerebral artery.

Therefore, the data collected in patients with gunshot wounds
are particularly relevant (cf. Russell & Espir, 1961). As a rule, the
localization of the brain lesion is made in these subjects by plotting
the bony defect and intracerebral metallic fragments on a reference
chart indicating the standard topographical relations between
prominent structures of the skull and the brain underneath. This
method allows a fairly precise localization, although it obviously
is not reliable for the assessment of the distant effects of brain
wounds.

While the routine neurological examination and the usual
ancillary methods (i.e., EEG, air encephalography, and carotid
angiography) are too crude to allow a precise localization of a
cerebral lesion, the method of radioactive scanning appears to be
suited to fill a considerable gap in neurological diagnosis. This
technique has recently been applied by Benson (1967), who
classified the clinical features of his patients on the basis of their
verbal output, one group being "speechless or nearly so" (Jackson), i.e., nonfluent, and the other group verbose or fluent in their
language production. Benson was able to establish a correlation
between fluent aphasia and lesions having a posterior localization,
while nonfluent aphasia was correlated with anterior lesions, the
reference being the Rolandic fissure. This new approach to the
study of cerebral localization appears to be promising, since it
circumvents the necessity for post-mortem study to delineate the
locus and extent of the cerebral lesion.

The most significant progress in the research on aphasia has
been made by applying linguistic methods to the study of aphasic
speech, particularly spontaneous and conversational speech.
Linguistic analysis has allowed us to recognize certain rules in the
seemingly disordered way in which the patients deal with verbal
symbols. Furthermore, it has given much more insight into the

grammar of aphasic language than clinical description permits. It appears that, on the basis of linguistic analysis, distinct syndromes can be described that eventually might be correlated with anatomical findings. It is likely that this approach will also be helpful in the formidable task mentioned above, namely to define more sharply aphasic as opposed to nonaphasic types of language disturbance.

Another group of neurological symptoms that has been studied extensively in recent years are the so-called *disturbances of the body schema*. This concept was developed by Head (1920) to provide a physiological basis for the understanding of both motor control and awareness of one's own body. In Head's terms, the body schema was defined operationally, as a function of the central nervous system and in particular of the cerebral cortex.

Subsequent use (and misuse) has changed this concept to the extent that its actual significance has been seriously questioned (Poeck, 1965). This is not the place to discuss in detail the many theoretical problems inherent in the doctrine of the body schema nor can we review all the symptoms that have been considered as disturbances of this hypothesized somatognostic function. However, we will consider certain symptoms in this category in order to exemplify the contribution of careful neuropsychological analysis to the elucidation of behavioral disturbances in brain-damaged patients.

The first symptom to be discussed is *autotopagnosia*, described by Pick in 1908. The patients are unable to indicate on verbal command, or to denominate on indication by the examiner, parts of their own body or, frequently, parts of the body of another person or of a design or model of a man.

Autotopagnosia is still considered a symptom in its own right, although it is not observed without manifold other behavioral disturbances. These usually include aphasia and/or overall mental deterioration. Analyzing the reports described in the literature, it is striking to note that until now no attempt has been made to evaluate the obvious significance of aphasia and general mental impairment for the patient's behavior in a test situation calling on verbal comprehension, naming, attention, short-term memory, and related factors.

In my opinion, it appears likely that the symptom of auto-topagnosia in the great majority of the cases is in fact nothing else than one of the many psychological disturbances that are language dependent, provided it is not simply due to mental impairment. There are, however, some very rare cases not explained by this assumption. A very instructive case of this type has been published by De Renzi and Faglioni (1963). Their patient exhibited a severe disorder of "orientation to one's own body" that could not be explained in terms of aphasia or dementia. The patient was slightly aphasic but was nevertheless able to *describe* with sufficient accuracy the parts of his own body and to name them when indicated by the examiner. In contrast to this correct performance, he failed seriously when the examination required him to *indicate* parts of his body on verbal command.

Here, then, the deficit did not pertain to the denomination but rather to the *localization* of body parts. It was shown by De Renzi and Faglioni that the patient committed equally serious errors when the task was to localize parts of his car, although he was an engineer by profession. Further examination revealed other spatial disturbances in the relevant tasks of designing, writing, and calculating. While in the first-mentioned cases autotopag-nosia appears to be an aphasic symptom, in the case described by De Renzi and Faglioni it was obviously a symptom of spatial disorientation.

Everyday clinical experience will confirm that these are the principal two sets of disorders that bring about "autotopagnosia"; the third one is mental deterioration and the last is neglect of one side of the body, which belongs to still another category of symptoms.

This analysis is reported here at some length because it illustrates some points that are of importance in modern neuro-psychological work:

1. The introduction of a new procedure of examining brain-damaged patients is likely to bring to light a certain behavioral deficit that depends primarily on the requirement of the task. It is not necessarily useful to describe this deficit as a particular disorder of psychological function. If this were justified, it would depend on the examiner's imagination to create new syndromes by applying new methods of testing.

2. Any observation of a behavioral disturbance described in neuropsychology should be submitted to rigid testing with regard to the following questions: Is it a symptom in its own right or merely the expression of one or more underlying disturbances, such as, for example, aphasia or spatial disorientation? To what extent does the observed symptom depend on general variables, such as intelligence, attention or memory and can it be explained as the resultant of one or several of these specific and unspecific factors?

3. Only those symptoms should be accepted as circumscribed disorders which fulfil the requirements implicit in the above-mentioned questions.

4. It would be desirable to describe a neuropsychological disorder as a disturbance of a normal psychological function. Aphasia is a disturbance of normal speech; spatial disorientation has a correlate in topographical orientation. In this way, the diagnosis of aphasia or spatial disorientation becomes meaningful from the standpoint of normal psychology. On the other hand, a symptom like "autotopagnosia" calls for further analysis, as indicated above. It is unlikely that there exists such a basic normal psychological function as "somatognosis." The practical use of body parts does not depend on the ability to name them or to understand their names. On the other hand, failure in dealing with the names of body parts does by no means implicate any nonverbal, "gnostic," or praxic impairment with respect to one's own body. This holds true not only for the case of

cerebral pathology but also for the developmental aspect
(Benton, 1959; Poeck & Orgass, 1964). It is possible to train
a child $2\frac{1}{2}$ years old to name and understand the name even
of functionally insignificant body parts, such as elbow or
ear lobe. This underlines the view that "somatognosis"
is mainly a language problem.

The same type of analysis has been applied to other alleged
disturbances of the body schema, for instance "right-left disorientation" (impairment in distinguishing the two lateral sides on the
patient's own body and/or in external space) as well as to "finger
agnosia" (impairment in the identification of the fingers). We
have been able to demonstrate that these symptoms are equally
nonhomogenous in their appearance and genetic condition, the
most frequent underlying cause being again aphasia. The results
of these studies have been reported in detail elsewhere (Orgass &
Poeck, 1968; Poeck & Orgass, 1966, 1967a, 1967b, 1969).

Among the group of disturbances of the body schema there is
the very peculiar phenomenon of the *phantom*. In the older literature, this was defined as the vivid feeling that a missing part of
the body is still present. A widely accepted theory assumed that
the phantom was an expression of the activity of the body schema.
Given the hypothetical nature of the schema, this explanation
cannot be very satisfactory. Moreover, it is difficult to understand
why the phantom should be a disturbance of the body schema and
not one of its physiological properties.

In recent years several extensive studies have been carried out
in order to assemble systematically new facts that might eventually give more insight into the nature and pathogenetic conditions of the phantom. Poeck (1963) has studied two problems:
the apparent mobility and the sensory phenomena that can be
found in the majority of phantoms and the psychological situation
of amputees who do, as opposed to those who do not, experience
a phantom.

It has long been known that many amputees can perform

apparent movements with their missing limbs, sometimes in a quite similar way as with the normal limbs. It was shown that the phantom frequently exhibits a very distinct, reproducible, and sometimes peculiar behavior pattern in relation to objects. For instance, when the phantom is brought close to a wall or a similar obstacle, it may give way by flection in the virtual joints and extend again when the stump is taken back. Another pattern in the same experimental situation is the telescopic shrinkage of the phantom into the stump until it completely disappears at the very moment that the wall is touched. When the stump is taken away from the wall, many patients experience, *pari passu*, a lengthening of the phantom until it reaches its former shape and extent. The most peculiar pattern is the penetration of the phantom into the wall without any subjective experience of conflict.

For the examination of the sensory side, the examiner can put his hand "on the phantom," i.e., on the place where the patient feels his virtual limb. In some cases, this leads to a fading of the phantom experience, *beginning when the hand comes close to the phantom*, not only when the hand reaches its actual place. In other cases, the phantom retracts into the stump in a similar way as described above. A brisk slap "on the phantom" is experienced by some amputees as painful.

These motor and sensory patterns were demonstrated in the majority of a group of forty cases. The composition of this group permitted ruling out the possibility that these were hysterical phenomena induced in particularly susceptible subjects.

These complex experiences shed some new light on the old question whether phantoms are of peripheral or central origin, a problem that was vigorously debated in the literature. Some authors had been inclined to suggest that phantoms are the result of altered excitatory processes in peripheral nerves, consecutive to the amputation or a previous trauma.

It is true that under certain circumstances peripheral manipulations such as cooling the stump, local anesthesia, and the like are followed by increase or decrease in the subjects's awareness of his phantom. However, many other properties of the phantom cannot satisfactorily be explained on the basis of altered activity of peripheral nerves but call instead for some central mechanism. Among these properties is the described behavior of the phantom in front of an object.

These central mechanisms have been assumed by some authors to be psychological in nature, while others have postulated physiological processes. The psychological theory is prepared to equate the phantom experience with some kind of nostalgia or, more specifically, to consider the phantom as the psychodynamic expression of a subconscious tendency to deny the mutiliaton. This view is somewhat akin to Schilder's concept of "organic repression."

It is understood that any theory suggesting acceptance or refusal of the amputation must have recourse to the amputee's dreams because conscious experience is not likely to reveal his psychological situation. It has been customary in this respect to refer to Charcot's (1888) famous remark that some amputees appear intact in their dreams. This observation stimulated the theory that the presence or absence of the phantom corresponds to the psychological situation of acceptance or refusal of the amputation. It was taken for granted that denial of the amputation was expressed by a wishful intact dream image and acceptance of the amputation by the realistic image of the amputated limb.

In the examination of our forty subjects, we were able to show that this is by no means the case. The results, which have been extended in recent years to further cases, clearly indicate that there is no correlation between the presence or absence of a phantom and the dream image of the amputee as reported in the interview. Furthermore, a closer analysis reveals a vivid conflict with regard to the bodily defect even in seemingly uncomplicated dreams. Without confirmation by the subconscious experience of the subjects themselves, however, every psychodynamic theory must be regarded as purely speculative.

The problems of the phantom have been further elucidated by the studies of Weinstein and his associates (Weinstein, 1963a; Weinstein & Sersen, 1961; Weinstein, Sersen & Vetter, 1964, 1967, 1968). First, he has liberated the problem from the restriction to phantom experiences after amputation of limbs. Instead, he has studied extensively phantoms of other body parts such as the female breast as well as phantoms in paraplegia and—most important—in congenital absence of limbs. Weinstein's findings of phantoms in congenital aplasia have provided a new empirical basis for a physiological theory of the phantom. Furthermore, his results have proven most stimulating for discussion of the doctrine of the body schema in general. When a phantom of a congenitally absent limb is experienced with the same vivid intensity as phantoms after amputation of limbs, then the "body schema" or, in broader terms, the cerebral organization underlying the awareness of structure and position of the body cannot depend in any crucial way on afferent information originating in the peripheral receptors of that limb.

The experimental investigations reported so far as examples for modern neuropsychological research have one characteristic trait in common: they are all based on the classical syndromes described in the old neurological literature. Unquestionably, there is a strong need for the re-examination of old concepts with the aim of determining which of these are still valid today and which must be subject to revision. This type of research, however, has one serious problem: presupposing the existence of the classical syndromes in a way means to confirm them even though certain results might be at variance with the original descriptions. Another possibility is to assume a completely unprejudiced behavioral attitude, to abandon more or less the traditional classification together with the interpretation of symptoms, and to examine performances that can be clearly defined by modern standards. This approach has been chosen recently by De Renzi and his co-workers in Milan. These authors have studied such problems as the recognition of sounds and noises and the recognition of meaningful *vs.* nonmeaningful sounds, the recognition of physiognomical traits with regard to human faces and other objects, the handling of color tasks, visual memory, and the performance of transitive and intransitive movements.

One might object that the Milan group is not studying the classical syndromes but only more or less related phenomena. However, it seems to me that this is a very promising way of studying the effect of brain lesions on behavior. The detachment from the classical concepts is justified because the classical syndromes are conspicuously rare and, more often than not, the original cases did not correspond to their describer's definition, let alone their interpretation. On the other hand, the pragmatic approach of examining performances, making a firm analysis of the findings, especially with regard to interdependence with other specific and nonspecific behavioral disorders is a safe way to collect "hard" data. Only on the basis of "hard" data will there eventually emerge certain syndromes confirmed by rigorous testing. In addition, this approach offers the opportunity to compare in some situations the results of experimentation on brain-damaged patients and on animals.

If one is to make a prediction, it seems likely that the line of research, briefly reviewed in this chapter, will contribute a great deal to clarify the puzzling variety of disorders that are clinically recognized today. It is possible that eventually the present descriptive classification will be replaced by a genetic one.

As mentioned above, one prerequisite for a rational classification of the psychological effects of brain lesions is the clear distinction between *symptoms* and *disorders*. This distinction is a matter of fact in clinical neurology: nobody would consider action tremor (a symptom) and cerebellar ataxia (a syndrome) to belong to the same category of phenomena. Nobody would deny that the finding of an impairment in precise alternating finger movements (an equivocal symptom) requires further classification as to its under-lying cause (disorder, syndrome), e.g., spastic paresis, cerebellar ataxia, extrapyramidal motor disturbance, or severe sensory loss.

Remarkably enough, this necessary distinction is still widely lacking in neuropsychology. Phenomena such as ideomotor apraxia and apraxia for dressing, for example, are diagnosed, described, and discussed on the same level. An analysis of these phenomena, however, reveals that they are not comparable: ideomotor apraxia is a clear-cut homogeneous disorder even though it may be considered as a language-dependent motor dis-turbance. Dressing apraxia, on the other hand, is not an apraxia at all, but an ambiguous symptom reflecting one or more of several underlying disorders (Critchley, 1953). Among these are ideomotor apraxia, overall spatial disorientation, and neglect of one side of personal and extrapersonal space, the last one possibly also nonhomogeneous in nature.

Experimental work carried out in the last decade has furnished enough data to make possible the required new formulation of old concepts. The picture emerging from many of the recent neuro-psychological studies is that of very few basic factors underlying the wealth of neuropsychological symptoms. Among these are disturbances of language, spatial orientation, motor and somato-sensory functions, vision, and audition. Relevant general factors are disturbances of consciousness, recall, orientation, intelligence, drive, and emotion.

By combining this assumption with Geschwind's disconnection doctrine, we find it possible to formulate the following hypo-thesis: Pure syndromes (i.e., disturbance of one isolated function) are very rare. The great majority of neuropsychological syndromes are the result of an interaction between two or more basic dis-orders with or without one or several general disturbances. This interaction depends upon the anatomical locus of lesion, that is, on the interruption of pathways connecting specific association areas with one another.

The Functional Asymmetry of the Cerebral Hemispheres

In subhuman species, the two cerebral hemispheres are equivalent not only with respect to anatomical structure but also to function. Only in man does there exist a functional asymmetry between the two halves of the brain. The best known example for this asymmetry is the lateralization of the speech area.

Neuropsychological studies in this field were long focused almost exclusively on the problem of cerebral dominance for language and its relation to handedness. The hemisphere harboring the language area was termed dominant or major. In the majority of the population, this is the left half of the brain and, in these instances, left-sided cerebral dominance for language is very strongly correlated with right-handedness. The other hemisphere, usually the right one, was only negatively defined as nondominant or minor (cf. Benton, 1965; Benton & Fogel, 1962; Branch, Milner, & Rasmussen, 1964; Hécaen & Ajuriaguerra, 1964).[1]

The critical role of the left hemisphere is not confined to overt language behavior, such as speaking or understanding language, reading or the linguistic aspect of writing. It is recognized increasingly that a broad spectrum of behavioral disturbances that are correlated with lesions in the left hemisphere are language dependent in a wider sense of the word. These problems have been briefly discussed above.

On the other hand, it has been demonstrated that certain nonverbal activities, particularly spatial perception and orientation, depend on the integrity of the temporal and parietal areas of the right hemisphere. Yet, if one is to assess the functional significance of each hemisphere, it is evident that there are important differences in degree. In the normal right-handed person, impairment of verbal activities in the broader sense for all practical purposes

1. Exceptions to this rule, as well as the problems of left-handedness, are not discussed here.

indicates with certainty a lesion of the left hemisphere. However, a deficit in tasks requiring spatial orientation, constructional praxis, or visual and tactile perception of complex nonverbal patterns is observed after lesions in either hemisphere, even though these symptoms appear to be more frequent and more severe after right sided lesions. On the basis of these observations, Piercy, Hécaen and Ajuriaguerra (1960) have put forward the hypothesis that certain functions have a bilateral but asymmetrical cerebral representation. These findings indicate that the "non-dominant" hemisphere is involved in a particular group of psychological activities. But they do not necessarily call for a basic revision of the concept that the left hemisphere plays the leading role and is rightly regarded as "dominant."

Recently, however, important results have been obtained with new techniques of examining auditory and visual perception. The evidence from these experiments suggests that there does exist a differential functional organization of the human brain in which each hemisphere plays its part in a particular field and makes a separate contribution to human experience and behavior.

Auditory Recognition

The organ of Corti, i.e., the peripheral receptive organ of audition of either ear is connected by crossed and uncrossed pathways with both temporal lobes. Evidence from animal experiments (Rosenzweig, 1951; Tunturi, 1946) suggests that the crossed pathway is functionally stronger than the uncrossed one. When both ears are stimulated simultaneously, a mechanism of occlusion may occur, enhancing the functional superiority of the crossed pathway.

In patients with temporal lobectomy for the relief of intractable epilepsy, Milner (1962) has demonstrated a dissociation with respect to various kinds of auditory recognition. Presenting verbal stimuli through earphones, she found patients with left-sided lobectomy to be significantly more impaired than patients with right-sided lobectomy, although in the left-sided cases the language area had remained intact and the patients had no manifest aphasic disturbance. In contrast, patients with right-sided lobectomy were definitely inferior to the recognition of tonal patterns and in the discrimination of tonal qualities (Milner, 1962; Shankweiler, 1966a). These results suggested that the right temporal lobe plays a critical role in the perception of certain nonverbal stimuli.

This assumption was borne out by examining normal subjects with the dichotic listening technique involving the simultaneous application of two different auditory stimuli (Broadbent, 1954). In this experimental situation, a series of pairs of different stimuli is presented, and the subject is asked to report all the stimuli he has heard. Using this technique, Kimura (1961a,b, 1964, 1967) has studied the interaction of the two ears in normal healthy persons and in subjects with organic brain damage of diverse localization. When *verbal stimuli* were applied (e.g., numbers or nonsense syllables), the subjects reported much more frequently the number given into the ear contralateral to the (language-) dominant hemisphere. This result was reproduced also under multiple-choice conditions, when no expressive speech was required that might have activated particular functions of the left hemisphere. This differential effect did not depend upon the extent or localization of the brain damage. When *nonverbal* stimuli were applied e.g., melodies (Kimura, 1964, 1967) or familiar sounds (Curry, 1967), the ear contralateral to the minor hemisphere proved to be superior.

It follows from these and similar experiments that in auditory perception there is a functional asymmetry of the two halves of the brain that is dependent on the quality of the stimulus. The left hemisphere seems to play a leading role in the perception and analysis of verbal stimuli while the right hemisphere apparently is superior for nonverbal stimuli, such as melodies and noises. It could be demonstrated that this asymmetry was not correlated to the greater or lesser familiarity of the stimulus (Kimura, 1967).

The quality of the verbal stimulus necessary to demonstrate right-ear (i.e., left hemisphere) superiority has been further clarified by Shankweiler and Studdert-Kennedy (1967). These authors found that vowels have only a very low right-left gradient while syllables consisting of vowels and consonants produced the ear asymmetry described above. These results seem to indicate the importance of articulatory experiences for the superiority of the left hemisphere in dichotic listening of verbal stimuli.

In left-handed subjects, the functional asymmetry of the two hemispheres in these experiments is less clear-cut. There is a marked equipotentiality of the two halves of the brain in left-handers, which had been known before on the grounds of other experiments and of clinical observation.

Apart from their theoretical implications, these results have a very obvious practical significance. The method appears suited to establish reliably and without risk the hemisphere that is dominant for language. This would be a great advantage compared to the technique described by Wada and Rasmussen (1960), which requires the injection of sodium amytal into at least one carotid artery. The new technique lends itself also to the study of the development of the functional asymmetry of the brain. The left hemisphere proved superior in the task of dichotic listening of numbers as early as age 4 (Kimura, 1963b). Based on the results of hemispherectomy, most authors had been in agreement that the lateralization of the language area takes place only at a later age, at about 8 or 9 years.

Visual Recognition

Similar experiments have been carried out on visual recognition. Here, two different visual stimuli are presented tachistoscopically, one to each half-field of both eyes. Either signal is projected to the corresponding receiving area in the occipital

lobe (striate area). As described above, the right half-fields
project to the left striate area and vice versa. However, the signals
do not remain confined to the respective hemisphere. Both
striate cortices are connected by way of the surrounding association cortex via commissural pathways in the posterior portion
(splenium) of corpus callosum. This pathway includes one
synapse which makes for a measurable delay in transmission as
compared to the direct, uncrossed route.

In patients with unilateral brain damage, an asymmetry
between the two halves of the brain can be demonstrated already
by the usual method of presenting one visual stimulus to both
eyes simultaneously. It is everyday knowledge in neurology
that *left-sided* damage to the parieto-occipital region leads to an
impairment in the recognition of words or letters (alexia).
Damage to the *right* temporal lobe will interfere with the recognition of nonverbal stimuli such as single geometric forms (Kimura,
1963a; Milner, 1958) or groups of dots and of overlapping
meaningless figures (Kimura, 1966) as well as other complex
visual stimuli (De Renzi & Spinnler, 1966; Warrington & James,
1967).

This differential effect is shown still more clearly when the
stimuli are presented, as described above, to both left or right
visual half-fields, respectively. Under these experimental conditions, in normal, healthy subjects the right half-fields are
superior for words (Mishkin & Forgays, 1952), for letters (Heron,
1957), and for concrete objects lending themselves to ready
verbalization (Wyke & Ettlinger, 1961). The left half-fields,
on the other hand, are superior in the recognition of meaningless figures (Heron, 1957) and of other nonverbal visual tasks
(Kimura, 1966).

Any attempt to interpret these experimental results in terms of
hemispheric specialization must allow for the fact that the para-
visual association areas of both hemispheres are connected by
commissural pathways. Consequently, an optic stimulus
presented in any part of the visual field is transmitted to both

hemispheres. This fact makes somewhat problematic the assumption that the differential effect in the periphery reflects differences in hemispheric organization. It is reasonable, however, to presume that a visual signal will arrive earlier in the corresponding striate area than in the contralateral one, the latency being due to the commissural pathway involving one more synapse. Kimura (1966) has advanced the hypothesis that a visual signal arriving in the corresponding striate area might activate intrinsic association processes: verbal association in the left and spatial integration in the right hemispheres. This would explain why hemispheric mechanisms come into play in spite of transcallosal transfer of signals.

In contrast to the situation in auditory recognition, there is one more factor to be considered. Visual discrimination involves scanning movements of the eyes, organized in the oculomotor area lying close to the visual association areas. Some observations suggest that reading habits might play an important role in bringing about the field (and hemispheric) differences.

The most important of these are: (1) The right-left gradient becomes stronger with length of schooling (Forgays, 1952). (2) Hebrew, which is read from the right to the left side, is recognized better in the left visual half-fields (Orbach, 1952). (3) If the ocular scanning habit is eliminated by presenting Hebrew words in vertical order, the right half-fields are again superior (Barton, Goodglass, & Shai, 1965). (4) It has been reported that mirror writing of English words will reverse the usual field superiority (Harcum & Filion, 1963). Oculomotor influences, however, cannot be the only relevant factor to make up for the field differences, as pointed out recently by Braine (1968).

Summing up, it has been demonstrated that the posterior portion of the left hemisphere is critical for the recognition of verbal patterns, while the corresponding part of the right hemisphere appears critical for the recognition of complex nonverbal patterns. These findings have an interesting parallel in certain clinical syndromes. Visual object agnosia, for example, seems to be correlated with lesions in the left occipito-parietal region. The disorder essentially consists in defective naming of visually presented realistic objects. The data reported here on the role of the left hemisphere in visual recognition support the hypothesis that visual object agnosia is due to a disconnection between the visual and the language areas.

On the other hand, visual spatial disorientation is a characteristic disturbance in posterior right hemisphere lesions. The role of the right hemisphere in the visual recognition of complex nonverbal figures and of spatial relationships, as demonstrated in normal subjects, indicates the neural mechanism that is probably affected in spatial disorientation.

Finally, it has been demonstrated that both temporal lobes make an important extrastriate contribution to visual recognition in general. These findings give a clue to the understanding of "psychic blindness" (i.e., visual agnosia), which is one of the cardinal symptoms of the Klüver-Bucy syndrome. This complex syndrome is observed after bilateral temporal lobe damage not only in animals but also in man (Pilleri, 1966).

It is interesting that comparable results have been obtained in tasks requiring visual as well as auditory recognition. The data reported here suggest a differential organization of both cerebral hemispheres, each half of the brain having its particular functional significance. The logical consequence of these findings is to abandon the assumption that one hemisphere is the dominant one in favor of the concept of a functional asymmetry between the two cerebral hemispheres.

Conclusion

In this introductory chapter we have discussed several aspects of neuropsychological research in man. It must be stressed, however, that there is no strict boundary separating neuropsychology from related fields of the physiological sciences. For example, the important work on somatosensory changes observed in cases of penetrating brain wounds in man (Semmes, Weinstein, Ghent, & Teuber, 1960) has added another dimension to the knowledge of hemispheric asymmetry. It has been shown that even basic functions of somatosensitivity (touch, two-point discrimination, point localization) are differentially organized in the two halves of the brain: there is diffuse representation in the right hemisphere and circumscribed representation in the left one. This difference is possibly the consequence of the large extension of the language area in the left hemisphere, as suggested by Milner (1962) in another context.

Still more important appears to be the finding that left-sided lesions led to bilateral, right-sided lesions only to contralateral somatosensory defect. This would mean that the left half of the brain is superior not only at the high level of language dependent psychological activities but also at a physiological level.

Another point worth mentioning is the increasing overlap between human neuropsychology and animal physiological psychology. It is likely that many of the nonverbal behavioral changes observed after brain lesions in man can be studied in animals, particularly in primates. This means that the experiments can be carried out under controlled conditions and not influenced by the many motivational factors that have created so much ambiguity in neuropsychological work on patients.

2

The Behavioral Effects of
Commissural Section

George Ettlinger
and Colin B. Blakemore

It is now more than forty years since Bykov (1924–1925) reported that transection of the corpus callosum in dogs prevents
the irradiation of the conditioned response between corresponding
points on the left and right sides of the body. The subsequent
work falls into two periods. First, there was what might be called
the "negative" period. A large number of investigations were
carried out during this period, for the most part on patients with
surgical section or disease of the corpus callosum, notably by
Akelaitis (1944) and his colleagues and also by others. The bulk
of the findings were interpreted as "negative," that is, as tending

to show no behavioral alterations that could be specifically ascribed to the commissural damage. However, even during this so-called "negative" period certain subtle deficits of the kind that might be expected to follow commissural damage, for example, the inability to read letters in the left half-field of vision, came to light (cf. Maspes, 1948; Smith, 1951; Trescher & Ford, 1937). The second or "positive" period took its origin from the animal experiments of Myers (1956), Myers and Sperry (1953, 1956), and Sperry, Stamm, and Miner (1956). These and the many subsequent experimental investigations have demonstrated beyond doubt that the forebrain commissures can participate actively in the exchange of information between the cerebral hemispheres. The application of new and more sensitive testing methods soon gave evidence also in man of manifold behavioral defects consequent upon commissural damage (cf. Gazzaniga, Bogen, & Sperry, 1962; Geschwind & Kaplan, 1962).

It is not our purpose to review comprehensively the many cases in the older neurological literature in which possible commissural dysfunction was discussed, nor yet the many direct investigations of commissural function. Various such reviews are already available (cf. Bremer, Brihaye, & Andre-Baliseaux, 1956; Myers, 1965, pp 1–17; Sperry, 1961, 1964). Rather we intend to use the findings of selected studies of commissural function to illustrate a general property of the mammalian brain: its plasticity in the organization of behavior. In justification, we shall endeavor to resolve by this approach what would otherwise appear to be discrepant and irreconcilable findings of the behavioral effects of commissure section.

In the main subsection of this chapter we shall illustrate the brain's plasticity by considering sucessively the findings relating to vision, audition, touch, motor functions, emotions, and dominance, insofar as they apply to mammals and particularly primates. In a subsequent section we shall deal with selected variables (such as set, age) and examine to what extent they can be shown to influence the outcome of commissural section. But first, we shall briefly describe the connections between the left and right halves of the brain.

The Neural Connections across the Midline of the Brain

There are two kinds of structure that interconnect the left and right halves of the brain. At some levels the nerve fibers run haphazardly across the midline in many directions and lie intermingled with nerve cells. In other cases the fibers are gathered together into a discrete transverse bundle to the exclusion of all nerve cells; such a fiber tract is then called a "commissure."

By far the largest commissure is the "corpus callosum" (see Fig. 2.1), which forms the connecting pathway between extensive regions of the left and right hemispheres. The corpus callosum is itself conventionally further subdivided anteriorly into the "rostrum" and "genu." Its major constituent part is designated the "body" of the corpus callosum; at its posterior end the body becomes the "splenium." Located separately, ventral to the anterior end of the body of the corpus callosum, but functionally interdependent with some parts of the corpus callosum is the "anterior commissure," which (except in marsupials) is much smaller than the corpus callosum. It is the pathway that predominantly connects certain areas of the temporal cortex and limbic system across the midline, providing also a small connection between the left and right frontal lobes in some species.

Likewise much smaller than the corpus callosum (but nonetheless important in the neural organization of behavior) are the following commissures: the "interthalamic" commissure, which is situated ventrally in the thalamus of certain, but not all, mammalian species and connects the left and right somatosensory projection systems; the "hippocampal" commissure (also called the "psalterium"), which lies immediately ventral to the posterior body of the corpus callosum and interconnects the left and right limbic systems; the "posterior" commissure, which, like the

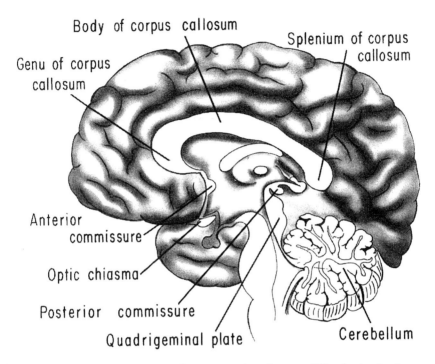

Figure 2.1   *A semidiagrammatic representation of some midline brain structures of the monkey brain.*

"commissure of the superior colliculi," belongs to the upper midbrain connecting various structures including the visual system across the midline; and the "commissure of the inferior colliculi," which is concerned with audition.[1]

Apart from the commissures proper, connections across the midline are formed by fibers running diffusely in the "massa intermedia" of the thalamus (in many, but not all, individuals); in

1. Another commissure, connecting the habenular nuclei across the midline, is located immediately ventral to the splenium of the corpus callosum; so far this and other minor commissures have not been shown to have behavioral significance in mammals.

the "quadrigeminal plate," which continues ventral to the corpora quadrigemina of the midbrain; in the cerebellum; and in the tegmentum. (The variable presence of the massa intermedia is unlikely to be of importance in experiments on man, as it has then been sectioned whenever present. Cf. Sperry & Gazzaniga, 1967.)

It should also be recalled that each eye normally projects to both left and right cerebral hemispheres. The fibers leaving the left eye and destined for the right hemisphere cross in the optic chiasma with the equivalent fibers from right eye to left hemisphere. If the optic chiasma is divided along the midline, all crossing fibers are destroyed, so that visual fibers now pass from each eye only to the ipsilateral hemisphere (but cf. some suggestive evidence to the contrary for the cat: Glickstein, 1965). In consequence, the animal is blind in both temporal fields, that is, to the left in the left eye and to the right in the right eye. In man, the eyes can be directed onto a fixation mark and exposure of a visual stimulus to the left half-field of either eye then restricts transmission of the visual response to the right hemisphere and conversely with right-sided stimulation to the left hemisphere.

Each ear likewise normally projects to both cerebral hemispheres, but fibers cross the midline at many levels in the afferent auditory system. It is therefore not feasible to restrict the auditory inflow from one ear entirely to a single hemisphere. In the case of the limbs there is both behavioral and physiological evidence to support suggestions that there is a limited ipsilateral projection of somatosensory inflow such as could form the basis for certain kinds of tactile discrimination performance. The main somatosensory afferent projection passes from each limb to the contralateral hemisphere, so there is again no practical way of insuring that *all* relevant sensory inflow reaches only a single hemisphere.[2]

2. Auditory and somatosensory inflow can, of course, be restricted to a single hemisphere in animals by drastic surgical procedures (e.g., unilateral destruction of a sensory relay nucleus). Any such procedure, however, would preclude behavioral testing of commissure function because only one hemisphere remains available for training and testing.

But whereas the ipsilateral projection is substantial in audition, certain lines of evidence (from experiments to be described on transfer of training between the hands after callosal section) indicate that it is of only minor importance in tactile function.

The anatomical connections and physiological properties of the neural pathways that cross the midline of the brain have been studied in some detail. Here we shall touch upon only those experiments that are directly relevant. We refer the reader who requires further anatomical information to Myers' (1965, pp. 133–143) recent review and for physiological information to Bremer (1958, 1966), Rutledge and Kennedy (1960), and Whitteridge (1965, pp. 115–120).

The Plasticity of the Neural Organization of Behavior

It is well known that over the years many investigators of the mammalian brain have been impressed by its "plasticity," in the general sense of this term that a particular kind of behavior can be sustained by various neural substrates. Naturally, the majority of such workers were concerned principally with neural structures other than those that cross the midline. Take, for example, Lashley who derived the concept of "equipotentiality" from cortical ablation experiments. Equipotentiality, together with the less restricted concepts of "vicarious function," "compensation," and "reconstitution of function" can be regarded merely as special cases of the general principle of plasticity. Plasticity has also been invoked in studies of commissure function to account for certain limited findings, for instance by Trevarthen (1965, pp. 34–35). To this extent our approach is not new. Following such precedents, we shall now consider under six headings a variety of clinical and experimental observations, and attempt to understand them more fully as an expression of a brain that is a plastic, nonrigid instrument of behavior.

Vision

Gazzaniga, Bogen, and Sperry (1965) mention briefly that their patients with transection of the forebrain commissures (i.e., corpus callosum, anterior commissure, hippocampal commissure, and massa intermedia if present) are impaired on certain non-verbal visual tasks that require interaction between the two half-fields of vision (and therefore between the two hemispheres). "So far, we have found no evidence that what is perceived in the right half-field has any influence on the perception or comprehension of what is seen in the left half-field" (Gazzaniga et al., 1965, p. 232). In effect, this confirms the original finding by Myers (1956) of deficient interocular transfer of learned pattern discrimination problems in "split-brain" cats (i.e., cats having section of the optic chiasma as well as of the forebrain commissures). In the same investigation (Myers, 1956), split-brain cats were trained to make opposite responses to one pair of stimulus patterns seen successively through the left or right eye and did not show the interference between such conflicting habits that occurs when only the chiasma has been cut (Myers, 1955). Subsequently, Trevarthen's (1962) split-brain monkeys learned (see Fig. 2.2) simultaneously to make two contradictory responses to a single pair of visual patterns when, by the elegant use of polarized light, the two eyes were presented concurrently on each trial with opposite tasks. Monkeys having their forebrain commissures intact were not able to acquire simultaneously these conflicting habits. In yet another type of experiment, Trevarthen (1965, p. 145) failed to teach the split-brain monkey to perform a binocular visual conditional task. In this task, the "figure" consisted of vertical and horizontal bars presented to the one eye, but seen in the context of a "ground" of either vertical or horizontal stripes presented to the other eye.

These and other investigations not described by us give a clear-cut, positive answer: in the absence of the forebrain commissures

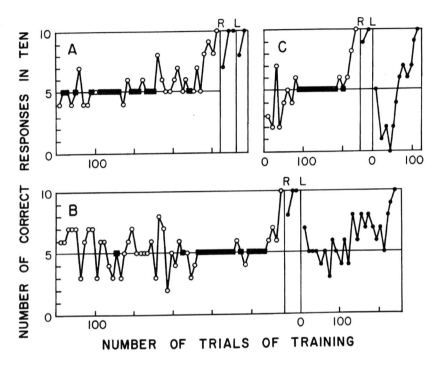

Figure 2.2 *Sample learning curves for three different tasks. A. Simultaneous learning of contradictory "circle vs. plus" discriminations by the two eyes. B. Monocular learning of another task and interference of performance with the other eye. C. Monocular learning and interocular transfer of learning with contradictory brightness discriminations. Each hollow circle (binocular learning) or solid circle (monocular tests) represents ten trials. R = right eye test, L = left eye test. Position habits by which all ten trials of a group were made to one response screen are shown by black horizontal bars. (From Trevarthen, 1962, p. 258)*

the subject is unable to solve visual pattern discrimination tasks that require interchange of information between the hemispheres and can learn contradictory tasks in a way not possible by the intact individual. We can therefore infer that the forebrain commissures are normally able to effect an interchange of information between the hemispheres.[3] Myers (1965, pp. 4–8) has reviewed the evidence for the cat as to how effective the neo-cortical commissures are in the interchange of visual information under various test conditions.

Different results are, however, obtained if the animal[4] is given a visual task not requiring the discrimination of pattern. With stimuli differing in intensity, color, or frequency of intermission there is good interocular transfer, despite prior section of the optic chiasma and forebrain commissures, in the cat (Meikle, 1964; Meikle & Sechzer, 1960; Voneida, 1963), in the monkey (Trevarthen, 1962), and in the chimpanzee (Myers, 1965, p. 43). Voneida (1963) and Meikle (1964) have presented evidence that such residual visual transfer may be mediated by the posterior commissure and/or the commissure of the superior colliculi in cats, and Thompson (1965), working with the rat, has also stressed the importance of these midbrain commissures. With stimuli differing grossly in size, Trevarthen (1965, p. 145) has succeeded in retraining the split-brain monkey to make inter-ocular comparisons (when each eye sees one of a number of differ-ent sized circles). From these various lines of evidence we can conclude that provided intensities, colors, frequencies of inter-mission, or sizes are to be discriminated, the forebrain commissures are not essential for the exchange of visual information between the two halves of the brain.

Having formulated the general rule that the forebrain com-missures are necessary for the interocular transfer of pattern but the midbrain is capable of transferring other visual dimensions, we can now consider some instructive exceptions. First, split-brain cats do show interocular transfer of certain simple visual

3. An intact individual would, of course, normally scan a visual display with his eyes so as to stimulate both left and right half-fields; in consequence both hemispheres would receive very similar visual inflow directly along the afferent pathways.

4. We can find no mention of relevant observations in patients after com-missure section. But note that case II of Gazzaniga et al. (1965) was unable to match colors across the midline.

pattern discriminations if electric shock (for errors) is substituted for food reward (Sechzer, 1964). Subcortical pathways can, therefore, transmit information related to patterns under certain test conditions. At present it is not certain whether the critical factor is the degree of motivation or the different distribution of the fiber pathways concerned on the one hand with shock motivation and on the other with food motivation (Sechzer, 1964).[5]

A more dramatic example of plasticity has been given by Trevarthen (1965, p. 30). Two split-brain monkeys were trained to respond through one eye to the more intense stimulus of a pair, while concurrently they could learn to choose through the other eye the less intense stimulus of the same pair. After the two animals were performing well with both eyes open, they were tested for learning through each eye separately (see Fig. 2.3). Tested first through the eye contralateral to the preferred hand, both animals performed almost perfectly. Next, this eye was covered and the monkeys were tested through the second eye. The performance of both animals fell at first to a level significantly below chance, indicating that the animals had learned the same and not the conflicting response through the second eye. So, unlike the results with visual patterns, contradictory habits had not been formed, and the learning in the hemisphere contralateral to the preferred hand had transferred to the other hemisphere. However, performance through the second eye soon improved and the two animals then learned a contradictory habit with this eye. When they were retested through the first eye, the original habit for that eye was rapidly reestablished within between 40 and 120 trials. So, despite this evidence of initial transfer, opposite habits were subsequently acquired without reciprocal interference. As Trevarthen puts it: "Apparently a

---

5. It has been shown that monkeys can readily learn a successive auditory discrimination task with shock motivation but scarcely with food motivation after bilateral frontal ablations; here the degree and not the pathway of the motivation is likely to be the important variable.

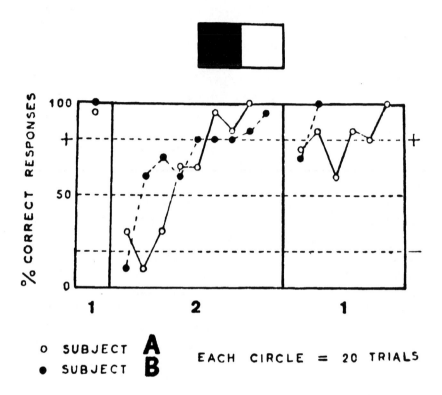

Figure 2.3 *Monocular retention of a brightness discrimination task after binocular learning with conflicting stimuli. The first eye tested (1) was contralateral to the hand used for the initial learning. The second eye (2) showed different degrees of retention. The left stimulus in each pair was correct for the left eye. (From Trevarthen, 1965, p. 29)*

pathway of communication had been closed or a common memory mechanism suppressed."

Another illustration of plasticity can be considered briefly. We have already seen that learned discriminations of intensity and color transfer from eye to eye in the split-brain animal (with midbrain commissures intact). Now in the split-brain cat the method of testing does not seem to be critical. However, in the split-brain monkey simultaneous training of the two eyes with conflicting tasks apparently facilitates transfer (Trevarthen, 1962), whereas successive monocular training apparently impedes if not prevents transfer (Hamilton & Gazzaniga, 1964). Trevarthen (1965, p. 31) has suggested that "testing one side at a time leads to attentional or other adjustments which keep the two halves of the visual system apart, even when, in other circumstances, they can converge in undivided brainstem systems."[6]

Audition

Very little is known about the effects of commissure section on the performance of auditory tasks. This may be due in part to the many connections across the midline in the auditory system and in part to the practical difficulties inherent in work on audition. Wegener (1965, pp. 69–72) has provided us with a useful summary of what is known as a result of animal experiments. We are aware of no recent work on auditory capacities after commissure section in man.

Touch

"In a few tests involving the learning of simple tactile discriminations with right or left hand, the learning did not carry over to the opposite hand" (Gazzaniga, Bogen, and Sperry, 1962, p. 1768). Although these authors at first reported that learning of a stylus maze did transfer from either hand to the other in the same patient after commissure section, they subsequently considered that this could be attributed "in part at least to the nature and size of the maze and the consequent shoulder movement and

6. The good transfer of intensity and color discriminations in split-brain chimpanzees (presumably) tested successively (Myers, 1965, p. 43) is not consistent with this interpretation.

trunk adjustments (not confined to one side) involved in its performance" (Gazzaniga et al., 1963, p. 213). The patient was unable to indicate with his right hand where he had been lightly touched or pricked on the left side of the body, although he was able to do so with his left hand; similarly he could find only with the right hand and not with the left a light touch, a thermal stimulus or a painful prick applied to the right side of the body.[7] He was able to describe (verbally) the locus of a right-sided somatic stimulus but not of any left-sided stimulation, except on the head and face. These findings imply that the neocortical commissures are essential for the exchange of tactile information between the hemispheres in man and also that the ipsilateral tactile projection can not serve as a substitute.

Recently, however, different results were obtained (Gazzaniga & Sperry, 1967) with two of five further patients studied after commissure section. These two cases were presumed to have little or no cortical damage, and therefore their performance could reflect more directly the effects of commissure section un-complicated by additional pathology. Both showed some limited ability to draw correctly with the one hand shapes palpated by the other (Gazzaniga & Sperry, 1967, p. 146) although unable to match shapes held in different hands (p. 142). Both could report (verbally) the site of a tactile stimulus to the left side of the body (but not to the left hand or foot) and were able to write with the left hand. These new findings are difficult to evaluate at present. It is possible to attribute some of the tactile impairment in the remaining cases to the effects of additional cortical damage when combined with commissure section.[8] Alternatively, the ipsilateral somatosensory projection may have been exceptionally strong in the two unimpaired patients. Or individual differences

7. Cross-localization was accurate for stimulation of any kind on the head or face.

8. It must be recalled that commissure section in man is undertaken for the relief of incapacitating epilepsy; this could be symptomatic of a cortical lesion which might impair the patient's performance more severely after than before commissure section (see p. 66).

in brain organization may account for the discrepant findings. A final possibility, namely that the commissure section was incomplete in the two exceptional cases, can be largely discounted on the evidence of Gazzaniga and Sperry (1967): these patients were able to write with the left hand the name of an object presented to the right hand, but not to the left; and again, if the name of an object was flashed to their left half-field, then they were able to find the object from a selection with the left hand but not with the right.

Turning now to animal experiments, the outcome of transection of the forebrain commissures is again variable. Although Stamm and Sperry (1957) showed that intermanual transfer of training is abolished in the split-brain cat, the subsequent work with monkeys by Glickstein and Sperry (1960) was less conclusive, there being some evidence of transfer in about one-third of possible instances. Ebner and Myers (1962a) found no evidence of intermanual transfer (see Fig. 2.4) in monkeys having all the forebrain commissures cut and trained to solve difficult tasks in an automatic apparatus. However, Ettlinger and Morton (1966) observed virtually perfect intermanual transfer. The anterior commissure[9] had not been divided in their monkeys, and training without special apparatus had been given on easy or moderately difficult problems. Lee-Teng and Sperry (1966) have carefully assessed the retention of intermanual size comparisons and size matches after total forebrain commissure section in monkeys. Performance was no better than chance when absolute judgments were precluded from the comparisons; and intermanual matching of even large differences in size was impossible, whereas unimanual matching remained efficient.

Perhaps a clue is provided by Semmes and Mishkin (1965a) who studied intermanual transfer in monkeys having section of all the forebrain commissures and employed special apparatus to restrict the use of one or the other hand. They state (in their

9. The anterior commissure has no known connections with the somatosensory projection or association systems.

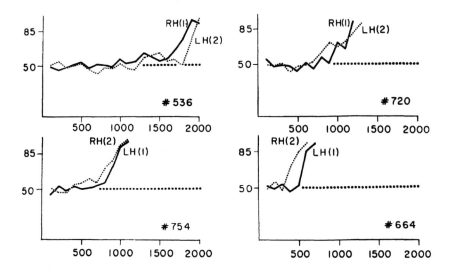

Figure 2.4   *First and second hand learning curves on the groove-smooth problem in four corpus callosum sectioned monkeys. Similarity of learning through the two hands is striking. (From Ebner & Myers, 1962a)*

footnote, p. 61) that "even a normal animal may show poor transfer if the second hand is not given the preliminary easy discriminations before testing for recall of the difficult one. The transfer results on these preliminary discriminations failed to give clear evidence of impairment in any operated group. . . ." There are here two separate points. First, to secure optimal performance with the second hand it is necessary to adapt the animal to working with this hand. (This point is, perhaps, reminiscent of an earlier observation by Meikle, Sechzer, and Stellar, 1962: a few trials of shock reinforcement to the second paw insured good transfer in the split-brain cat of the respiratory response—although, strangely, not of the limb flection response—conditioned to unilateral tactile stimulation.) Second, Semmes and Mishkin's split-brain monkeys performed as well as unoperated animals on transfer tests with easy tactile discrimination problems, although with a difficult discrimination task the same animals gave no evidence of intermanual transfer.

A new interpretation of the inconsistent findings on intermanual transfer is due to M. F. Piercy (personal communication). In an unpublished experiment, Piercy has found that intermanual transfer generally does not take place in split-brain monkeys with tasks requiring the discrimination of differences in size (i.e., with differential proprioceptive input); whereas the same animals often give evidence of good transfer with shape or roughness discrimination tasks (i.e., with differential input from the touch receptors in the skin). Such a different outcome of callosal section, depending upon the nature of the tactile task, has not previously been obtained; and, as already mentioned, intermanual transfer has been found to be absent in certain of the earlier studies even when the split-brain monkeys were required to discriminate between shapes or grades of roughness. However, Semmes and Mishkin (1965b) have shown that large unilateral removals of sensorimotor and posterior parietal cortex can give rise to impairment in the ipsilateral hand on tasks of shape or roughness but not of size discrimination. Therefore Piercy's findings with shapes and roughness, as also the good transfer in the experiment of Ettlinger and Morton (1966), may be due to an ipsilateral as well as contralateral projection from the touch receptors in the skin, and the rarity of transfer with sizes may reflect a more completely crossed projection from the proprioceptive receptors in the joints.

As a final illustration of the variable capacity of the commissures to transmit tactile information we refer to an instructive experiment on contradictory learning by Myers (1965, pp. 13–16). Unoperated monkeys were trained to discriminate between two grades of roughness with the right (first) hand, then to learn the *opposite* discrimination with the left (second) hand, and finally were tested once again for the original habit with the right (first) hand. One monkey showed good (negative) transfer from the first to the second hand (performing below chance for over 100 trials), and again from the second back to the first hand (performing below chance for 40 trials and requiring 150 trials to relearn the original habit with the first hand). Another animal, tested under identical conditions, showed no transfer from the first to the second hand, and again no transfer initially from the second back to the first hand (although on trials 21–80 the performance fell below chance, indicating some transient [negative] transfer from the second back to the first hand). Other animals gave similar or intermediate results. A certain variability of intermanual transfer in unoperated monkeys had also been reported by Ettlinger and Elithorn (1962): monkeys were trained to discriminate between two laterally inverted (i.e. mirror-image) shapes with the one hand; these animals then showed variable (but always positive) transfer when tested for the *opposite* response with the second hand; but all retained the original habit well when finally tested once again with the first hand.

Combining these results of Myers and of Ettlinger and Elithorn, we can conclude that the intact monkey does not readily learn opposite responses through the two hands except with laterally inverted shapes, when there is no evidence of interference between the contradictory habits. However, Glickstein and Sperry (1960) have shown that the splitbrain monkey can acquire conflicting responses to ordinary tactile test objects through the two hands without reciprocal interference. Finally, all these studies agree in reporting variability between subjects.

Motor Functions

A great deal of work has been done on various aspects of motor function after commissure section. We shall consider successively the findings relating to: bimanual skills, transfer between the hands of unimanual skills, the effect of changing hands on the performance of visual discrimination tasks, the accuracy of reaching for visual targets, and reaction times. However, we certainly do not wish to imply that these kinds of motor activity can be clearly differentiated.

The left hand also works well along with the right in other habitual tasks such as tying a knot in the belt of his robe, folding towels, putting on and removing clothes. [The patient's wife, nevertheless, had] also noted antagonism between the actions of the right and left hands, e.g. the patient would pick up the evening paper with the right hand, but put it down abruptly with the left and then have to pick it up again with the right. Similar contradictory movements were observed occasionally in the course of dressing and undressing, and in other daily activities (Gazzaniga et al., 1962, p. 1767).

So it would appear that learned movements requiring the simultaneous activity of both hands can generally, but not always, be fully realized in the absence of the forebrain commissures in man.

Very similar results obtain also for the split-brain animal. There is evidence from the work of Ettlinger and Morton (1963), Myers (1965, p. 109), and Trevarthen (1965, p. 111) that bimanual skills and movements made under visual guidance generally remain unimpaired in cats, monkeys, and chimpanzees after commissure section. Nonetheless, Trevarthen (1965, pp. 103–105) has described various examples of clumsy, "apraxic," and even conflicting responses by the two hands in commissure sectioned monkeys that were performing a bimanual task. These examples of discoordination were described as subtle rather than gross; and they were precipitated either when visual attention was directed elsewhere (p. 105), or, with a puzzle box, when close attention was needed for simultaneous and separate movements of the two hands (p. 111).

Turning now to transfer between the hands of a learned

unimanual motor skill or manipulation,[10] there is clear agreement: such transfer is impaired after transection of the fore-brain commissures in chimpanzees (Black & Myers, 1965, pp. 47–59; Myers & Henson, 1960) and monkeys (Trevarthen, 1965, p. 105). However, when the time required for four chimpanzees (having section either of all the forebrain commissures or retaining the anterior commissure intact) to learn the skill under visual guidance with the first hand was compared with the time taken for them to relearn it under similar conditions with the second hand, the least "savings" was found to be 60 per cent and the most was 76 per cent (Black & Myers, 1965, p. 55). These findings indicate either that subcortical pathways can participate within certain limits but not entirely with the forebrain commissures in the intermanual transfer of motor learning or that the second hemisphere to be tested received some relevant information during training of the first hand.

In their analysis of the intermanual transfer of a learned skill, Black and Myers (1965) have shown that it is immaterial for the performance of the split-brain chimpanzee whether it can see the task (i.e., the puzzle box and its hand) through the eye that was open during training or through the other eye: the critical factor determining the level of performance is whether the manipulations are made with the trained or untrained hand. Now previously (p. 36) we have seen that the split-brain animal generally can not solve a visual pattern discrimination problem through the untrained eye without relearning. Gazzaniga (1964) has carefully studied the performance of split-brain monkeys that were initially trained to make a visual pattern discrimination through a particular eye-hand combination and were then tested while forced to respond with the other hand—but still through the

10. The distinction between intermanual transfer of a tactile discrimination habit and of a motor skill is often arbitrary (for instance, in the case of a stylus maze). Black and Myers (1965, p. 58) state, "There is also strong evidence, from present work in the laboratory, that the same neural systems support transfer of both 'motor' skill and tactual learning."

same eye. He found an asymmetrical effect: good performance if training was through an ipsilateral eye-hand pair and the same eye but contralateral hand was tested; in contrast, no retention of the task if training was through a contralateral eye-hand pair and then the same eye but ipsilateral hand was tested. These results amplify and extend the earlier findings of Downer (1959).

Trevarthen (1965, p. 32) has likewise reported that performance on a visual discrimination task became defective for some hundreds of trials when a split-brain monkey, fully trained with both contralateral eye-hand combinations, was forced to use either ipsilateral eye-hand pair, even though the animal retained good proficiency on the same task with both contralateral eye-hand pairs. Such impaired performance when ipsilateral eye-hand combinations are tested is not seen in chiasma-sectioned monkeys having the forebrain commissures intact (Downer, 1959; Gazzaniga, 1964).

After practising on several tasks for a long period of time there was clear improvement. Eventually the split-brain subjects had compensated for the deficiencies of ipsilateral eye-hand co-ordination, and they then behaved, with all eye-hand combinations, about as well as normal animals (Trevarthen, 1965, p. 32).

So here again there is evidence that the fore-brain commissures are largely necessary for the control of the ipsilateral hand in the execution of a visual pattern discrimination learned in one hemisphere; but that alternative pathways can progressively assume this function. "The brain can change after surgery so as to prolong, and perhaps even to increase, the effects of separating the hemispheres, or else it can compensate for them almost completely" (Trevarthen, 1965, p. 34).

Similar observations have been made when the subject with commissure section is required to use one hand to locate a target seen in the opposite half-field of vision. Gazzaniga, Bogen, and

Sperry (1965, p. 224) describe how their patient was initially able to locate a left-sided visual stimulus only with the left hand and a stimulus falling into the right half-field only with the right hand (or verbally). However, "tests similar to the foregoing, repeated at 24 months after surgery, show the patient now is able to use either hand to locate the visual target in either half-field, indicating an increased control of the secondary hand" (p. 224).

In split-brain animals there is also some evidence of transient misreaching with ipsilateral eye-hand combinations. For example, Black and Myers (1965, p. 50) describe how one chimpanzee with section of all forebrain commissures "exhibited some initial imperfection in reaching for the reward on the wire and in placing his hand on the rotating turntable. The clumsiness occurred only in the ipsilateral eye-hand combinations and disappeared after several trials." Nevertheless, all their remaining split-brain animals performed the visuomotor pursuit tasks successfully from the outset, regardless of the eye and hand tested, and irrespective of the extent of their commissure sections. Gazzaniga (1964, p. 150) also found no inaccuracy of reaching with ipsilateral eye-hand pairs in the same split-brain monkeys that, with visual pattern discrimination problems, showed defective transfer from the contralateral to the ipsilateral eye-hand combinations. Accurate reaching and tracking performance, irrespective of the combination of eye and hand tested, was likewise reported by Myers, Sperry, and McCurdy (1962) in the split-brain monkey, a result obtained under quite different test conditions also by Bossom and Hamilton (1963). Gazzaniga (1966c) has shown that the ipsilateral motor efferent fibers are not necessary for ipsilateral eye-hand movements in the split-brain monkey, and has implicated nonvisual feedback systems resulting from eye, head and neck orientation movements.

Lastly, we have information from Gazzaniga, Bogen, and Sperry (1965, p. 224) that reaction times (RTs) are slowed to all visual stimuli after commissure section in their case I.[11] It is not recorded whether the RTs improved in the course of time in this patient. Trevarthen (1965, pp. 105–106) has observed that initially RTs were slowed in the split-brain monkey; but later, the RTs returned to their preoperative levels except that, when vision was restricted to the eye ipsilateral to the responding limb, the RTs remained longer and more varied.

If now we survey motor functions broadly, it appears that only in special circumstances is there severe deficit in the commissure-sectioned subject (e.g., in the intermanual transfer of skills, and in the change from contralateral to ipsilateral eye-hand pairs with visual pattern discriminations); and even then, such deficit is subtotal or impermanent. In most activities there are only occasional and transitory instances of motor defect (e.g. in bimanual skills, and in reaching). So we may conclude that the forebrain commissures are essential for some but largely dispensable for other kinds of visuomotor activity involving the left and right limbs.

Emotion

Gazzaniga (1966b) has investigated the emotional reactions of split-brain monkeys. The stimulus arousing the emotion (a toy snake) was presented briefly through one eye while the

11. We have not been able to include in our review findings on cases of callosal agenesis (a developmental absence of the corpus callosum); however, Jeeves (1965, pp. 88–90) has reported marked increases of RTs for crossed when compared with uncrossed stimulus-response conditions in each of two cases of agenesis. No differences between these two conditions were found by Gazzaniga et al. (1965, p. 232) for their second patient, and no comparative results are reported for their first patient. In evaluating all of these findings on RTs, it should be borne in mind that good evidence exists to suggest that any form of cerebral lesion can be associated with a lengthening of RTs, increased variability and with certain differential effects (Benton, Sutton, Kennedy, & Brokaw, 1962; Blackburn & Benton, 1955; Costa, 1962).

unrestricted animal was required to continue performing a visual pattern discrimination task seen only through the other eye. Initially, the emotive stimulus disrupted the visuomotor activity of the opposite hemisphere, but after 8 to 50 repeated presentations there was little or no interference with the opposite brain half. In a somewhat different situation, the split-brain monkey was shown the snake repeatedly through one eye so that the animal refused to continue with the discrimination problem when seen through that eye even after the snake had been removed; but when, after presentation of the snake, the discrimination problem was immediately switched to the other eye, the monkey either became more placid (if it had not been very severely aroused) or continued to show extreme emotional agitation (if it had previously been totally aroused). Gazzaniga (1965) has described similar investigations after commissure section in man. For example, presentation of emotionally arousing pictures to the minor hemisphere, within a series of emotionally neutral pictures presented to the major hemisphere, is followed by emotionally reactive behavior, such as a grin and change of voice, even when the patient is unable to verbalize the basis of this behavior. In discussing the results for the monkey he says (1966b, p. 34) that "emotionally traumatic stimulation of one half brain renders the opposite disconnected hemisphere equally disturbed and aroused. On the other hand, less vigorous presentation of such stimuli appears not to precipitate identical strong reactions in the unstimulated hemisphere." So there is both a threshold effect[12] related to the degree of arousal and, independently, an habituating or adapting effect related to the number of times the stimulus has been presented.

Downer (1961) has performed a different experiment. In two split-brain monkeys he made additional ablations of the right temporal pole and right amygdaloid complex respectively. Each

12. It will be recalled that Sechzer (1964) observed interocular transfer of learned visual pattern discriminations in the split-brain cat with shock but not with food reinforcement.

animal became tame and placid[13] when it could see only through the right eye but reacted in its naturally aggressive manner when it could see only through the left eye or when both eyes were opened. Animals lacking the forebrain commissures therefore have, within certain limits, two separate neural substrates for emotional reactions, each sensitive to stimulation in terms of its residual capacities.

Dominance

The usage of the term "cerebral dominance" has changed dramatically during the course of the last twelve years. Whereas traditionally speech, praxis, and gnosis were thought to be located exclusively in one (the major) hemisphere in man—namely the one opposite to the preferred hand—we now have evidence for the asymmetrical localization (to a varying extent) of many additional aspects of behavior and of many exceptions to the importance of hand preference. In this fresh light, we shall now discuss the evidence from commissure-sectioned subjects for the asymmetrical organization of speech, praxis, and visual-spatial functions in the human brain and then consider briefly some hints of a rudimentary kind of asymmetrical organization also in the monkey.

A case can be made both for and against the exclusive localization of speech in the major hemisphere on the original evidence presented by Gazzaniga, Bogen, and Sperry (1965) in respect of their cases I and II of commissure section. For while both patients were permanently unable to name any object seen in the left half-field or palpated in the left hand, the second patient showed progressive improvement during several months after the operation

13. Klüver and Bucy (1938) have shown that bilateral removal of the temporal lobes gives rise to a characteristic syndrome, one component of which is placidity.

at writing[14] with the left hand (p. 232). Moreover, this second patient could correctly select with the left hand from a series of objects or pictures the one that corresponded to an object-name briefly exposed as a word only in the left half-field of vision even though the word could not be reproduced verbally. Conversely, if an object was palpated in the left hand or its picture briefly flashed in the left half-field, the patient could correctly select the name corresponding to the object from a series of names printed on cards.

Though able to comprehend written material in either field, case II showed no ability at all to put together a longer word or a compound word that fell half in one field and half in the other. . . . With such a word as "heart" for example, with the fixation point falling between "he" and the "art," she would describe only the word "art" (Gazzaniga *et al.*, 1965, p. 233).

It seems from the reports of Gazzaniga, Bogen, and Sperry (1965) and Gazzaniga and Sperry (1967) that two of six cases of commissure section have shown the ability to comprehend verbal material through the minor hemisphere although neither patient could express the comprehension other than through a matching procedure (i.e., direct verbal expression of the word was not possible). Perhaps, then, the major hemisphere can sustain all speech functions (including verbal expression) while the minor hemisphere can support only the comprehension of speech[15] (and of course other nonverbal functions). However, as Gazzaniga, Bogen, and Sperry (1965, p. 234) put it: "lateral specialization including language functions . . . would appear to be subject to a

14. As will be described below, this patient was also able in the course of time to execute verbal commands with the left hand, so it could be that her writing with the left hand was controlled exclusively from the left hemisphere.

15. Our personal clinical experiences lead us to believe that severe and lasting expressive dysphasia is much more commonly seen than severe and lasting receptive dysphasia (i.e. comprehension defect) in cases of left-sided cerebral lesion. Moreover, Smith (1966) has reported a remarkable preservation of speech after left-sided hemispherectomy in a right-handed adult—with verbal comprehension less impaired than expression.

considerable range of individual variation." The brains of the two exceptional cases showing verbal comprehension through the minor hemisphere may, for reasons that can not yet be specified, have developed exceptional forms of organization that have no general implications.[16] Alternatively, the remaining cases of commissure section may have failed on being tested for comprehension of verbal material through the minor hemisphere because of damage to noncommissural brain structures (presumably in the minor hemisphere). Finally, despite the very strong behavioral evidence to the contrary presented by Sperry and Gazzaniga (1967), a remote possibility does remain, in the absence of post mortem verification, that part of the body of the corpus callosum was left intact in each of the two exceptional cases.[17]

Turning now to praxis, the coordination of so-called voluntary movements, we find a slightly different general outcome. As might be expected, no patient was impaired on any motor task with the right hand after commissure section. However, case I of Gazzaniga, Bogen, and Sperry (1962) was initially severely apraxic with the left hand. If he was asked "to repeat on command with the left hand any of these motor performances or even to make much simpler movements, the left arm and hand may fail to respond at all or the responses may be spasmodic and grossly inadequate. . . . In the early tests especially, a profound apraxia was apparent with respect to any independent movements of the left hand in response to a purely verbal command" (p. 1767). Nonetheless, starting about three months after the operation, there was some progressive improvement in executing verbal commands with the left hand, particularly if the experimenter demonstrated the movement (p. 1767); and after two years, considerable improvement in responding with the left hand and arm

16. It is unlikely on several lines of evidence (although this possibility can not be absolutely rejected) that the two exceptional patients learned only after surgery to comprehend verbal material through the minor hemisphere.

17. This proposal would not explain a variety of findings. However, it would successfully account for the various other residual abilities possessed only by these two and not the other cases of commissure section.

to test patterns flashed to the right half-field (Gazzaniga *et al.*, 1965, p. 225). These same authors report (p. 231) for case II that "the severe apraxia to verbal commands that has persisted in the preceding case was apparent here only in the early post-operative weeks."

Division of the forebrain commissures then reveals in both cases I and II a somewhat greater residual facility to execute movements than to produce speech when direct control by and access to the major hemisphere are precluded. As the left hand of case I was even from the outset after surgery "capable of refined inviduated finger movements and generally (was) adept and dextrous enough in the performance of familiar automatic activities such as handling and smoking a cigarette, lifting a coffee cup, putting on glasses, and the like" (Gazzaniga *et al.*, 1962, p. 1767), we consider it unlikely that any cortical damage to the minor hemisphere would lead before surgery to an unnatural dependence upon the commissures and major hemisphere for the control of the left hand. Moreover, there is no independent evidence whatsoever that the commissures were not completely transected in case I. The slow recovery of motor control of the left hand in this patient may then be the result of relearning either with the minor hemisphere or along the ipsilateral motor efferent pathways to the left hand from the major hemisphere.[18] The much more rapid recovery in the second patient may reflect in this particular case either a greater facility by the minor hemisphere to control movements to command of the left hand independently of the major hemisphere; or a stronger ipsilateral efferent projection from the left hemisphere; or some cross-communication between the hemispheres if (as has already been tentatively suggested for this patient) all the commissural fibers were not transected. At any rate, as in many other aspects of behavior, commissure section has again revealed a variable outcome that is inconstant in time.

18. It should be noted, however, that many of the so-called "uncrossed" motor efferent fibers do in fact decussate in the cord.

There is suggestive evidence from lesion studies in man that the minor hemisphere is more particularly concerned than the major hemisphere with visual-spatial functions, and also in a qualitatively different way (cf. Arrigoni & De Renzi, 1964, for a recent review). Referring to case I, Gazzaniga, Bogen, and Sperry (1965) write: "Following the commissurotomy, when he copied sample figures that suggested spatial perspective like the Necker cube, his performance with the left hand was considerably better than that with the right [see Fig. 2.5]. . . . The subject was always able to reconstruct standard patterns in a block design test and to assemble complex object puzzles with the left hand. Those patterns that were correctly reconstructed with the right hand were always extremely simple and done so only after much practice" (p. 227). This difference between the ability of the two hands persisted in case I but diminished over a period of seven months in case II.[19] Of interest, likewise, is the qualitative account given by Gazzaniga, Bogen, and Sperry (1965, p. 235): even though both patients were impaired at constructing designs with the right hand, they could use this hand to indicate which of five alternative designs was the correct one. "This shows that the primary perceptual capacity of the left dominant hemisphere is capable of discriminating between correct and incorrect reconstructions," that is, it can correctly match visual-spatial designs which it cannot construct.[20] So we have suggestive evidence of the lateralization of visual-spatial constructional abilities, but in this instance in favor of the minor hemisphere; and an unequivocal implication that the corpus callosum participates in the visual-spatial constructive performance of the right hand in the intact subject.

If now we consider the monkey, it is well established that the

19. We have seen that in the execution of verbal commands the right hand was more skillful than the left in both patients.

20. These findings would not have been predicted as a result of lesion studies, since the major hemisphere has been implicated in the executive aspects of construction and the minor hemisphere in the perceptual aspects by Arrigoni and De Renzi (1964), McFie and Zangwill (1960), and by Piercy, Hécaen, and Ajuriaguerra (1960).

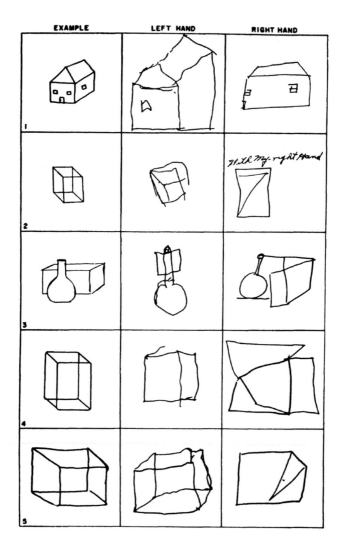

Figure 2.5 *Samples of the performance of case I with right and left hand in copying example figures, each trial being limited to three minutes. (From Gazzaniga, Bogen, & Sperry, 1965)*

majority of animals develop natural hand preferences (Brook-shire & Warren, 1962; Ettlinger & Moffett, 1964). It could there-fore be supposed that unilateral ablations from the hemisphere opposite the preferred hand might give rise to a different degree and/or kind of discrimination defect than comparable unilateral removals from the hemisphere on the same side as the preferred hand. We are not aware of any such findings. However, Gazzaniga (1963) has devised a most instructive alternative experiment. Three unoperated monkeys, with a natural preference for the right hand, were trained to perform a visual pattern discrimina-tion task. The two patterns, matched for light intensity, were located side by side and were seen during the initial training through both eyes. Only one hand could be used on any trial, but over a session equal use was secured of both hands by forced alternation every twenty or forty trials. After the animals had reached a standard level of performance, the various eye-hand combinations were separately tested: all the animals continued to perform at a high level irrespective of the eye-hand pair being used. Then the optic chiasma and forebrain commissures were divided and (after an interval) the animals were once again tested with each eye-hand combination. In every instance, the per-formance deteriorated considerably except when the right eye and left hand were tested. With this one particular combination, two of the three monkeys showed excellent performance throughout, and the third animal made rapid improvement coincidental with the disappearance of some initial moderate paralysis of the left arm.

Considering these findings on their own, we might be tempted to conclude that visual pattern learning takes place predomi-nantly in the hemisphere on the same side as the preferred hand in the monkey.[21] However, Gazzaniga (1963) provides grounds for

21. Applying the method of commissure section *after* training (see p. 69), Myers (1961) found that the changes consequent upon visual learning take place to some extent in both hemispheres in the cat; Ebner and Myers (1962b) and Semmes and Mishkin (1965a) have confirmed this result with tactile training in the monkey.

extreme caution: when two of the original three monkeys were taught to perform two new discrimination tasks binocularly and after surgery, testing with the four individual eye-hand pairs again indicated that learning had been confined to one hemisphere, but not necessarily the right hemisphere. In fact, in three of these four instances, learning took place predominantly in the left hemisphere. Further experiments along these lines are obviously needed with some urgency.[22] Meanwhile, it would be premature to conclude that dominance or lateral specialization in the hemispheres is an absolutely unique property of the human brain.

Important Variables

When first in the mid-1950's the animal work of Myers and Sperry heralded what we have called (p. 31) the "positive" period, the major variables to be examined in research on the functions of the commissures were (1) the sense-modality of the task (e.g., visual or tactile); (2) the dimension of stimulation (e.g., visual patterns or intensities); and (3) the level in the brain of the commissures concerned with a particular stimulus dimension in a particular sense-modality. By the end of the decade 1950–1960, a fourth major variable was also being evaluated: the species of the experimental subject. In the preceding section we have already

22. Despite Gazzaniga's own caution, it can be argued that his initial result, implicating the right hemisphere in right-handed monkeys, is valid, for the right hemisphere was retracted during surgery, and this might not have greatly affected learning that had already taken place but nonetheless might have increased the probability of any postoperative new learning taking place in the other, left-sided hemisphere. Trevarthen (1965, pp. 30–32) has pointed out that in most of his experiments with polarized light, learning took place in only one hemisphere even though both eyes were open; but the commissures were already divided before learning in his experiments, and there was no forced alternation between the hands.

considered these variables and seen how they can interact.[23]

More recently, increased emphasis has been falling on certain additional variables. Granted that we envisage a neural organization of behavior that is plastic as opposed to fixed, we nonetheless would wish to be able to specify all the factors that determine when a particular neural system does or does not sustain a particular kind of behavior. Now, whereas the general principles of the neural organization underlying the transmission of information between the hemispheres have already become manifest (and are unlikely to require any substantial modification), the more detailed and precise specification of the factors that determine the exceptions to the rules or principles has hardly begun. It is to be hoped that in the course of time we shall gain a full understanding of how these factors operate. Then observations that we now have to regard as exceptions to the rules will become examples of new and additional rules, governing not so much the basic organization of the brain, but rather what we have termed its "plasticity." In the meantime, following an earlier precedent (Ettlinger, 1965, p. 148; Myers, 1965, p. 148), we can only hint at some of the additional factors that may prove to be important in determining the behavioral outcome of commissure section.

Set

It is possible to gain some understanding of the importance of set from an experiment by Ettlinger and Morton (1966). They trained unoperated monkeys and monkeys having cortical ablations to solve in the dark a tactile size-discrimination problem.

23. For example it was noted (on pp. 38–41) that the interocular transfer of simultaneous visual intensity discriminations may be more closely dependent upon the forebrain commissures in the chiasma-sectioned monkey than cat; but there is no such species difference with pattern discriminations. We have not been able to discuss one important phylogenetic effect: learning through one hemisphere alone in the split-brain animal when compared with learning through both hemispheres in the intact animal is often impaired in the rat and cat but not in the monkey or chimpanzee.

During this training the animals were not restricted in the use of either hand, but subsequently in half of the animals the preferred hand (in the other half the nonpreferred hand) was restrained by attaching a weighted rubber ball to a bracelet on one wrist. The performance of some animals on the size-discrimination task then deteriorated substantially over 10–40 trials even though the first hand to be tested was the previously preferred hand in certain animals. The animals next learned a tactile object-discrimination problem with the first hand. Then this hand was restrained and the animals were tested on the original size-discrimination problem for forty trials with the second hand. Again certain animals showed initial impairment even though some might be using the originally preferred hand. However, all animals next showed excellent immediate intermanual transfer on the object discrimination task.

These findings indicate that alteration of the test conditions, only to the extent of restraining one and then the other hand, can in some animals produce suboptimal performance, at least transiently. Since poor initial performance with the second hand can be misinterpreted as due to the absence of immediate intermanual transfer, it seems important to provide a "set" for optimal performance in these new conditions. Semmes and Mishkin (1965a, p. 62) have also reported occasional poor transfer in unoperated monkeys when the second hand had not first been adapted on preliminary easy tasks. In vision, Gazzaniga (1966a) has recent findings of poor interocular transfer in chiasma-sectioned monkeys having their callosum intact.

No real confusion is likely to ensue, however, if in the absence of an appropriate set, there is equal impairment in control and commissure sectioned animals. If, on the other hand, some kind of interaction were to occur between the lack of set and the commissure section, then poor performance with the second hand could (and most probably would) be attributed directly to the commissure section. As noted above (p. 44), Meikle, Sechzer, and Stellar (1962) have shown that a few shock reinforcements to the second limb are needed to promote good intermanual transfer under certain conditions in the split-brain cat. Similarly, Russell and Ochs (1963) found in the rat that a lever-pressing response learned through only one hemisphere is transferred when tested through only the other hemisphere, provided that reinforcement is given on a single trial while both hemispheres are functional.[24] We might interpret these findings as resulting from the lack, after training through only one hemisphere, of a rather specific set to utilize a limited degree of learning that has taken place in the second hemisphere (i.e., as an interaction between an inadequate set and a surgical or functional dissociation of the hemispheres).

So far we have considered some illustrations of the specific influence of set on transfer behavior. Glickstein and Sperry (1960) have shown how a much more general set (called by them a "tactile-testing habit," or the acquired set to compare test objects by palpation in particular test conditions) can transfer intermanually in the split-brain monkeys even when there is little or no transfer of a specific discrimination habit. These authors have also devised a procedure for distinguishing between such general and the more specific transfer. Ranging even more widely, it may also be that the cumulative past training history of a split-brain animal could influence its degree of dependence upon a particular commissural system. However, we know of no evidence bearing conclusively on this point.

Age

At present we have no published results of the comparative effects of commissure section in neonatal and adult animals. This problem

24. These experiments were not performed on split-brain rats but on animals having first one and then the other hemisphere "depressed" by the application of a chemical agent; it is possible that the single reinforcement may have acted not on both hemispheres together but particularly on the untrained hemisphere (which was tested for transfer by the method of extinction, not of reinforcement), so that there might still be transfer to the second hemisphere even if the first hemisphere were to be depressed during the single trial of reinforcement.

has been explicitly raised by Ettlinger (1965, p. 148), Jeeves (1965, p. 107), and Myers (1965, p. 148). Extrapolating from the results of ablation experiments, it might be predicted that section of the forebrain commissures in neonatal animals will impair the exchange of information between the hemispheres less severely than in adult (or adolescent) animals. However, such a prediction cannot be made with real confidence. First, there may be a lesser degree of equipotentiality between the several commissures than between individual cortical regions in the neonate. Second, we have largely positive evidence of deficit in cases of callosal agenesis (Jeeves, 1965).[25] There is, then, an obvious need for an empirical, as opposed to speculative, solution to this problem.[26]

Not, strictly speaking, related to age but rather to the simple passage of time, is the evidence of recovery of function after surgery. In discussing cases I and II of Gazzaniga, Bogen, and Sperry (1965) we have already cited (see pp. 53–57) examples of improvement on a variety of tasks during the course of the initial two years after surgery. Geschwind (1965, pp. 101–102) has noted that the findings in the cases of Akelaitis (1944) may have been negative partly because the testing was carried out after a degree of recovery had already taken place. It is not clear at present whether we can explain the progressive recovery of cases I and II in terms of improved functioning of subcortical commissures or of ipsilateral pathways or of cortical systems in the other hemisphere (or by a combination of these for different kinds of performance). It would not be difficult in animal experiments to identify the neural system responsible for the recovery. However, there is as yet no solid evidence (as far as we are aware) of progressive recovery

25. This point is not compelling, as there has been much discussion of how far the behavioral defects reported in cases of agenesis may reflect associated brain pathology instead of the simple absence of commissural pathways.

26. Geschwind (1965b, p. 102) has raised a related but not identical problem: to what extent the onset of epilepsy in *early childhood* may have contributed to the largely negative results reported after callosal section in *adult* patients by Akelaitis (1944).

after commissure section in animals. Perhaps a careful comparative analysis would reveal relatively more recovery in the chimpanzee than in the monkey, so that the relevant experiments could then be performed in this species.

Difficulty

We have already recorded (see p. 38) that the interocular transfer of intensity and color discriminations generally survives, whereas the transfer of pattern discriminations generally fails in split-brain animals. The learning scores, however, tend to be greater with pattern than with other kinds of visual discrimination, implying that the former is more difficult. Also Meikle and Sechzer (1960) and Meikle (1960) have found little or no transfer with difficult (i.e., near threshold) as compared with easy intensity discriminations in the split-brain cat. Perhaps, then, the dimension of visual stimulation per se is unimportant while the critical variable is task difficulty: the subcortical commissures (on this argument) would be capable of transmitting information related to easy but not to difficult visual-discrimination tasks, whatsoever the dimension. We still lack conclusive experiments on this point. With tactile learning, it appears from the report of Semmes and Mishkin (1965a, p. 62) that the intermanual transfer of easy but not difficult discrimination problems survives transection of the forebrain commissures. Similarly, Ettlinger and Morton (1966) concluded that the good intermanual transfer of their split-brain monkeys could be related, at least in part, to the low level of task difficulty employed. On the other hand, the findings of Gazzaniga, Bogen, and Sperry (1965) for man do not support this line of argument. For instance, their case II could not indicate whether two colors flashed to the two half-fields were the same (p. 232). Therefore it would be premature to conclude that the level of task difficulty is by itself a major determinant of the survival of transfer after section of the forebrain commissures.[27]

In ablation experiments, Orbach and Fantz (1958) have established that overtraining reduces the discrimination defect otherwise expected to follow a cortical removal. Ettlinger (1962) has argued that with training to a standard level (i.e., until a given proportion of a fixed number of trials is correct), the animal is bound to receive more overtraining during performance at criterion on easy rather than on difficult discrimination problems. Therefore experiments are needed to examine transfer in split-brain animals when (1) stimulus dimension, (2) level of task difficulty, and (3) degree of overtraining are varied independently of each other. Following a similar line of reasoning, it also seems important to inquire whether more commissural fibers are necessary for the efficient transfer of a difficult compared with an easy discrimination task—by making partial transections of varying extent within the forebrain commissural system.

Additional Pathology

Gazzaniga, Bogen, and Sperry (1965) and also Sperry and Gazzaniga (1967) have repeatedly warned that certain kinds of impairment in some of their human patients may not have resulted directly from transection of the forebrain commissures. It is difficult to exclude the possibility that certain new postoperative defects are a consequence of damage to the hemispheres even when such damage has preceded the commissure section. For preoperatively the patient's behavior may have remained unimpaired (despite the presence of pathology) because the commissures were intact and able to participate in the functioning of an alternative or substitute neural system; such a substitute system may have been deprived of its input or output connections

27. Myers (1965, pp. 4–6) has reviewed compelling evidence in the cat of less effective transmission of information across the forebrain commissures when task difficulty is increased *within* one dimension (visual patterns).

or otherwise isolated by the commissure section, so that the behavioral consequences of the preoperative pathology then became manifest in addition to the direct effects of transecting the commissures. Damage to the hemispheres can also occur during the surgical procedure for commissure section. A rapid and uncomplicated postoperative recovery would tend to exclude this, whereas a stormy course during the first few days after surgery might give rise to suspicion.

Even so the role of additional pathology is complex. Glickstein and Sperry (1960) have suggested that unilateral cortical damage may promote transfer in the split-brain monkey because the animal might both learn and be tested for transfer through the single intact hemisphere, irrespective of the laterality of the inflow. Also Geschwind (1965b, p. 102) has proposed that their long-standing epilepsy may have opened up alternative routes of communication across the midline in the cases of Akelaitis (1944) and that such routes could then, in part, support the exchange of information after commissure section. So the various modes of operation of hemispheric damage of different kinds and durations remain to be further explored.

Other Variables

We have not completely exhausted the list of factors that can influence the outcome of commissure section. For example, Trevarthen (1965, pp. 35–38) has stressed the importance of oculomotor orienting reactions in connection with the reduced visual fields of animals having the optic chiasma sectioned. And there are yet other variables that may prove to be important but at the moment are still poorly understood. We shall not pursue them further now because we have already given sufficient indication of the complexity of such variables, and because as a result of future experiments these remaining factors may come to be understood as further examples of the important variables we have already discussed.[28]

Problems of Localization

We can formulate the following three basic questions: (1) Which commissures are necessary for the exchange of particular kinds of information? (2) Is one particular subdivision or sector of a commissure (or commissural system) especially important for the exchange of a particular kind of information? (3) How far do investigations utilizing commissure section contribute to an identification of the neural structures that sustain various kinds of behavior?

In connection with the first question, we have already seen that there is no constant relationship between the task and the level in the brain at which the information is transferred across the midline. The particular test conditions may be as important as the task in determining the capacity of the individual commissures to transfer information. We might also note that as yet there are no experiments in animals to distinguish between the roles of the posterior commissure and commissure of the superior colliculi; that in man no midbrain commissures have been cut in association with transection of the forebrain commissures; that as yet the midbrain commissures have not been cut without section of the forebrain commissures; and that it has so far not been found practicable to divide the hippocampal commissure without involvement of the corpus callosum.

As regards the second question, Myers and his colleagues have examined in a series of careful analyses the contribution made by various subdivisions of the forebrain commissural system to the exchange of visual, tactile, and motor information in a variety of

28. Perhaps an oculomotor orienting reaction should be considered as a specific set (cf. p. 61) that must be acquired for adequate performance in the presence of a field defect.

species. The interested reader can be referred to their work on this topic in primates: Myers and Ebner (1962), Black and Myers (1964, 1965), as well as to Gazzaniga (1966a). The functions of the anterior body of the corpus callosum and of the genu are still totally unknown.

In the context of our predominant emphasis on the brain's plasticity, we cannot give even as much as a thumbnail sketch of the many investigations undertaken to identify the structural basis of various forms of behavior and employing commissural section to achieve that end. In any case, a sharp distinction cannot be drawn between experiments directed at elucidating commissure function and experiments utilizing commissure section to explore the function of related structures. Fortunately, a comprehensive review by Sperry (1961) already exists. We shall therefore deal with only a single problem that will be seen to be very closely related to other issues already raised by us: how far have studies involving the section of commissures advanced our knowledge of the neural basis of learning?

It will be recalled that in simple transfer tests the subject learns a problem through one hemisphere after commissure section, and his performance is then assessed on the same problem through the other hemisphere. Myers (1957, 1961) has devised a complementary procedure: he trained animals on a problem while the sensory inflow was restricted to one hemisphere, only then sectioned the forebrain commissures, and finally tested for transfer on the same problem with the inflow confined to the other hemisphere. This training paradigm has been adopted also by Ebner and Myers (1962b), Meikle, Sechzer, and Stellar (1962), and Semmes and Mishkin (1965a). The outcome varies with the level of the task difficulty. With difficult discrimination problems, the neural changes underlying the "memory trace" are laid down during the original learning for the most part only in the hemisphere that received the afferent inflow. If, subsequently, transfer is tested through the second hemisphere after an intervening commissural section, performance is generally poor, indicating that only a very weak memory trace was laid down in this hemisphere during the original training through the other hemisphere;[29] but if transfer is tested through the untrained hemisphere without any intervening commissure section, performance is good, indicating presumably a capacity of the untrained hemisphere to "refer back" through the commissural pathways to the memory trace laid down in the trained hemisphere. However, with easy discrimination problems, almost equivalent memory traces are laid down in both hemispheres during learning, so that performance is adequate after commissure section even through the untrained hemisphere.[30]

A different procedure can be adopted to answer the same question. Animals can be trained to perform a discrimination problem with the sensory inflow restricted to one hemisphere. Subsequently, various structures can be destroyed in the trained hemisphere. Performance can then be tested either through the trained hemisphere or, if blindness or paralysis resulting from the destruction prevents this, through the untrained hemisphere that is still connected to the trained hemisphere by the intact commissural pathways. This kind of experiment has been undertaken, with various unilateral cortical removals, by Myers and Sperry (1958) for vision in the cat, by Semmes and Mishkin (1965a) for touch in the monkey, and by Butler (1966) for vision in the monkey. Because animal species, sense-modality, and level of task difficulty have been confounded we cannot yet draw any firm conclusions except that the memory trace is laid down predominantly in the trained hemisphere, at least with difficult discrimination problems. Using a modified procedure, commissure section has been combined with unilateral destruction of parts of the limbic system. On testing the animal through the damaged

29. If the trained hemisphere is tested for retention after commissure section, performance is excellent.

30. It will be seen that the "double" learning under these conditions is in conflict with the evidence that learning is confined to a single hemisphere, discussed at length earlier, unless task difficulty ultimately emerges as a critical variable.

hemisphere an impairment of tactile reversal learning has been reported in cats by Teitelbaum (1964) and Webster and Voneida (1964) and of tactile discrimination learning in monkeys by Ettlinger and Morton (1966).

It should be feasible to teach a human subject to make visual and tactile discriminations of unfamiliar nonverbal material through one half-field and one hand before surgical section of the commissures, and then test for transfer through the other hemisphere after surgery. To our knowledge this has not yet been done.

Summary and Conclusions

We have tried to give some indication of the progress made in a rapidly expanding field during the past fifteen years. It should be evident that no one would now seriously inquire whether the commissures are of functional importance in the neural organization of behavior[31]—because Myers and Sperry have given us a conclusive "yes." Nor are we still asking which tasks can and which cannot be effectively transferred after section of the forebrain commissures—because we now know or suspect that motivation, set, age, and dimension and difficulty of the task as well as other factors can determine the outcome of a transfer experiment. We have regarded such variations in outcome as illustrations of the brain's "plasticity": under certain conditions the subcortical commissures acquire the capacity to take over some of the functions normally sustained by the forebrain commissures, or the ipsilateral projection systems can attain greater functional importance, or cortical systems in an isolated hemisphere come to function in a way previously not possible. Such plasticity is not a consequence uniquely of commissure section, nor can studies of

31. It is true that the direct evidence of commissure function has been derived (at least in the animal experiments) as a result of unnatural restrictions of the sensory inflow; but if the commissures can function in the exchange of information under these unnatural conditions it is probable that they perform similar functions in the intact subject.

commissure function be meaningfully distinguished from experiments that make use of commissure section to investigate other problems of brain function, for example, the course and localization of the formation of the memory trace.

We have become aware that considerable gaps still remain. This applies in particular to our knowledge of commissural functioning in man. There exists a real need for additional kinds of clinical testing. Certain discrepancies may ultimately be explained by invoking cortical damage (that varies from patient to patient) or even more basic interindividual differences in brain organization, but we have also raised the remote possibility of subtotal commissure section in some patients when post mortem verification is lacking. Despite the lacunae and discrepancies, the broad principles of commissure function seem securely established.

As in other branches of neuropsychology, we have now reached the stage of systematic and quantitative manipulation of selected variables that we know to be important for the outcome of commissure section. We should be prepared for complex interactions among these variables, and scrupulous attention may have to be given to control procedures. In this way we would hope to be able to add substantially to the general picture of commissure function as we see it today, by focusing bit by bit on the finer structure. It is unlikely that we shall see any important modification of the general theme, but much detail remains to be filled in.

3

Neuropsychological
Studies of the Phantom

Sidney Weinstein

Phantoms following amputations have been long known and extensively reported, but, unfortunately, little studied. In the first published description of the phantom limb, Ambroise Paré wrote in 1551, "Verily it is a thing wondrous strange and prodigious, and which will scarse be credited, unlesse by such as have seene

The research of the author and his associates described in this chapter was supported by grants from the Vocational Rehabilitation Administration (RD–1495-M), the National Institute of Neurological Diseases and Stroke (NB07404–01), and the National Aeronautics and Space Administration (NsG 489). The author is also grateful to the Korein Foundation for supporting the preparation of this manuscript.

with their eyes, and heard with their eares the patients who have many moneths after the cutting away of the Legge, greviously complained that they yet felt exceeding great paine of the Leg so cut of . . ." (Paré, 1952, p. 147).

Before we discuss our studies of the phantom, the question may arise: why does a neuropsychologist study phantoms? The answer, given by the eminent British neurologist, Sir Henry Head, to which we subscribe is that we study disease processes, not for their intrinsic interest, but rather for the information they provide us in laying bare the normal processes of the organism. The relationship between somatosensation and phantoms may not be apparent. However, if we understand how an individual can report sensation in a missing or deafferent limb, we have increased our understanding of the sensory process in general.

Kipling wrote in *Kim*, "Chela know this. There are a great many lies in the world and not a few liars, but there are no liars like our bodies, except it be the sensations of our bodies." The phantom, albeit such a lie, is nevertheless a valuable one to the psychologist; in the process of misinforming us that a missing appendage is present, we learn that the limbs we perceive are literally unnecessary for the perception of those limbs.

Our understanding of the relationship between brain mechanisms and behavior, the ultimate goal of the neuropsychologist, has been enhanced by our studies of the phantom. In the course of our research, we have studied the phantom after total or partial amputation of upper or lower extremities, orchiectomy, peotomy, mastectomy, para- and quadriplegia, and congenital absence of limbs. We have studied preference for bodily parts in normal men and women, as well as after mastectomy, and have studied somatic sensation in normal individuals and on the stumps and homologous areas in individuals after amputation. The program of research dealing with these interrelated topics is described below.

History of the Phantom

Literary References to the Phantom

Phantoms have not been unknown in folklore or the popular literature. That a considerable literary mystique has developed about the phantom is not surprising, since it is a phenomenon widely believed to be apparently delusional and hallucinatory in individuals who are otherwise mentally competent.

Literature, historical and fictional, abounds with references to men who have lost limbs. We all recall Captain Hook, Long John Silver, Peter Stuyvesant, and Hemingway's fishing boat captain. Lord Nelson expressed the belief that his experience of a phantom arm constituted proof of the soul.

The treatment by Remarque in *All Quiet on the Western Front* of a painful phantom, experienced by a wounded soldier who had awakened unaware that his leg had been amputated, remains one of the most graphic literary and cinematic portrayals of the phantom.

Melville's protagonist, Captain Ahab, had a vivid phantom which he picturesquely describes:

Look ye carpenter, I dare say thou callest thyself a right good workmanlike workman, eh? Well, then, will it speak thoroughly well for thy work, if, when I come to mount this leg thou makest, I shall nevertheless feel another leg in the same identical place with it; that is, carpenter, my old lost leg; the flesh and blood one, I mean. Canst thou not drive that old Adam away?

Truly, sir, I begin to understand somewhat now. Yes, I have heard something curious on that score, sir; how that a mismasted man never entirely loses the feeling of his old spar, but it will be still pricking him at times. May I humbly ask if it be really so, sir?

It is man. Look, put thy live leg here in the place where mine was; so now, here is only one distinct leg to the eye, yet two to the soul. Where thou feelest tingling life, there, exactly there, there to a hair, do I. Is't it a riddle?

I should humbly call it a poser, sir.

Scientific References to the Phantom

Despite Paré's early report, it was not until 1798 that the first systematic inquiry into the nature of the phantom was attempted (Lemos, 1798). Less than fifty years later, Valentin (1844) presented a rather sophisticated hypothesis, for that time, associating phantoms (of congenitally absent parts!) with cortical somatic representation. As we have documented (Vetter & Weinstein, 1967), Valentin's observations have, unfortunately, until now, been almost totally ignored. During the remainder of the nineteenth century an impressive array of papers containing excellent descriptions of phantoms appeared, along with some unique ideas as to their significance.

Guéniot (1861) first described what still appears to be the most unusual phenomenal character of the phantom, namely, its tendency to shorten with time. For him the presence of the phantom indicated that the wound was healing and that the patient was making a good recovery. In addition to coining the term "phantom," Mitchell (1871, 1872), the Civil War surgeon and novelist, provided the first extensive, accurate description of the phantom in the English language. One of his findings, e.g., that phantoms are almost universal (84 of his 90 cases) following major limb amputation, has since been repeatedly confirmed. In addition, his demonstration that electrical stimulation of the stump could evoke a phantom that had long since disappeared gave the first clear evidence relating the origin of phantoms to neurophysiological factors.

William James' (1887) description of phantoms closely parallels that of Mitchell's. In his typically concise manner he wrote that the phantom "varies from acute pain, pricking, itching, burning, cramp, uneasiness, numbness, etc., in the toes, heel, or other place, to feelings which are hardly perceptible. . . . The hand and foot are usually the only lost parts very distinctly felt, the intervening tracts seeming to disappear. A man, for example, whose arm was cut-off at the shoulder-joint told me that he felt his hand budding immediately from his shoulder" (p. 250). Although he studied a reasonably large sample ($N = 185$), the results were, in James' words, disappointing. That the data were obtained from a self-administered questionary was possibly one contributing factor. A second, possibly, more likely factor was that James chose a Darwinian-functionalistic philosophical approach. He commented, "The feeling of the lost foot tells us absolutely nothing which can practically be of use to us. It is a superfluous item in our conscious baggage. Why may it not be that some of us are able to cast it out of our mind on that account?" (p. 254).

Pitres (1897) must be credited for an early exposition of a basic physiological theory of the phantom. A popular theory at the time specified that "mental representation of movement" (e.g., hand-clenching) produced voluntary phantom movements of a limb. This concept, with its dependence upon central mechanisms, was rejected by Pitres, who after observations on the effects of stump stimulation concluded that "it is certain that the majority of the illusory sensations of amputees are subordinated to the irritation of the nerve fibers of the stump" (p. 179). The attribution of phantoms to irritation of the nerves of the stump may be considered one of the first expositions of phantom etiology based upon peripheral, rather than central nervous system, or mentalistic or emotional factors.

Today, opinions continue to differ on the origin of the phantom. Moreover, some investigators have unfortunately failed to differentiate between the phantom and the patient's reactions to it or to environmental stresses. Such failings are manifested chiefly in the theories of phantoms based upon psychoanalytic interpretation, and more appropriately termed "need" or "fantasy" theories. Thus, for example, one frequently finds statements such as "it seems more likely that its origin [phantom pain] is central, that is, intracranial, and most probably psychic. Some of the evidence in our cases suggests the probability that it is some form of obsession neurosis" (Bailey & Moersch, 1941, p. 42).

In contrast to phantoms of the limbs, the existence of such sensations for other appendages is less well documented. Nevertheless, phantoms do occur following amputation of the breast (e.g., Ackerly, Lhamon, & Fitts, 1955), male genitalia (e.g. Heusner, 1950), and facial parts (e.g., Hoffman, 1954). The literature on phantoms exclusive of amputations in adults is less extensive; however, it is worth citing. In chronological order of first reporting are the following observations: phantoms in cases of congenital aplasia (Valentin, 1836); limb phantom resulting from complete spinal cord transection (Riddoch, 1917) or anesthesia (Van Bogaert, 1934); phantom due to brachial plexus lesions (Mayer-Gross, 1929) or anesthesia (Tatlow & Oulton, 1955); phantom following amputation in infancy (18 months) (Critchley, 1955); finally the apparent lack of phantom following absorption of digits due to Hansen's disease (Simmel, 1956).

The earlier studies have shown clearly the pervasiveness of the phantom within certain patient groups. Also, some previous reports have shown that peripheral or central intervention (stump stimulation; plastic surgery of the stump, Kallio, 1949; or cerebrovascular accident, e.g., Head & Holmes, 1911) may drastically alter the phantom for an extended period of time. In addition, there have been systematic studies of one or more physiological parameters (e.g., Bors, 1951; Cronholm, 1951; Katz, 1920; Weinstein, 1963a).

The purpose of the continuing research program described below is the systematic and comprehensive study of the physiological and experiential events associated with phantoms, in large groups of subjects, and in varying sites of amputation or deafferentation.

Definition of the Phantom

As a first step in understanding the phantom, we have operationally defined it: *The phantom is the report of the awareness of a nonexistent or deafferent bodily part in a mentally competent individual.*

The word "report" has been used because, to date, the phantom is still an entirely subjective phenomenon. That is, we rely solely upon the patient's statement that he has sensations of the missing or deafferent parts. The word "awareness" was employed to distinguish the varieties of sensations found from the term "pain," which has commonly and uncritically been employed in the literature for all phantom sensations. At one time we might have used the word "amputated" where now we use the word "nonexistent," since a phantom is a sensation not only of amputated bodily parts but also of congenitally absent bodily parts. The word "deafferent" was employed since, as we have pointed out, it occurs in cases of paraplegia, brachial plexus injury, and indeed almost any functional or anatomical separation of receptors from the primary projection area in the cortex. We have employed the term "bodily part" rather than "limb" because there are many cases in which appendages such as the testes, the breast, the tongue, facial parts, etc., have yielded phantoms upon amputation. Finally, the definition has been qualified to restrict it to *mentally competent* individuals in order to exclude its use in cases of psychosis, or anosognosia, in which individuals with cerebral involvement deny the impairment of bodily parts. Although the latter phenomenon may be related to the phantom, it seems worthwhile from the vantage point of current research procedures to consider such phenomena separately, at this point.

Theories of the Phantom

In spite of the hundreds of papers on the subject of the phantom, there are only three basic theories: (1) the fantasy or need theory,

(2) the peripheral theory, and (3) the central theory. Let us consider each one briefly.

The Fantasy Theory

The fantasy theory proposes that the amputee so greatly needs the part that he unconsciously imagines that it is there (e.g., "represents a substitute for some desired wish as well as punishment"— Bressler, Cohen, & Magnussen, 1955). In rejecting this view the following abundant evidence is adduced.

1. Sensations are a most drastic manifestation of a need. There are no other psychological "needs" that result in hallucinations. Thus, orphans do not hallucinate their absent parent.

2. Phantoms are universal in some populations of patients; fantasies are never so consistent.

3. If phantoms are fantasies, it is difficult to understand why they are so often: (a) painful, (b) telescoped, (c) shrunken, and (d) misshapen. Fantasies typically involve wish-fulfilment rather than such undesirable distortion.

4. It seems evident that the "need" for a missing limb does not differ among young children. However, the proportion of phantoms of appendages in children of the same age is a monotonic function of the age at which the amputation occurred or whether it was congenital. If "need" were to dictate the existence of a phantom, one should expect that the age at which the amputation occurred would be irrelevant to the proportion perceiving it.

5. It has frequently been reported that phantoms of amputated limbs frequently tend to shrink, fade, or telescope in time; such phenomena are difficult to understand in the framework of a fantasy theory.

6. Finally, during spinal anesthesia, when the patient has no apparent reason to fantasy his anesthetic but otherwise normal legs, he often perceives phantoms of his legs in incorrect positions.

The Peripheral Theory

The peripheral theory ascribes the phantom to sensations that arise from stump nerve endings that are "triggered off" by irritants such as neuromata, scar tissue, anoxia, etc. Sensations are then "assigned" to parts originally supplied by those fibers. Although there is a rational basis for such a theory, it has been discredited today by most neurosurgeons (e.g., Livingston, 1945). Thus, most phantoms tend to return, or to persist, after corrective surgery, blocking of nerves, dorsal rhizotomy, sympathectomy, etc., and when they return, the order is opposite to that of telescoping. In addition, phantoms frequently occur immediately after amputation, long before neuromata can form, and exist in some cases of aplasia of limbs in which there are neither neuromata nor other peripheral irritants.

Central Theories

Central theories, in general, attribute the presence of the phantom to activity within the cortical projection areas which subserved the missing or deafferented bodily parts. Such activity is hypothesized as occurring spontaneously, in some states, or through excitatory processes from neighboring projection or other cortices (Weinstein & Sersen, 1961).

The evidence for these theories is good. First, the frequency, vividness, duration, etc., of the amputation phantom seem to be related to the actual size of the cortical sensory homunculus (the cortical representation of bodily parts). Penfield stimulated the cortex of an amputee during a craniotomy for the relief of epilepsy and thereby evoked a phantom of the missing part. He then excised that area of the cortex and found that the phantom was abolished (Hécaen, Penfield, Bertrand, & Malmo, 1956). The historical report of Head and Holmes (1911) and recently completed work (Weinstein, Vetter, Shapiro, and Sersen) have also demonstrated the effects of brain damage on the phantom.

In addition, our studies (Shapiro, 1966; Weinstein, Sersen, & Vetter, 1964) and those of Katz (1920), Teuber, Krieger, and Bender (1949), and Haber (1955) show greater tactual sensitivity (not hyperalgesia) of the stump in comparison to that of homologous contralateral regions. This increased sensitivity could result from the same factors that produce the denervation super-sensitivity described by Cannon and Rosenblueth (1949). A second possibility to account for such enhanced sensitivity is that the cortical regions which subserved sensation of amputated (or congenitally absent) parts no longer do so, and hence become "more available" for representation of bodily parts (i.e., stump of the limb) that are subserved by neighboring cortices.

Mountcastle and Powell (1959) have reported that stimulation of distal parts of a limb may inhibit cortical evoked potentials from stimulation of more proximal parts when both areas are simultaneously stimulated. A third alternative hypothesis to account for the fact that amputation results in enhanced sensitivity of stump areas, therefore, is that amputation may remove a potentially inhibitory region to more proximal ones and may thus effect greater sensitivity of the stump.

Having considered the three current major theories of the phantom, let us turn to some recent empirical studies, to determine how the resulting data conform to existing theories, and to demonstrate how they have led to a new theory of phantom etiology.

Recent Studies of the Phantom

Phantoms after Paraplegia or Quadriplegia

As part of our program of research on various causes of the phantom, we studied a group of 150 men with transection of the

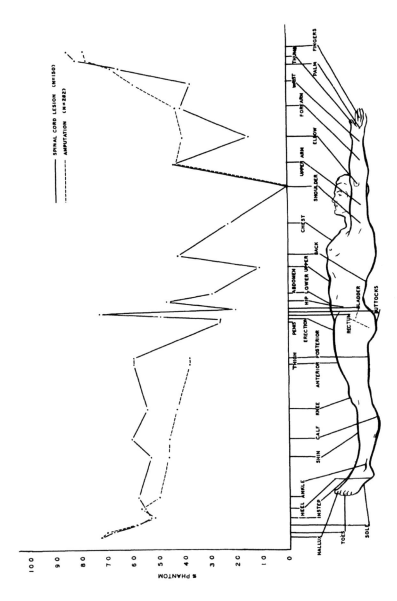

Figure 3.1   *Percentage of phantoms as a function of bodily part in 150 patients with spinal cord transection and 282 patients with various amputations.*

spinal cord (Weinstein, 1963a). The data were derived from responses to a comprehensive questionary individually administered as an interview.

Reinterviewing 42 of the men after a seven-month delay demonstrated predominantly statistically significant reliability of their reports and also gave an indication of the stability of the phenomena.

Figure 3.1 shows the percentage of phantoms of various bodily parts in all 150 cases of spinal cord injury and in 282 individuals with amputations.

First, it was rather interesting to learn that 100 per cent of the paraplegics studied had a phantom of one or more parts at some time after the injury. There were two patients who, although having lost their phantom, had experienced it at one time. Second, there was no single bodily part that was experienced as a phantom by all subjects.

We find a general tendency for bodily parts innervated by the sacral and caudal lumbar nerves to show a greater frequency of phantoms than those parts innervated by the rostral lumbar and thoracic areas. This trend holds true both for the paraplegics and those with amputations. There is also a large frequency of the phantom for the rectum and the buttocks. At present we cannot yet account for this reversal of the general tendency, except to note that these parts, as are the toes, are within the sacral and caudal lumbar dermatomes.

If the central theory is valid, then knowledge of the relationship of the phantom to the physiological variables should provide us with the chief means by which to predict (and ultimately control) the existence and character of the phantom (particularly the painful phantom).

Quality of the Phantom

Our study of adult paraplegics is a step in that direction. Let us consider, e.g., the quality of the phantom in paraplegics (Fig.

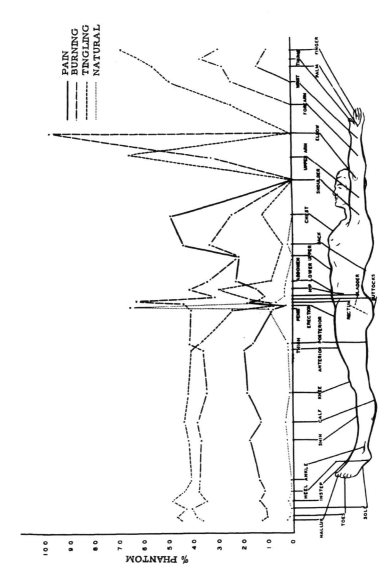

Figure 3.2 *Percentage of phantoms as a function of quality of sensation.*

3.2). First, note that for the lower extremity there is a consistent proportionality of the phantom for quality of the sensation perceived. That is, the curves representing tingling, burning, pain, and natural phantoms show a consistent relationship from the hallux to the posterior thigh. It can be seen that the most frequent sensation is tingling for these bodily parts, with burning sensations a close second. In general, however, the most frequent sensation obtained overall was burning (65.3%), the second, tingling (50.0%), the third, pain (42.0%), and finally, natural (21.3%). Other sensations including coldness, numbness, etc., were obtained, but much less frequently. Since the combination of burning and pain was perceived by the majority of patients, it is, therefore, not surprising to discover that 54 per cent of the patients had a "dislike attitude" for their phantom, whereas only 29 per cent were indifferent toward it, and only 17 per cent liked it.

Etiology of Paraplegia

Let us consider the causes of the paraplegia and their relationship to the phantom. The three etiological categories employed, roughly ranked in terms of speed of onset of injury, were: missile wounds, accident (fracture or compression), and disease process. Figure 3.3 shows the following highly significant relationships for quality of sensations among the etiologies studied: pain was produced most often by missile, next by accident, and least frequently by disease. There was a (nonsignificant) tendency, however, for burning to be produced most often by accident and tingling most often by disease.

Level of Lesion

One important question we asked was whether the level of the spinal cord lesion has any differential effects upon the phantoms.

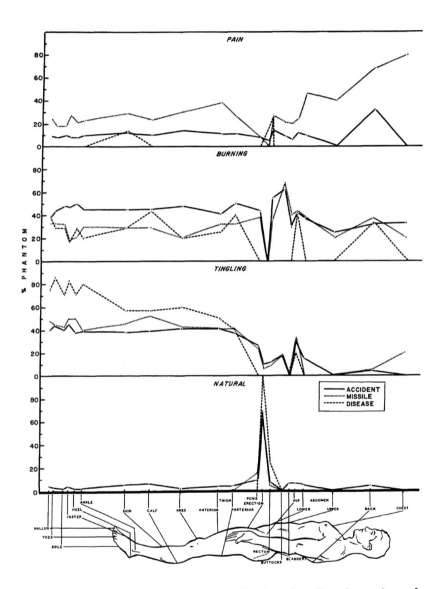

Figure 3.3   *Percentage of phantoms as a function of quality of sensation and nature of injury.*

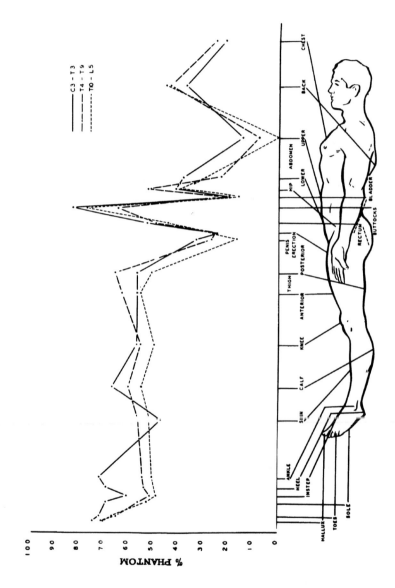

Figure 3.4 *Percentage of phantoms as a function of level of lesion.*

Figure 3.4 shows the percentage of phantoms as a function of three levels of lesion: (C3 to T3), (T4 to T9), and (T10 to L5). If we observe the lower extremities, it is apparent that phantoms occur in decreasing order of frequency after cervical, thoracic, and lumbar lesions. Although there are occasional reversals of this trend, there is a statistically significant overall difference for phantom frequency among the three levels.

The relationship between level of lesion and quality of phantom is shown in Figure 3.5. The lowest lesions (T10 to L5) produced the greatest frequency of painful phantoms, whereas the group with the highest lesions (C3 to T3) demonstrated a proportion of natural phantoms twice as great as either of the other groups. These findings find support in the fact that only high thoracic (T1 to T2) anterolateral cordotomy alleviates burning or pain in such patients (Freeman & Heimburger, 1947).

Duration of Paraplegia

Finally, of considerable theoretical significance are the consistent effects of duration of the paraplegia upon the phantom. Figure 3.6 shows the percentage of phantoms as a function of time elapsed since injury. In general, the proportion of phantoms increases significantly with time after injury. This finding is in direct opposition to reports based on patients with amputation in whom the phantom tends to fade with time (e.g., Cronholm, 1951). Similarly, there are few paraplegics who experience continual phantoms in the first years after injury; however, the proportion of patients who continually experience phantoms increases significantly with time after the injury. Not only do the continual phantoms increase, but the frequency of paraplegics reporting pain also increases significantly with time since injury.

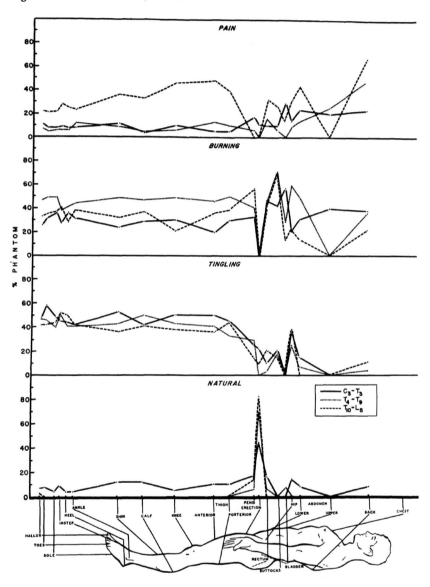

Figure 3.5   *Percentage of phantoms as a function of quality of sensation and level of lesion.*

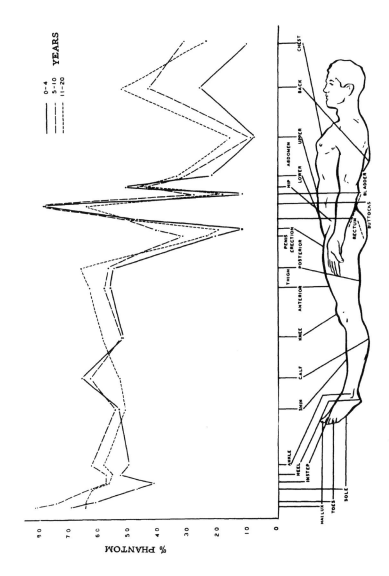

Figure 3.6 Percentage of phantoms as a function of time since injury.

Phantoms after Mastectomy

We extended our study of those patient populations evincing phantoms by testing 203 women with unilateral or bilateral mastectomies (Weinstein, Sersen, & Vetter, 1969). Of major interest was the question of whether "need" for this bodily part would produce a relatively large proportion of phantoms, or at least a larger proportion than for those parts for which lesser "needs" exist. The finding that only 33.5 per cent of the mastectomy cases reported phantoms does not appear to lend support to a "need" or "fantasy" theory.

Empirically, we solved many questions that arose from hypotheses concerning either phantom etiology or factors that might affect the phantom's course or presence. Thus, we learned that

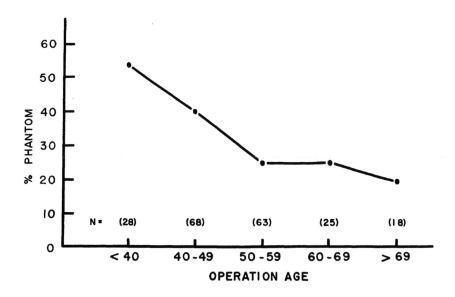

Figure 3.7   *Incidence of phantoms following mastectomy as a function of operation age.*

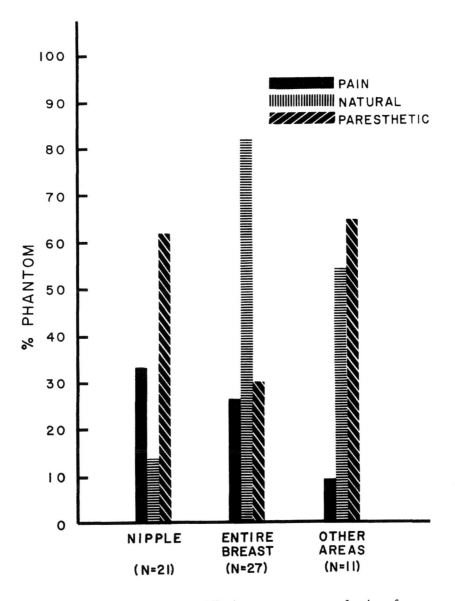

Figure 3.8   *Quality of phantom following mastectomy as a function of area perceived.*

mastectomy phantoms were *not* related to: (1) number of preg-
nancies or parturitions; (2) number of breastfed children; (3)
whether the mastectomy was simple or radical; (4) subsequent
ovariectomy; (5) duration of preoperative morbidity; or (6)
breast volume.

We did, however, find a number of interesting relationships.
Thus, there were significant decreases in phantom incidence (i.e.,
patients who evinced phantoms) both as a function of the age at
which the mastectomy was performed (see Fig. 3.7) and meno-
pausal status. Whatever the concomitant aspects of aging may be
that effect attenuation of phantom incidence, a gradual reduction
of sex hormones may certainly be among them since the likelihood

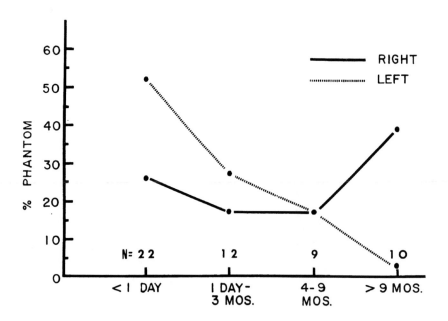

Figure 3.9   *Time of appearance of phantoms as a function of right or left
mastectomy.*

of phantoms was reduced if the mastectomy was performed subsequent to menopause. However, abrupt reduction of such hormones (ovariectomy) was without effect upon the phantom.

With respect to the quality of the sensation, for phantom experiences restricted to the nipple, "natural" sensations are significantly fewer than all others; however, such patients evinced significantly more sensations of a paresthetic or painful nature than patients whose phantom included the entire breast (Fig. 3.8).

Finally, with regard to the time the phantom first appeared (Fig. 3.9), left phantoms appeared significantly earlier after mastectomy than did right phantoms. Although we cannot consider the significance of this finding in detail at this time, it may be of interest to point out that left breasts have been found to have greater sensitivity to pressure than right breasts (Weinstein, 1963b).

Studies of Bodily Preference

Bodily Preference in Normal Individuals

Since, according to the fantasy or need theories of phantom etiology, the phantom is the emotional compensation for the loss, we attempted to determine the degree of emotional significance for various bodily parts in normal men and women. By relating the level of such emotional significance of bodily parts to the frequency of phantoms after loss of those parts, we believe we were able to assess the role that "need" for the part plays in the etiology of the phantom. To anticipate our exposition, we can point out here that there was no positive relationship obtained between the

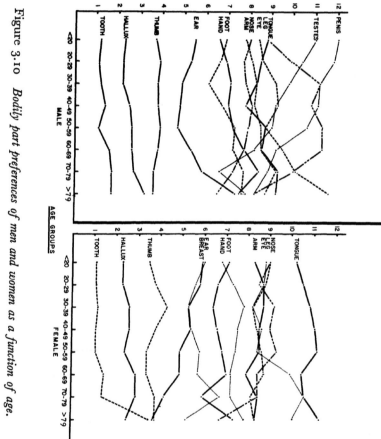

Figure 3.10 *Bodily part preferences of men and women as a function of age.*

psychological importance of the part and the probability that a phantom would be experienced after its loss.

In our first study of bodily preference (Weinstein, Sersen, Fisher, & Vetter, 1964), some 1,000 men and 1,000 women ranked various bodily parts according to the subjective value of those parts (Fig. 3.10). Although it is apparent that the subjective value of the penis remains relatively high as a function of age, it can be seen (refer to Fig. 3.1) that there is a low percentage of such phantoms among paraplegics. Furthermore, Crone-Münzebrock (1951) found that only 58 per cent of his peotomy cases experienced a phantom penis. The lack of association between the emotional significance of the part and the probability of occurrence of a phantom of that part is again seen in comparing the mean rank orders of the testes or the breast with the hallux. It may be observed that testes and the breast are rated much higher than the hallux. However, in a study of forty cases of bilateral orchiectomy (Weinstein, Sersen, & Vetter, 1968), only 22.5 per cent evinced phantoms, and, returning to the data of the mastectomy study, it may be recalled that only 33.5 per cent of the group evinced phantoms. These data are in distinct contrast to the greater than 70 per cent phantom incidence for the thumb or hallux in the groups with amputation or paraplegia (refer to Fig. 3.1). Yet, without exception, the testes and the breast were subjectively evaluated to be of greater significance than these digits.

Bodily Preference after Mastectomy

In order to validate the questionary and assess the reliability of our previous findings, we studied bodily preference in more than 550 women after mastectomy (Weinstein, Sersen, & Vetter, 1967; Fig. 3.11). We found a great (and significant) correspondence between the average rankings of the bodily parts for the

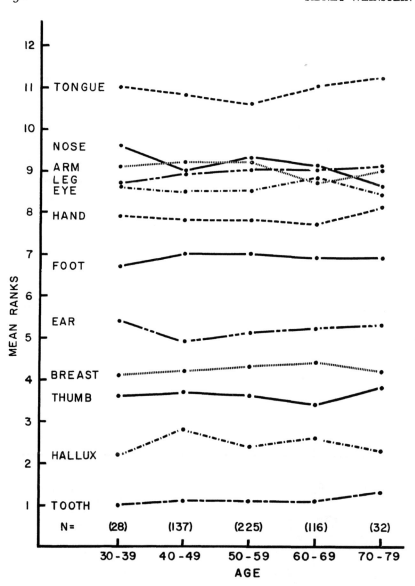

Figure 3.11   *Bodily part preferences after unilateral mastectomy as a function of age.*

women of both groups. Within the mastectomy group, the rankings also demonstrated very little change with age.

Phantoms and Emotional Significance of Bodily Parts

The major purpose of determining the emotional significance of bodily parts was to determine whether such a measure could help us to predict phantom incidence, and thereby contribute to our understanding of phantom etiology. Again, the data demonstrated the breast to be of greater emotional significance than, e.g., the hallux, in women after mastectomy, as it is in normal women. In addition, we decided to compute a correlation between bodily parts ranked on: (a) subjective importance versus (b) incidence of phantoms after amputation. The ranks of the emotional significance were taken from our bodily preference data; the ranks of phantom incidence were computed from our studies on phantoms after orchiectomy and mastectomy, and on (284 cases of) hallux, hand, foot, arm, and leg amputations. Additionally, data on peotomy cases (Crone-Münzebrock, 1951) were included.

The resulting correlation was slightly negative and not significantly greater than zero ($r_s = -.10$).

There were other data available on phantom incidence based upon the paraplegic sample which we were also able to relate to the emotional status of the parts. When the rank order correlation was computed between the ranked bodily preferences versus phantom incidence of these parts in the paraplegic group, the correlation was significant and negative ($r_s = -.79$, $p < .05$).

The correlations between emotional significance and phantom incidence, therefore, in yielding no relationship in amputees, and a negative relationship in paraplegics again cast grave doubt upon the validity of need theories of phantom etiology.

Central Nervous System Correlates
of the Phantom

The Cortical Homunculus

We continued to scrutinize our data with regard to theories of causation, this time rather specifically testing the validity of the "central" theory. First, we examined the relationship of the phantom to the degree of cortical representation of the bodily parts in question. Penfield and Rasmussen (1950) have prepared a homunculus which depicts the locus and degree of somato-sensory cortical projection areas which subserve given bodily parts. Thus, from this homunculus, it can be seen that the facial parts and distal limb parts—e.g., toe, foot, thumb, and hand— are subserved by relatively large cortical areas. We had, of course, been aware that distal parts evince the largest proportion of phantoms after loss. We therefore decided to quantify the relationship between the probability of phantoms of a given bodily part with the degree of cortical representation of that part, as we had done for the phantom versus the emotional significance of the part (see above).

We determined the degree of cortical representation of the part from the data of Penfield and Rasmussen (1950) and derived a rank order of size of cortical area from greatest to least. We computed a rank-order correlation between this rank and the rank of percentage phantoms for the same bodily parts from the data of the paraplegic group. The obtained correlation was positive and statistically significant ($r_s = .80, p < .01$), demonstrating a strong relationship between degree of cortical representation of a bodily part and the probability it would be perceived as a phantom after deafferentation.

Generality and meaning are imparted to this finding by the data of another study (Weinstein, 1968). Figure 3.12 gives the

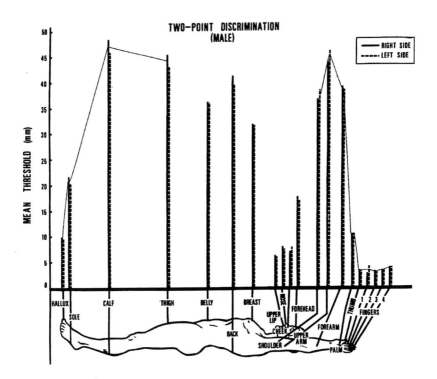

Figure 3.12   *Two-point discrimination thresholds for males.*

mean thresholds for two-point discrimination determined on 24 men for 20 pairs of bodily parts. The low thresholds for the hands, feet, and facial parts seem to indicate that some relationship exists between this measure and the size of the cortical somato-sensory areas representing the parts. Indeed, the correlation between the rank order of the size of the cortical representation and the mean two-point thresholds of the same bodily part was positive and significant ($r_s = .74$, $p < .001$) and similar to that reported above between this cortical measure and phantom incidence (.80). However, when an intensive measure of somatic sensation (pressure sensitivity) was similarly determined in the same group, and correlated with the cortical measure obtained, no relationship was found ($r_s = -.003$).

The results of these studies thus appear to indicate that phantom incidence, although not positively related to emotional significance, is related to the size of the cortical area representing the bodily part under consideration.

Phantoms in Congenital Aplasia

We have presented data, many of which could not be predicted from previous theories; let us shatter one final icon: that there are no phantoms for aplasic limbs. Although we have reviewed some historical evidence to the contrary, both prior and subsequent to the reports of Pick (1915), it has been customary to quote Pick's view that phantoms do not occur unless: (1) the limb was amputated, and (2) the amputation occurred no earlier than eight years of age.

It was left for us, however, to rediscover the facts. In a first report (Weinstein & Sersen, 1961), we demonstrated the existence of phantoms in five cases of aplasia. Subsequently (Weinstein, Sersen, & Vetter, 1964) we described a total of 18 cases of phantom in 101 aplasics. A recent review of the literature on this subject (Vetter & Weinstein, 1967) demonstrates that our discovery was, unfortunately, a rediscovery of a phenomenon reported several times in the past.

Figure 3.13 demonstrates that the stump is more sensitive than the homologous contralateral area in aplasia, a finding frequently demonstrated in individuals after amputation, as well.

Our data on aplasics too, therefore, support a central theory

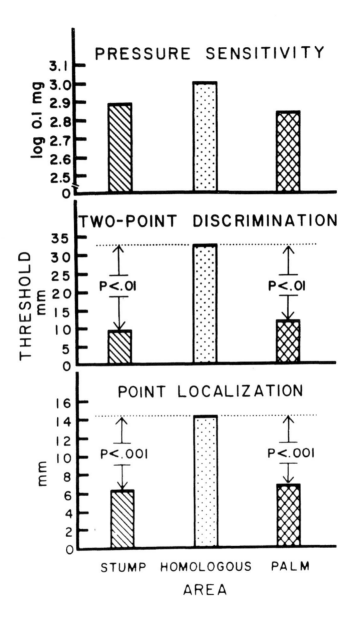

Figure 3.13 *Sensitivity thresholds of congenital aplasics on stump, homologous area, and palm.*

of the phantom on two grounds: (a) peripheral irritations (e.g., neuromata) are unlikely to be present in the aplasic stump, and (b) enhanced stump sensitivity is unlikely to occur in irritated stumps or as a function of fantasy. Furthermore, despite equivalence of the degree of need, a lower proportion of phantoms is evinced by aplasics, in comparison with those experiencing amputation sometime after birth.

Figure 3.14 demonstrates, from the data of two studies (Boeri & Negri, 1954; Weinstein, Sersen, & Vetter, 1964) and a survey

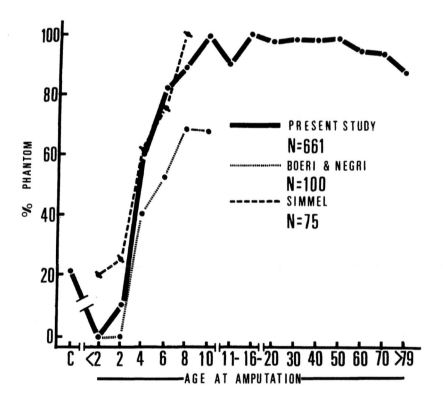

Figure 3.14   *Percentage of phantoms in terminal aplasia, and following limb amputations at various ages.*

of earlier reports (Simmel, 1962) that the incidence of phantoms is a function of the age at which the loss occurred, despite equation of the age at which the individual was interviewed. These data seem to indicate that for a need theory of phantom etiology to be valid it must incorporate a conception of such need that increases as a function of the age of the child at the time of the operation. A peripheral theory must likewise account for the fact of differential phantom incidence with age.

A Theory of Phantom Etiology

We have recently expressed the following theory of phantom causation:

We believe that the nucleus of the adult body schema may have its origin in a neural substrate which is the framework for the potential adult sensory homunculus. The neural "framework" may be modified by multimodal sensory experiences during the lifetime of the organism. In amputees, evoked activity in sensory cortices may then activate those close cortical regions representing the amputated part and thus evoke a phantom proportional in vividness to the magnitude of stimulation and to the period of time during which the engrams had been deposited. According to this idea, emotional reactions in the adult amputee might evoke the most vivid phantoms and random "irradiations" from neighboring regions in cases of congenital aplasia, the least vivid and least frequent phantoms (Weinstein & Sersen, 1961, p. 911).

This theory of phantom etiology, based upon neurophysiological mechanisms and incorporating both genetic and experiential factors, accounts for: enhanced sensitivity of the stump, increased phantom incidence as a function of age at amputation, the relation of phantom incidence to the area of sensory projection cortex, phantoms of aplasic limbs, and, indeed, much of the phenomenology of the phantom experience.

Comment

We have raised questions concerning the validity of the peripheral theory of phantoms, have cast grave doubts upon the "fantasy" or "need" theories, have adduced data that negate many of the dogmas, e.g., concerning nonexistence of the aplasic phantom. Furthermore, we have reported empirical findings on: the physiological concomitant of phantoms in paraplegia and various sites of amputation, on sensory changes on the stump, and on the relationships of phantoms both to bodily preferences and to cortical projection areas of the brain.

We have also presented a central theory of the phantom that has its origin in antiquity, that has been nurtured by astute neurologists and psychologists, and that is supported by abundant recent neuropsychological data.

4
Problems in the Anatomical Understanding of the Aphasias

Norman Geschwind

In the classical period that ended approximately with World War I, the approach to the aphasias and other disturbances of the so-called higher functions of the nervous system relied heavily on anatomical knowledge. Broca's (1861) paper, which revealed for the first time that localized lesions of the nervous system could lead to disorders of language, stimulated an

The personal researches cited in this chapter were supported in part by Grant NB–06209 from the National Institute of Neurological Diseases and Stroke.

enormous interest in the founders of the infant specialty of clinical neurology. Wernicke's (1874) paper published thirteen years later opened the period of the great investigations that continued for another half-century. Stimulated by Meynert's sketch of the major outlines of the cortical connections, he attempted to account for the syndromes of aphasia. A major portion of the advances in the field were made by either his assistants or students in Breslau, or by others following his theoretical approaches (Geschwind, 1966, 1967b). This approach was the only one extensively capable of generating predictions. The other two approaches—i.e., the holistic approach and the mosaicist approach—each had protagonists who made important contributions but neither of these approaches ever matched the successful predictive capacity of the connectionist approach of Wernicke. Although it is commonly believed that the teachings of Wernicke's school were seriously challenged, particularly by the holists, none of the opponents could advance major evidence which threatened the general outlines of aphasia as developed by the Breslau school. Thus Kurt Goldstein (1917) pointed out that his disagreements with the classical localizationist teachings extended only to finer aspects of localization too subtle to be dealt with by current anatomical techniques. As has been pointed out elsewhere (Geschwind, 1964), Goldstein not only accepted the major tenets of Wernicke but made major contributions in the same theoretical tradition. Head (1926) totally rejected this approach, but in his own work ended up with a series of localizations that agreed with those of his classical predecessors.

Although the connectionist approach to disturbances of the higher functions of the nervous system has been highly successful, it should by no means be thought that it has led to more than an initial understanding of the problems posed by these disorders. Even among those generally committed to this approach, there has always been heated controversy, and the supporters of the opposing mosaicist and holistic schools repeatedly pointed out other areas in which the classical approaches led to predictions at variance with the observed data or phenomena and which they were incapable of handling. It is the purpose of this paper to stress not the successes of the classical anatomical interpretation but rather the areas in which it encounters difficulties. We will begin with a brief outline of the current state of theory and then devote most of our discussion to these problem areas that constitute some of the chief challenges for future research.

The Anatomical Basis of the Higher Functions

Let us for a moment omit any discussion of the problem of cerebral dominance and consider that the functions we are concerned with are present to a significant degree only in the left hemisphere. We will summarize broadly the functions of certain areas (Fig. 4.1). The angular gyrus region (or more correctly, the region of the temporo-parieto-occipital junction) may be thought of as containing the rules for associating stimuli in two modalities, e.g., visual and auditory. Thus a visual stimulus can evoke an auditory association by means of the pathway: visual cortex—visual association cortex—angular gyrus—auditory association cortex. The auditory association cortex shown here is the classical Wernicke's area. Broca's area is a region of motor association cortex lying anterior to the face region of the classical motor cortex. It may be thought of as containing the learned rules for translating a particular heard sound pattern into a motor sequence.

In the light of the above scheme let us consider how we name a seen object. A stimulus reaches the visual cortex, goes to the visual association cortex, then to the angular gyrus. This in turn arouses the name in Wernicke's area. From here the impulse is transferred over the arcuate fasciculus to Broca's area where the muscular pattern corresponding to the sound is aroused. From here the impulse reaches the motor cortex and is then conveyed downward.

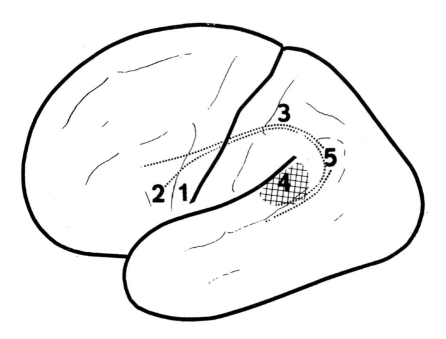

Figure 4.1   *Lateral surface of left hemisphere. 1. Face area of motor cortex;
2. Broca's area; 3. Lesion involving arcuate fasciculus (dotted lines); 4. Wernicke's area; 5. Angular gyrus.*

This simple diagram immediately permits us to make certain
predictions. Assume a lesion of Wernicke's area. A word may
reach the auditory cortex but can arouse no response in Wernicke's
area and thus fails to arouse associations elsewhere in the brain.
Hence it is not understood, nor can it be repeated. The patient
will not be able to describe his environment since a stimulus
from visual cortex will not eventually reach Broca's area. The
patient fails to understand written language since the seen words
can no longer arouse their auditory forms. A contrasting lesion
in Broca's area produces a different pattern. Speech is abnormal
but comprehension of spoken and written language is preserved.
A lesion in the arcuate fasciculus also leads to abnormality in

speech by breaking the pathway from Wernicke's to Broca's area but comprehension of spoken and written language is retained. The disturbance produced by a lesion in this location is called conduction aphasia.

All of the lesions mentioned above lead to abnormal speech, but the disturbances vary with the localization. Thus in the lesion of Broca's area little speech is produced and what is produced is halting and dysarthric. In the other two forms mentioned above, there is often copious production of abnormal speech. It is clear that the integrity of Broca's area is necessary for the production of this type of fluent aphasia. It seems reasonable to hypothesize that this fluent abnormality represents the running on of the relatively isolated Broca's area. Some support for this view comes from the fact that in children fluent aphasias either are never seen or are extremely rare. This would appear to be the result of the fact that Broca's area has not had the overlearning necessary to permit its running on in isolation.

Other syndromes can also be predicted from this model. Consider a lesion that destroys the left auditory radiation or cortex and that also destroys the callosal fibers from the opposite auditory region. Wernicke's area, although intact, can now receive no auditory stimulation. The patient does not understand spoken language although he speaks normally since Wernicke's area is intact. An analogous situation is seen when a lesion destroys the left visual cortex and the splenium of the corpus callosum. The patient can see words in the left visual field, but these are not capable of reaching the speech areas and the patient can no longer understand written language, although he speaks and writes correctly.

A similar analysis enables us to understand a related group of disturbances, i.e., the apraxias. Consider how a patient carries out motor responses to auditory command. It is necessary to use the pathway from Wernicke's area to the left motor association cortex and from there to the motor cortex. To carry out auditory commands with the left hand, it is necessary to go by way of Wernicke's area, left motor association cortex, then over the corpus callosum to the right motor association cortex, and the right motor cortex.

A lesion of the corpus callosum thus causes the patient to be incapable of carrying out motor commands with the left hand while he is still capable of performing them with the right. A lesion of the left motor association cortex will have the same effect, although the praxic difficulty in the right hand is often masked by a right hemiplegia. A lesion in the arcuate fasciculus will lead to a bilateral difficulty in carrying out verbal commands.

Difficulties in Anatomical Interpretation

We may divide our difficulties of interpretation into three categories.

1. There exist certain regular features of the syndromes listed above that do not appear to be readily explained by the anatomical model.

2. There exist certain syndromes whose existence is not predicted by the model.

3. There exist certain cases where the expected syndromes do not appear despite an apparently adequate lesion.

The occurrence of difficulties of any of the above types has led many authors to dismiss all localizationist approaches as incorrect, but without offering an adequate substitute. Despite its shortcomings, an anatomical approach most closely meets the criteria of efficiency in explaining the known data, efficiency in predicting new phenomena, or in design of important experiments and susceptibility to refinements that can be checked by observation or experiment. In some instances the discrepancies between theory and observation are only apparent. Thus Wernicke himself discussed the syndrome to be expected from a lesion disconnecting Wernicke's area from Broca's area. His predictions were apparently not borne out, but subsequent studies showed that there were two reasons for this: (1) Wernicke had incorrectly assumed that the pathway between these two regions traversed the insula; (2) he had incorrectly interpreted his own diagram in determining what the effects of such a lesion should be.

Let us now consider some of the specific difficulties that arise. The objection might be raised that the expressive disturbance should be the same in the case of Wernicke's, conduction, and Broca's aphasias. As we have already noted, this is not the case since the two former varieties lead frequently to fluent aphasias while Broca's aphasia is nonfluent. This is probably accounted for by the hypothesis mentioned earlier that the fluent aphasias represent situations in which Broca's area runs on by itself. However, certain features of these syndromes are not predicted by the approach given above, although they are not inconsistent with it.

Thus the linguistic production is different in the fluent and the nonfluent cases. The nonfluent cases tend to have relatively less trouble in naming but marked difficulty in producing sentences, while the fluent group may produce "empty" sentences that are well constructed but lacking specific words and have great difficulty in naming. This possibility suggests that the anterior speech region is involved in some special way in the grammatical structuring of speech, but the mechanism of this is not at all clear at this time. Why should naming often be relatively well preserved in the Broca's aphasic? There are at least two alternative explanations available to us. Let us assume that in the posterior speech regions we have a system for finding the word appropriate to a given physical stimulus. A partial lesion will result in either failure to find the word or selection of the wrong "bin" that will contain an incorrect word. Assuming this posterior region to be intact, then the correct auditory form of the word is aroused in Wernicke's area and is then transferred forward. What reaches Broca's area is thus the correct "sound-pattern" which must arouse the appropriate muscular patterns. A partial lesion in this region will result in inaccuracy of these patterns but the word may be correct. It should be stressed, however, that the only effect of Broca's area lesion is not an inaccurate sound pattern since the grammatical structure is also distorted for reasons that are not clear and that are certainly not clarified by our present anatomical knowledge.

An alternative explanation of the relative preservation of naming in Broca's aphasics is that the right hemisphere can carry out naming tasks. This, however, probably cannot explain the fact that this preservation of naming is relatively common with left anterior lesions but not with posterior ones. A difference in the form of coding anteriorly and posteriorly as outlined above seems more likely. Hence, right hemisphere substitution, while possible in certain situations (as we will discuss below), is at least not a general explanation for the preservation of naming in Broca's aphasics.

If the model given is correct then why does not a lesion of the left internal capsule lead to some permanent abnormality of speech, even if it is only dysarthria or mutism? Yet the evidence seems to point to good recovery of speech after left purely capsular lesions. The reason for this is the fact that an alternative pathway exists. If Broca's area is intact as well as the callosal fibers from it to the corresponding region in the right hemisphere, then the impulse can cross to the right side and eventually the motor impulses may be transmitted down the right internal capsule. Since each Rolandic face area controls nearly all of the articulatory system bilaterally, the speech will be normal. This explanation is supported by the case of Bonhoeffer (1914) who was thought to have a Broca's aphasia in life but who at postmortem had a callosal lesion as well as a left capsular lesion. It is also supported by the fact the Broca's aphasia can be produced by subcortical lesions that simultaneously involve the callosal fibers from Broca's area and the descending fibers from the left face area.

A more serious problem is that raised by disturbances of writing. How does one write the name of a seen object? Some of the classical authors were inclined to feel that the sight of the object could directly arouse the written production, just as they felt that the production of the spoken name could take place over a direct pathway from the visual region to Broca's area. But what makes this supposition unlikely is that writing is *invariably* abnormal in patients with the speech *pattern* of Wernicke's aphasia,[1] while one might expect it to be spared at least occasionally if this were the case. Hence it appears that to write the word, the spoken form must be aroused first. But what is the next step? It seems possible that it is necessary to go from Wernicke's area back to the angular gyrus again since one can get an isolated alexia and agraphia from angular gyrus lesions, an agraphia that involves even the writing of dictated words.

Even this complicated arrangement leads to difficulties. Is there a separate pathway forward from the angular gyrus to the motor region? If this is the case, then how do we account for the fact that patients with Broca's aphasia have, in my experience, invariably manifested a writing disturbance of generally comparable degree to their speech disturbance.[2] It would seem reasonable, at first glance, that writing should not depend on Broca's area, which appears to be association cortex for the face region of the Rolandic cortex. Why then should writing be affected in these cases? The assumption that somehow the "heard word" passes from Wernicke's area to Broca's area, there to be turned into written as well as spoken form, does not appear to fit in with the already mentioned fact that pure alexia with apraphia can be produced by angular gyrus lesions. One can make conjectures that are as yet not verified. If the pathway

1. I have never seen a patient with grossly fluent and paraphasic speech who produced normal written language, although the orthography may be quite normal, nor have I seen a convincing report of such a case.

2. There are occasional reports in the literature of "pure motor aphasias" involving only speech and not writing. My own experience, however, has been that patients who are mute but write normally manifest normal language production as soon as they have any speech although they may be extremely dysarthric. Patients with the clear-cut linguistic pattern of Broca's aphasia in speech but with normal writing must be extremely rare, if they exist at all. Certainly some degree of discrepancy between written and verbal production is common but is not dramatic.

from the angular gyrus runs forward and mixes in the lower parietal lobe with the fibers from Wernicke's area, then one would expect agraphia with conduction aphasia, which is indeed always the case. One could further assume that the face and hand area overlap considerably in the premotor region so that any lesion large enough to produce aphasia will also produce agraphia. Yet this overlap cannot be complete since while pure Broca's aphasias are not seen, it seems to be the case that an occasional patient does develop agraphia without disturbance of speech from a lesion in front of the hand area of the cortex.

It can be seen that we have a reasonable knowledge of which lesions produce writing disturbances, whether in isolation or in association with other difficulties, but we have only a poor notion of the possible mechanisms.

Another anatomical mystery is afforded by the transient aphasias that come from lesions of the supplementary motor cortex. This region is not shown in Figure 4.1. It is, however, striking that this is the only cortical region outside of the classical speech areas from which aphasic phenomena are obtained on stimulation (Penfield & Roberts, 1959). My colleague, Dr. Deepak Pandya (personal communication), has shown in his anatomical studies in the monkey that the face portion of the supplementary motor area is clearly connected with the face portion of the classical motor cortex.

The first suggestion of the importance of the parasagittal region for speech is found in the work of Schwab and Foerster (Schwab, 1927), who found that 14 out of 21 patients with parasagittal cortical excisions, well remote from Broca's area, developed an aphasia beginning about the third postoperative day and lasting for two weeks or even longer. Transient speech disturbances from lesions in this area are mentioned by several authors (see Penfield & Roberts, 1959). The fact that these aphasias are transient has probably led to a neglect of this region. What role this area plays in speech still remains to be determined.

One of the hardest syndromes to account for, oddly enough, is classical anomic aphasia. One would be tempted to say that a lesion in the angular gyrus produces a visual-auditory disconnection and hence a disturbance of naming. But this explanation affords great difficulties, which have been discussed elsewhere in some detail (Geschwind, 1967a). The first problem is that classical anomic aphasia is predominantly a one-way disorder, i.e., the patient finds it difficult to find the name of a seen object but usually recognizes the name readily when it is offered by the examiner. This contrasts with the color-naming disturbance seen in many cases of pure alexia without agraphia, which appears to depend clearly on visual-auditory disconnection. Here the patient can neither give the correct name of a seen color nor recognize the name when it is offered. He clearly suffers from the inability to match the heard word to the visual stimulus, but this match fails in both directions, as one would expect in an audio-visual disconnection.

A clue to the problem, although not a solution, is given by consideration of another fact. It is frequently stated that lesions of the second temporal gyrus are involved in anomic aphasia, while other authors stress the angular gyrus. Indeed, these are not necessarily conflicting views, since the second temporal gyrus is in fact continuous with the angular gyrus. Like the angular gyrus of man, the second temporal gyrus is very late in its maturation (Flechsig, 1901). It is conceivable that we may have simplified too much in assuming that there was a simple step from angular gyrus to Wernicke's area for arousing the name of a seen object. We frequently must find a "name" in speech, using several cues, each one inadequate by itself. It is like the question: "What is an animal, found in India, savage, with stripes?" The word "tiger" is easily found, yet none of the clues alone is adequate, and omitting even one might still leave difficulties. Presumably the process of word-finding in spontaneous speech may well be similar. All sorts of partial information, sometimes even in different modalities, must come in and be used to find the right word. Conversely, given the word, finding the attributes is easy. It would appear to me reasonable that anomia is not the result of auditory-visual disconnection (which is probably not present in the anomic) but rather a disturbance of a well-organized "filing system" that perhaps is present in the angular gyrus and second temporal gyrus. But we need much further information to support this view. Isolated vascular lesions of the second temporal gyrus are remarkably uncommon and hence clinical information is lacking. Unfortunately we know very little of the connections of this region.

Even in the purer forms of aphasic disturbance we run into difficulties. Consider the syndrome of pure alexia without agraphia. The lesion involves the left visual cortex plus the splenium of the corpus callosum. It seems clear that this lesion isolates the right visual cortex from the speech area and the seen word cannot arouse the auditory form. How then do we account for the ability of the patient to name objects that must surely also require a connection from right visual region to the speech area? This question is dealt with elsewhere in some detail (Geschwind, 1965a) and will be discussed briefly here. One possible explanation is that object-naming is preserved by means of arousal of tactile associations in the right hemisphere which can then get across the callosum in its intact portions. Consistent with this explanation is the fact that in many of these patients the ability to name colors is impaired along with the disturbance of reading. Colors, unlike objects, will not have distinctive tactile associations and hence may well be disturbed along with reading.

Another problem not accounted for adequately by this model is the curious syndrome of aphemia. A typical case is that of a patient who suddenly becomes mute in association with a right hemiplegia. The patient, although mute, can write. Pseudo-bulbar mutism appears to be excluded by the absence of other pseudo bulbar signs. The hemiplegia may clear almost completely. As soon as the patient has some speech, it is usually evident that his language production is normal although his speech is slow and effortful. He may recover to the point where speech is produced readily enough for the purposes of ordinary life, but the patient remains markedly dysprosodic. The designation of this syndrome as "subcortical motor aphasia" appears to be inappropriate, since it seems highly unlikely that a lesion cutting off Broca's area from the Rolandic face area could frequently do so without a permanent hemiplegia. This syndrome for the time being remains a mystery.

The usual ability of the aphasic patient to sing on key correctly is another unsolved problem. This is particularly dramatic in the case of the classical Broca's aphasic whose spontaneous speech output is so limited and yet who generally sings melodies well. Even more striking is the occasional situation when words as well as music are produced in this situation, this being sometimes the only circumstance in which the patient produces any words. The interpretation that "music is in the right hemisphere," although possibly correct, is not very helpful if one is attempting to understand mechanisms. If Broca's area is in some sense a storehouse of motor patterns corresponding to auditory patterns, then why should music not be affected? We would have to assume that the nervous system separates the musical auditory stimuli by some set of criteria into the right hemisphere. This is certainly possible but it would be interesting to know what set of criteria would be used by the nervous system. In any case this problem remains unsolved.

Another difficult problem is posed by the anatomical model given above. How do we carry out certain commands such as "Pick up the ball"? A connection from auditory region to motor region alone would not suffice for this task since visual information is also necessary. This implies that perhaps the auditory and the visual information are "mixed" somewhere before being relayed to the motor region. This would of necessity involve some modification of our ideas of the apraxias. It would suggest that, rather than a direct auditory-motor pathway being involved, we use a pathway with a synapse in it. On the basis of anatomical studies in primates carried out by Pandya (personal communication), it seems reasonable that this region lies in the inferior parietal lobule, but much more investigation will be required to establish this view.

Lack of Expected Effects of Lesions

Let us now turn to another problem. As we have pointed out, we lack the ability to account for some of the common features of syndromes whose anatomical basis appears to be well established. Nor can we yet account for some syndromes such as aphemia that are not accounted for on the basis of the anatomical structure outlined above. We now turn to a different problem. How do we account for the situations where an apparently adequate lesion fails to produce the expected syndrome? Thus Kleist (1962) describes a patient with a destructive lesion that would have been expected to produce a Wernicke's aphasia, yet it produced no comprehension disturbance, although repetition was impaired. The problem is, therefore, why are some of the expected elements lacking or, indeed, why in some instances is there a total lack of the expected syndrome?

It should be pointed out that this is not the argument against localization that it is sometimes purported to be. The problem posed here is why certain lesions are necessary but not sufficient conditions for the existence of certain syndromes. Yet any reasonable theory must eventually account for the exceptions in a testable manner. We will consider here some of the possible explanations for this type of situation. For some of these good evidence exists, while others are speculative but subject to eventual test.

Of course one of the obvious reasons for discrepancy is inadequate examination. Thus patients are sometimes asserted to have difficulty reading as a result of Broca's area lesions (Nielsen, 1939). While it is certainly possible that such cases exist, the evidence is by no means clear, and it is quite evident that some of the cases so described have had difficulty in reading aloud with preserved comprehension of reading. Another common error is to diagnose difficulty in comprehension in patients who fail to carry out commands on the basis of apractic disturbances. This error is a frequent one, since most clinical tests for examining comprehension employ only the ability to carry out commands.

Another reason for apparent discrepancies is reliance on cases of cerebral tumor. As is well known, there are often marked discrepancies between the site of a tumor and its clinical symptomatology; these may often be the result of distant effects of distortion of the brain, traction on blood vessels, and obstructions of the ventricular system. Similarly, one can expect discrepancies in cases of cerebral infarction who die early in their course, since edema around the area of destruction may mislead one as to the effects of the destruction itself.

Another problem that may lead to apparent discrepancies is the transient syndromes such as those mentioned earlier from the supplementary motor area. There are probably other such syndromes that have been overlooked because of their transiency. Thus it is our belief that frontal lesions in man commonly lead to transient but not permanent unilateral inattention syndromes just as they do in animals (Welch & Stuteville, 1958).

Let us now turn from these cases of what we may call apparent discrepancy to cases of true discrepancy.

One of the oldest theories is that the way a task is learned will affect its performance. Thus one can theoretically conceive of a congenitally deaf person who has learned to read but has never learned spoken language. Since he has not learned to read by translating the written words into auditory form, he should not lose reading as a normal person would from a Wernicke's area lesion. Could one apply this type of reasoning to normals? Wernicke (1874) himself argued that one should see different aphasic pictures in the highly educated. One can imagine that eventually one might "free" himself from translating written language into auditory form and thus not lose reading with a Wernicke's area lesion. Similarly many older authors argued that the poorly educated who read aloud could become alexic with a Broca's area lesion. Unfortunately no one has yet published an adequate study of alexia from a Broca's area lesion. All of the above suppositions are possible but as yet unproven. At least one hypothesis of this type is probably incorrect. Thus some authors have argued that unilateral cerebral dominance for speech is the *secondary* result of having learned to write with one hand, usually the right. On the basis of this, it has been argued that speech would be less localized in the illiterate and hence their aphasias would be milder. Many lines of evidence argue against these hypotheses. The overwhelming predominance of left hemisphere lesions in the aphasias appears to have been as marked in France and Germany of the late 1800's, when illiteracy was common, as it is today. Despite the fact that nearly all left-handers of the late nineteenth century on the Continent were taught to write with the right hand, aphasias in association with left hemiplegias were frequently observed in such patients. At least half of those who today do write with the left hand become aphasic with right hemiplegias. There is further evidence against this thesis from callosal lesions in left-handers. It seems unlikely that the use of one hand for writing controls cerebral dominance for speech.

A second mechanism for incomplete or absent syndromes is duplication of function in the right hemisphere, either because the function was always duplicated or because of relearning. The evidence for duplication of function in varying degrees is quite strong. Thus the child who becomes aphasic frequently recovers very good speech within a few months. The period is clearly too short to permit relearning. Hence, language must have been in the right hemisphere before the lesion. Why is recovery not always immediate? It seems most likely that the right hemisphere is normally inhibited and that some period is required to release this inhibition. There are many analogs to this even in normal life. The "savings" technique, one of the classic methods of study of memory, is frequently used to show that there is some preservation of memory despite even gross failures in recall.

The conclusion that the child in many instances does not relearn with the right hemisphere but rather must somehow bring to the surface learning already present has some important implications. It necessitates recasting of some conventional ideas of cerebral dominance. We are often accustomed to thinking of dominance as the predominant *possession* by one hemisphere of a certain skill. Perhaps a more reasonable view is that learning takes place, at least in childhood, on both sides in roughly equal degrees, but that retrieval is readily effected only from one side.

The second important implication is that it is conceivable that, if language was once present on both sides, it is always present on both sides but that in the adult the retrieval problem is not fully overcome. Certainly if retrieval often takes a few months in the child, the period might extend to years and in some cases retrieval might never be achieved in the adult. It is my belief that the major hope for the eventual effective rehabilitation of the type of aphasic for whom we can do so little now lies in the possibility that language is present but inaccessible in the minor hemisphere.

Similar situations to those seen in childhood do exist in varying degrees in adult life. The left-handed patient of Dejerine and André-Thomas (1912) became aphasic with a left hemiplegia and then had a slow recovery. By the time of her death about five years later, speech was nearly normal. Relearning could probably be excluded by the patient's ability to deal with discussions of matters that she would hardly have dealt with during her illness, and by the high character of the performance. At postmortem the patient had nearly total destruction of the right hemisphere so that she must have been using her left hemisphere for recovery of speech. Cases similar to this one, although not perhaps so dramatic, are seen by everyone who works with aphasic patients. In ordinary practice, it is not unusual to see a patient who a year after the onset of aphasia is still severely impaired, yet who two years later shows a marked improvement. Lesser degrees of obvious right hemisphere substitution are also seen. Thus the patient studied by Smith and Burklund (Smith, 1966) who underwent a total left hemispherectomy for a glioma was severely aphasic, but he did have some speech and this was obviously coming from the right hemisphere. This certainly must suggest that, in other patients with severe aphasias, some of the retained speech comes from the right hemisphere. It seems likely that there is a great deal of variation in the extent of right hemisphere substitution.

The thesis of right hemisphere substitution need not be regarded as simply an *ad hoc* explanation, since there are means for studying this problem. Wada tests on the right carotid artery in aphasics at different stages of recovery would help to show how much speech was in the right hemisphere. We have, however, been reluctant to carry out arterial punctures for this purpose alone. Even this technique could not demonstrate the full potential of the right hemisphere but only its actual performance at any given moment.

A third possibility to account for incomplete or absent syndromes is not a shift to another cortical region but rather the use of alternative pathways to perform the function. There are two possibilities here. One is that of circumventing a disconnecting lesion by means of other pathways. An example is seen in animal work. Thus Black and Myers (1964) showed that, with lesions of the splenium of the corpus callosum in monkeys, a minority of the animals could effect transfer of visual learning between the hemispheres as long as anterior commissure was intact. This makes sense anatomically since the visual association areas (which are linked to their opposite numbers by means of the splenium) project to the lateral and basal temporal lobe which connects to the opposite side via the anterior commissure. We see similar situations in man. Thus as Bonhoeffer (1914) pointed out, a left capsular lesion does not produce aphasia because one can use the connections from the left Broca's area to its analog on the right. Bonhoeffer described a patient who became aphasic with the combination of a left capsular lesion plus a callosal lesion. It seems likely that the commissural pathway from Broca's area is commonly used in man when there is a capsular lesion. There may well be other situations where some humans can make use of a commissural connection (like the minority of monkeys who use the anterior commissure when the splenium is cut) that others fail to use. This will clearly lead to variation in clinical pictures with the same lesion. Notice that this is not the same as substitution by the right side. Substitution can conceivably occur when the left hemisphere is totally destroyed. In the type of situation we are talking about here connections from the intact portions of the left side are required. Substitution implies that a cortical region on the right can carry out the function. The type of compensation we are discussing here may merely mean that the right side is being run passively from the left. Obviously combinations of the two mechanisms could occur.

Still another type of mechanism involving alternative pathways must be considered. It is clear from anatomical studies that large motor outflows exist from regions other than the frontal lobe. Kuypers has laid special emphasis on this fact (Lawrence & Kuypers, 1965). These directly descending motor systems seem to arise primarily from the sensory association cortices and descend subcortically, in particular to the collicular or pretectal regions and to the cerebellum via the pontine nuclei (Jansen & Brodal, 1954). These pathways are probably not the complete equivalent of the pyramidal pathway. They are, however, capable of the delicate control of eye movements. The eye movements are in fact probably all controlled by this type of system, since there seems to be no representation of eye movement in the pyramidal system. On the other hand, these systems appear to be capable of less finesse in fine distal limb movements and seem to control mostly axial musclature. These nonpyramidal systems are probably much older phylogenetically than the pyramidal system.

There is a certain amount of evidence to show that at least in primates the direct descending pathways from the sensory association cortices may be less important in the normal animal than the transcortical pathway via the frontal lobe. With removal of the transcortical pathway, however, the animal can compensate to a great extent by means of the direct descending systems but the compensation may not be perfect. Thus Glickstein, Arora, and Sperry (1963) showed that for delayed response tasks it is still necessary to use the transcortical pathway. The important point, however, is that such direct descending pathways from sensory association cortices can often produce a significant degree of compensation in the primate. We must ask how great a role they play in man.

Some activities in man probably use directly descending pathways normally. Thus, even after destruction of the corpus callosum, walking is carried out normally. It seems unlikely that this activity need be coordinated via the corpus callosum but probably depends on these directly descending pathways. The better preservation of walking and other whole-body movements in many patients with apraxias resulting from destruction of cortico-cortical connections is compatible with this view.

There is other evidence for the participation of direct descending pathways in man. They may well account for the return of some movements of the left arm to verbal command in patients with callosal lesions. Thus we have had the opportunity, through the kindness of Drs. Bogen, Gazzaniga, and Sperry, to examine the first patient who underwent callosal section in Los Angeles. He failed to carry out many commands with the left hand but did succeed in a minority of instances. How can we account for this partial performance? Direct ipsilateral pathways from the left hemisphere appear to be the most likely explanation. Such ipsilateral pathways are most likely to be from the "medial" motor system of Kuypers (Lawrence & Kuypers, 1965) rather than from the "lateral" system whose connections are more strongly contralateral. Further evidence for the participation of these medial systems in this patient is that he carried out the commands in a different way in the left and right arms. With the left arm he tended to lose the finer distal components of movements but not with the right, findings compatible with the notion that the "medial" system was playing a greater role in the performances of the left hand. The same situation of partial carrying out of the commands with loss of the finer distal components is seen not only in lesions of the callosum proper but also in the apraxias of the left arm accompanying Broca's aphasia. It seems reasonable that here, too, the participation of direct descending "medial" motor systems can be invoked.

Could such direct descending pathways be adequate for the restoration of motor speech in the Broca's aphasic? I should think that this could give at best a partial restoration since the articulatory pattern of normal speech is so refined that I doubt the capacity of the medial system to achieve it. This problem, however, deserves further study. Conceivably, the relative and often dramatic preservation of naming in the Broca's aphasic might depend on such direct descending pathways from the posterior speech regions. Whether such pathways can maintain fully normal speech is an open question.

Let us now turn to the last of the mechanisms of the preservation of performance in the face of lesions which seem adequate to prevent it. This is the mechanism of "external" signaling, i.e., where one portion of the patient's nervous system stimulates visually or mechanically another part of the nervous system to which it does not have access by means of nervous connections. Let me cite two examples. A patient with facial apraxia, on being asked how he would blow out a match, may make the motion of striking a match and then carry his hand up to his face. He may then carry out the blowing movement. If he is prevented from using the arm, he will not carry out the blowing movement. It is clear that the command has been understood and that the patient is capable of carrying it out, but he can do so only by means of stimulating visually a portion of the nervous system that cannot be reached by internal connections from the left auditory

region. Similarly, a patient with a callosal lesion, on being asked
to salute with the left hand, may first carry out the movement
with the right hand and then with the left. If the right hand is
restrained, he is incapable of the action. Again it seems likely
that the left hemisphere, which understands language, is signaling
the "aphasic" right hemisphere nonverbally.

This concludes our discussion of the problems involved in
anatomical interpretations of the higher functions of the nervous
system. It has by no means exhausted them and only further
anatomical and physiological knowledge, coupled with clinical
observation and testing, will serve to unravel the difficulties
presented here.

5

Constructional Apraxia: Some Unanswered Questions

Arthur L. Benton

In this chapter, I should like to consider certain unresolved questions having to do with the disability designated as "constructional apraxia" that is observed in a fair proportion of patients with cerebral disease. Some prefatory remarks about the characteristics of the disorder and the development of thinking about it may be offered to provide a framework for the main discussion.

Constructional praxis refers to behavior in which parts are put

The personal researches cited in this chapter were supported by Research Grant NB–00616 and Program Project Grant NB–03354 from the National Institute of Neurological Diseases and Stroke.

together or articulated to make a single entity or object. Thus it denotes combinatory or organizing activity in which the relationships among the component parts of the entity must be apprehended if the desired synthesis of them is to be achieved. Its pathological counterpart—i.e., the specific deficit in constructional activity that is designated as *constructional apraxia*—was defined by Kleist as a disturbance in "formative activities such as assembling, building and drawing, in which the spatial form of the product proves to be unsuccessful, without there being an apraxia of single movements" (cited by Strauss, 1924). Moreover, Kleist specified that constructional apraxia was to be distinguished from rather similar psychomotor deficits that were clearly the result of visuoperceptive disabilities, and he conceived of a rupture in the connections between visual and kinesthetic processes as being the essential basis for the disorder.

The concept of constructional apraxia developed out of the much broader concept of "optic apraxia" employed by earlier authors to designate virtually any disturbance in action that was referable to defective visual guidance of responses. For example, Poppelreuter (1917), in his discussion of optic apraxia, described awkwardness in the execution of acts requiring manual dexterity, limitations in maintaining one's balance in tests of locomotion, defective imitation of unfamiliar movements, and certain types of disorientation in external space, as well as constructional deficits, under this heading. Kleist abstracted constructional apraxia as a *particular type* of optic apraxia because of his observation that it could occur independently of any other form of apraxia and his conviction that it possessed a distinctive neuropathologic significance. A definitive description of the disorder was then presented in 1924 by Kleist's student, Hans Strauss.

According to Strauss, the pure case of constructional apraxia shows adequate visual form perception and discrimination, preserved capacity to localize objects in visual space, and no signs of ideomotor apraxia. The constructional deficit of the patient may be shown in a variety of ways, e.g., block-building, mosaic-assembling, drawing from a model. The essential deficit is spatial in nature: the patient fails to orient the constructed object, design, or drawing as a whole in a correct spatial position or fails to align its parts in correct spatial relationship to each other. With respect to the question of the localization of the lesion responsible for the constructional apraxia, he stated that the posterior parietal region of the dominant hemisphere was the critical area mediating the integration of visual and kinesthetic processes necessary for successful constructional activity. Most older authors had been inclined to view constructional apraxia and similar deficits as a sign of widespread bilateral parieto-occipital disease. Strauss conceived of this visuomotor integration taking place in the left hemisphere and thence being conducted by way of the splenium of the corpus callosum to the right hemisphere in order to mediate bilateral constructional activity. Following the reasoning of Liepmann with respect to unilateral ideomotor apraxia, Strauss further postulated that a callosal lesion that interrupted the pathways from the dominant to the subordinate hemisphere could produce a unilateral constructional apraxia confined to the activities of the left hand.

After the publication of Strauss' paper, constructional apraxia was generally accepted as a specific category or type of "apraxia." However, while some observers appeared to agree with the Kleist-Strauss formulation that the deficit in pure form was neither visuoperceptive nor motor in nature but rather a disability in translating intact visual perceptions into appropriate overt actions, others seemed to regard constructional apraxia as a part-expression of a more pervasive visuospatial impairment that could be manifested in various ways. Nor was it clear that the responsible lesion necessarily involved the left hemisphere, despite the undoubted fact of a frequent association between constructional apraxia and other deficits referable to left hemisphere disease. Indeed, as clinical observations accumulated, increasing emphasis was placed on the role of disease of the right hemisphere in producing the clinical picture. Moreover, constructional apraxia rarely, if ever, presented in isolated form, but instead it constituted one aspect of a variable constellation of perceptual and cognitive deficits shown by the patients. This circumstance encouraged consideration of the possibility that one dealt here simply with one of the innumerable performance deficits shown by a mentally impaired patient and that there was no compelling reason for singling out this particular deficit for special attention.

Is "Constructional Apraxia" a Single Disability?

As we have seen, Kleist defined constructional apraxia in only the most general terms. One consequence of this circumstance is that many tasks, differing considerably in quality and complexity, have been used to probe for the presence of the deficit. Among these are: block-arranging in the horizontal dimension (cf. Strauss, 1924); block-building in the vertical dimension (cf. Poppelreuter, 1917); three-dimensional block-building (cf. Benton & Fogel, 1962; Critchley, 1953); stick-arranging (cf. Goldstein & Scheerer, 1941); construction of mosaic patterns from a model (cf. Goldstein & Scheerer, 1941; Wechsler, 1958); drawing from a model (cf. Benton, 1962); free or spontaneous drawing (cf. Piercy, Hécaen, & Ajuriaguerra, 1960)

These constructional tasks are sometimes extremely simple, as in stick-arranging, block-building in the vertical dimension, or copying single simple figures such as a square or a triangle. However, the level of difficulty can be augmented to practically any desired degree, e.g., by requiring three-dimensional construction instead of two-dimensional construction, by having the patient draw multiple figures with definite spatial and size relations among them, or by having him make his construction not from an actual model but from a more or less abstract representation of it. Thus, in the block-designs task, it would surely seem to make a difference whether the patient is required to copy an actual block model that shows the separation of the blocks or (as in the Kohs or WAIS block designs) a representation of it in reduced size that presents the global pattern but does not show the separation of the blocks.

TABLE 5.1   CONCURRENCE OF FAILURE ON FOUR TESTS
FOR CONSTRUCTIONAL APRAXIA

Pair of Tests	No. Failing Both	% Failing Both
Design Copying & 3-D Construction	7	41
Design Copying & Stick-Construction	7	41
Design Copying & Block Designs	5	29
3-D Construction & Stick Construction	9	53
3-D Construction & Block Designs	9	53
Stick-Construction & Block Designs	10	59

(From Benton, 1967a.)

For the most part, clinicians and investigators have used these various tasks indiscriminately in the evaluation of constructional praxis, the implicit assumption appearing to be that one deals here with a unitary deficit that may be disclosed by any one or more of these task performances. However, even a cursory review of the literature indicates that patients may show considerable intraindividual variation in performance, failing some types of constructional task but succeeding in other types. Thus the question is raised as to whether "constructional apraxia," as disclosed by failure on these tasks, is in fact a single deficit or whether the term comprises a number of discrete and distinguishable types of visuoconstructive disability.

The question remains essentially unanswered. The only empirical data bearing on it comes from a recent study that analyzed the interrelations among the performances of brain-damaged patients on four representative constructional praxis tests and that provided no strong support for the assumption of a unitary deficit

(Benton, 1967a). The four tasks (copying visual designs, stick-construction, three-dimensional block construction, block designs) were given to 100 brain-damaged patients and the seventeen poorest performances with respect to each test were identified. In the case of each test, this represented a performance level exceeded by 99–100 per cent of a group of 100 control patients which had been matched with the brain-damaged group for age and educational level.

The findings of the study are presented in Table 5.1. On the basis of chance and assuming no positive relationship among the tests, one would expect to find three patients failing a pair of tests. At the other extreme, if the tests are perfectly valid measures of a single ability, one would expect to find the same seventeen patients failing all the pairs of tests. As will be seen, in the case of one pair of tests (copying visual designs and block designs), the concurrence of failure is close to the chance level. In the case of the other pairs, the concurrence is above the chance level. However, the highest degree of concurrence (stick-construction and block designs) does not approach a perfect concordance.

Perhaps the most interesting result of these comparisons is that the degree of communality between failure in copying visual designs and the other three tests is consistently lower than the degree of communality of failure among the other three tests themselves. Evidently the graphomotor element in copying visual designs gives the test a specific character. Beyond this, since the degree of concurrence among the other tests is far from close (even though it is above the chance level), it is evident that considerable intraindividual variation in performance level on these tests is possible.

On the positive side, the results suggest that it is probably warranted to think in terms of at least two types of visuoconstructional activity. Performance on assembling tasks—such as stick-construction, three-dimensional block-construction, and block designs—appear to go together to form one type. On the other hand, the graphic performance of copying visual designs stands somewhat apart from these manual assembling tasks and perhaps should be considered as a second type of visuoconstructional activity.

But, of course, these limited findings do not provide definitive answers to the question of whether or not "constructional apraxia" is best conceived as a unitary type of impairment or to the further question of a possible typology of visuoconstructional performances. More extensive empirical study is required to provide these answers.

Is "Constructional Apraxia" a Reflection of General Mental Impairment?

As has been pointed out, constructional apraxia is not a rare finding in patients with cerebral disease. Indeed, a recent comparative study has shown that tests of constructional praxis generally identify a higher proportion of brain-damaged patients than do most WAIS subtests (Benton, 1967a). While these tests presumably do require spatial analysis and the specific ability to assemble components in correct spatial relations to each other, they also demand sustained attention and capacity for planned activity, which are abilities that are likely to be impaired in any patient suffering from general mental inefficiency. We may recall that tasks involving constructional praxis have long been utilized as tests of general intelligence. Block construction tasks—such as the building of a three-cube or a six-cube pyramid—and drawing tasks—such as the copying of a cross, square, or triangle—occupy a prominent place in intelligence scales for preschool children. At higher levels, there are bead-stringing and formboard tests as well as tasks involving the drawing of more complex figures. The Block Designs test of Kohs (1923) was originally devised as a nonverbal test of general intelligence and not as a measure of special ability. Kohs believed that his test assessed a broad and fundamental mental capacity that was not at all specifically associated with a

"spatial relations" factor but rather one that could well be considered as the very core of intelligence. Defining intelligence as the
capacity to analyze a situation, to discover methods for solving
it, and, finally, to synthesize details into a consistent unity, he
pointed out how the Block Designs test appeared to satisfy the
requirements of a valid test of general intelligence.

Considerations such as these raise the question as to whether
constructional apraxia, at least as reflected in failure on relatively
complex tasks, is not simply an expression of general mental impairment. The question is of some importance from a clinical
standpoint since, if constructional apraxia is *solely* an expression
of general mental impairment, it is difficult to see how it can have
a fundamental localizing significance despite the empirical indications of a relatively close relationship between the deficit and
lesions of the right hemisphere. At the same time, given the
presence of a significant general factor that pervades all mental
performances, it may be expected that constructional apraxia will
show some degree of relationship to general intellectual level. One
would be surprised if deteriorated patients were not inferior to
more intact patients on constructional praxis tasks (or, indeed, on
any other performance one might select). The crucial question
would seem to be whether the deteriorated patient is necessarily
apraxic.

We have tried to answer this question on the basis of our case
material by classifying our patients with cerebral disease as
"impaired" or "unimpaired" and determining the frequency of
failure on the tests in each group. We adopted as a criterion of
general mental impairment a WAIS Verbal Scale IQ score that
was 20 or more points below the IQ score to be expected on the
basis of the age and education of the patient. Our normative study
showed that, in a group of 100 control patients, one could expect
that two would show a discrepancy of 20 points between observed
IQ and expected IQ (cf. Fogel, 1964). In our group of 100
patients with cerebral disease, 35 showed discrepancy scores
ranging from 20 to 49 points. These formed the impaired group

and the remaining 65 patients (with discrepancy scores of 19 or less) formed the unimpaired group.

Table 5.2 shows the frequency of failure on the four constructional praxis tasks in the impaired and unimpaired subgroups of patients. It will be seen that the frequency of failure on each of the tasks is considerable in the impaired patients. This, of course, constitutes evidence for a positive association between constructional apraxia and the presence of general mental impairment. However, it is equally evident that a substantial proportion of the impaired patients were at least not grossly defective on the constructional praxis tasks. Thus the tentative conclusion that general mental impairment does not necessarily lead to defective constructional performance seems to be justified.

TABLE 5.2   FREQUENCY OF FAILURE BY IMPAIRED AND
UNIMPAIRED PATIENTS ON FOUR VISUOCONSTRUCTIVE TASKS

Task	Frequency of Failure %	
	IMPAIRED	UNIMPAIRED
Design Copying	40	9
Stick-Construction	37	12
Three-Dimensional Block Construction	46	15
Block Designs	46	8

However, this single comparison, which was of a rather limited nature, cannot be considered to have resolved the question. The criterion of constructional apraxia adopted (i.e., a performance level exceeded by that of 98–99 per cent of control patients) was a fairly rigorous one and, consequently, some patients who would appear from clinical observation to show at least moderate constructional difficulty were counted as normal. Moreover, our measure of general mental impairment was essentially a verbal one and thus was perhaps biased in the direction of poorer performance on the part of patients with language disabilities. Other presumptive measures of general mental impairment, such as reaction time (cf. Arrigoni & De Renzi, 1964) should be applied in arriving at a definitive answer to this question.

Is Constructional Apraxia Specifically Associated with Right Hemisphere Disease?

The question posed here involves the concept of hemispheric cerebral dominance, i.e., the idea that one cerebral hemisphere serves distinctive functions that are not shared, at least to the same degree, by the other hemisphere. The prime example of hemispheric cerebral dominance is, of course, the established role of the left hemisphere in the mediation of language.

As was mentioned earlier, Kleist and Strauss postulated a mediating mechanism in the posterior left hemisphere for constructional praxis but the cogency of this view was weakened by the observation of constructional disability in patients with lesions that were apparently confined to the right hemisphere. And, in fact, subsequent investigation has disclosed that constructional apraxia is shown with decidedly higher frequency by patients with disease of the right hemisphere than those with left hemisphere lesions (cf. Arrigoni & De Renzi, 1964; Benton, 1962; Benton & Fogel, 1962; Piercy, Hécaen, & Ajuriaguerra, 1960; Piercy & Smyth, 1962). However, defective performance on the part of patients with left hemisphere disease is not at all rare. Thus, if right hemisphere "dominance" for visuoconstructive performance does exist, it does not appear to be comparable to the "dominance" for language performance exercised by the left hemisphere. In samples of right-handed aphasic patients with unilateral lesions, one finds that about 95 per cent have left hemisphere lesions while the other 5 per cent have right hemisphere lesions, i.e., one finds a ratio of about 19 to 1 in favor of the left hemisphere group with respect to relative frequency of aphasic disorder. However, in comparisons of patients with unilateral lesions with respect to performance on constructional tasks, one finds that the relatively higher frequency of failure in patients with right hemisphere disease yields ratios of about 2 to 1, or, at best, 3 to 1.

Interpretation of these results is further complicated by the finding that the observed ratio varies as a function of the type of constructional task given to the patient and the particular definition of "deficit" adopted by the investigator. Table 5.3 presents the findings of a recent study addressed to this question (Benton, 1967a). In this investigation, the four constructional performances, the interrelations of which were cited earlier in this presentation, were analyzed with respect to the degree to which they discriminated between patients with right and left hemisphere disease when different criteria of defective performance were employed.

The results clearly suggested that the degree of bias in the direction of a higher relative frequency of deficit in patients with right hemisphere disease was related to the specific task employed. When failure was defined as a performance level exceeded by 95 per cent of control patients, defective performance on copying designs and three-dimensional block construction was more than twice as frequent in the right hemisphere group as in the left hemisphere group. In contrast, there were only minimal differences between the two groups with respect to the relative frequency of defective performance on stick-construction and block designs. It will be noted further that when a more stringent criterion of failure was employed—namely, a performance level below the distribution of scores of a group of control patients— the difference between right and left hemisphere cases increased in the case of each test. Conversely, when attention was restricted to what may be called "moderate deficit" (i.e., the range of scores exceeded by 95–99 per cent of control patients but exceeding that of the lowest 1 per cent of the controls), the differences between right and left hemisphere cases were attenuated.

It is evident from these findings that the degree of association between constructional apraxia and hemispheric locus of lesion

TABLE 5.3 VISUOCONSTRUCTIVE DEFICITS IN PATIENTS WITH LESIONS OF THE RIGHT
AND LEFT HEMISPHERES

Test	Deficit[a]			"Severe" Deficit[b]			"Moderate" Deficit[c]		
	RIGHT	LEFT	R/L RATIO	RIGHT	LEFT	L/R RATIO	RIGHT	LEFT	R/L RATIO
Design Copying	29%	14%	2.1	14.5%	5%	2.9	14.5%	9%	1.6
3-D Construction	54	23	2.3	23	9	2.6	31	14	2.2
Stick-Construction	34	26	1.3	14	7	2.0	20	19	1.1
Block Designs	34	30	1.1	20	14	1.4	14	16	.9

(From Benton, 1967a.)

[a] Performance level below that of 95–100 per cent of control patients (N = 100).
[b] Performance level below that of 100 per cent of control patients.
[c] Performance level below that of 95–99 per cent of control patients but above lowest 1 per cent.

may be determined by a number of factors. We lack precise definitions of these factors. It is not immediately obvious, for example, why a three-dimensional constructional task should provide a sharper differentiation between patients with right and left hemisphere disease than does stick-construction. Some of the findings are in accord with clinical observation. It is often stated that constructional apraxia is more severe, as well as more frequent, in patients with disease of the right hemisphere; our finding that hemispheric differences are augmented when a stringent criterion of deficit is adopted would support this impression. Similarly, the failure of block designs to differentiate between the hemispheric groups can be interpreted as supporting the widespread opinion that the test assesses an ability (or cluster of abilities) that is likely to be impaired by cerebral disease independently of the locus of the lesion. But, taken as a whole, the findings await satisfactory explanation and the answer to the question of whether "constructional apraxia" is specifically related to disease of the right hemisphere depends on such an explanation.

Concluding Comments

The three questions that have been posed concerning constructional apraxia—namely, whether the term covers one or more than one discrete deficit, the closeness of its association with general mental impairment and its relationship to hemispheric locus of cerebral lesion—are interrelated. The nature of the answer to each affects the answers to the others. The empirical data cited offer a number of suggestions but they scarcely provide definitive answers. Their chief virtue is the demonstration that these are unanswered questions of considerable importance. Our understanding of the neuropsychological significance of constructional apraxia is likely to remain quite limited until they are satisfactorily answered.

6

Protopathic and Epicritic Sensation: A Reappraisal

Josephine Semmes

In the early part of this century, Henry Head and his collaborators published a notable series of papers on altered somatic sensation after lesions at various levels of the nervous system (Head, 1920). These papers are a landmark in the history of sensory neuropsychology and provide a wealth of careful observations woven into a comprehensive, evolutionary theory. Although the meager anatomical and physiological knowledge available to Head led to serious errors in this theory, some of the ideas expressed continue to be influential. Indeed, during the last decade, one of Head's conceptions has received attention and favorable comment from leading anatomists and physiologists (Herrick & Bishop, 1958; Lele & Weddell, 1959; Nauta & Kuypers, 1958; Rose & Mountcastle, 1959). This conception is that the somatosensory apparatus is divisible, morphologically and functionally, into protopathic and epicritic components.

Head's idea grew out of observations on sensation at various stages following nerve section. He came to the conclusion that the skin is served by two separate systems of peripheral nerves, with each giving rise to its own peculiar quality of sensation. One system he called "protopathic" and considered this to be phylogenetically old and normally suppressed by the newer system. He held that after nerve section the protopathic fibers regenerated more quickly than the others, which unmasked their true nature. They responded only to intense stimuli and produced a diffuse, persistent, and, for the most part, extremely unpleasant quality of sensation, although under some stimulating conditions they were also capable of evoking extremely pleasant sensations. Activation of protopathic fibers was said to convey little or no information about the stimulating agent or its whereabouts, and consequently led only to a stereotyped response similar in some respects to the mass reflex in man after spinal cord transection. Contrasted to this nonspecific, unlocalized, and emotionally charged form of sensation was that mediated by the new "epicritic" peripheral nerves, which responded to gentle contact or thermal stimuli, producing a discrete, precisely localized, and affectively neutral form of sensation. This type of sensory experience, according to Head, was the basis for the perception of objects and permitted responses graded appropriately in intensity and disposed accurately in space.

In the light of subsequent criticism, it appears that Head's account of protopathic sensation, and the massive motor response it was said to evoke, can hardly be taken literally to represent a normal but phylogenetically early sensorimotor pattern. As Walshe (1942) and others have pointed out, the protopathic sensory experience described by Head was probably due in part to active pathological reactions of the injured tissues and in part to a quantitative rather than a qualitative reduction of the nerve supply. An even stronger argument advanced by Walshe against the phylogenetic aspect of Head's theory is that the hypothetical "protopathic animal"—i.e., an animal with no power of discriminating the intensity, position, or nature of a stimulus—does not exist and is almost inconceivable. Despite this criticism, the essentials of Head's distinction seem to be preserved in the modern view which contrasts the epicritic, or discriminative, type of sensation with the protopathic, or affective. Furthermore, Head's notion that two qualitatively different kinds of sensory experience are mediated by two anatomically distinct neural systems has also been preserved, although the locus has been shifted from the peripheral to the central nervous system. Specifically, it is now suggested that the new lemniscal system is responsible for the discriminative aspects of sensation, whereas the old extralemniscal system mediates the affective aspects.

Although Head's theory and this newer version are similar in form, it should be noted that they are not convergent. Thus, Head's own clinical findings in cases with central nervous system damage convinced him that the protopathic-epicritic dichotomy was not applicable to the central pathways. Conversely, the updated central theory does not apply to disorders of sensation resulting from peripheral nerve injury, the phenomena that first suggested the protopathic-epicritic distinction. In fact, whereas the two sets of ideas dichotomize sensation along the same lines and use the same labels, they have little in common of a substantive nature.

Despite the fundamental difference between the two theories, the modern version is subject to some of the same criticisms as those raised against Head. If one accepts Walshe's argument that protopathic sensation is a pathological form, then it cannot represent the normal function of any system, central or peripheral. Furthermore, if there has never been a "protopathic animal," it cannot be supposed that only the phylogenetically new central system is capable of mediating epicritic functions. Epicritic sensation, as judged by the presence of spatially accurate, graded responses, must have antedated the emergence of the new system.

These criticisms, which played a part in the rejection of Head's theory, seem to be equally damaging to the modern proposal. Since the development of a more adequate theory is likely to be hindered by continued speculation within the framework borrowed from Head, it is important to reexamine the evidence from which the newer version arose. This evidence, it should be pointed out, does *not* stem from a direct assessment of sensation after selective damage either to one system or the other. Rather, the support for the theory is indirect, consisting mainly of inferences about sensation that have been drawn from the differing anatomical and physiological properties of the lemniscal and extra-lemniscal pathways. In what follows, an attempt will be made to show that these inferences are open to question and reinterpretation. The argument will consider the phylogenetic history of the two systems, the evidence for their interdependence, and behavioral findings bearing directly on the inferences which have been made concerning their function.

Phylogenetically Old and New Afferent Systems

Comparative studies of the vertebrate nervous system (Bishop, 1959; Diamond, 1967; Herrick & Bishop, 1958) have broadened our conception of the central afferent apparatus and shed new light on the possible functional meaning of its various components. Perhaps the most important discovery in these studies is the relatively late emergence of the modality-specific sensory pathways and the thalamic and cortical centers in which they terminate. Thus, new sensory systems—visual, auditory, and somesthetic—were superimposed on those already existing in premammalian forms. Bishop (based on Herrick) describes three stages in the phylogenetic history of afferent representation in the cortex. In the first stage, the anterior pole of the nervous system consisted essentially of an olfactory center. Within this center, a general nonolfactory cortex developed, which was secondarily connected to the common thalamic pool serving all the remaining senses. The second stage was characterized by the beginning of specialization within the general cortex: islands developed with a more specific relation to parts of the thalamus which in turn received their respective inputs mainly from the visual, auditory, or somesthetic pathway. It was only later, in the third stage, that modality-specific projection areas in the cortex and corresponding relay nuclei in the thalamus emerged.

The development of these new systems, of course, does not imply the loss of the earlier form of afferent representation. Bishop sees the surrounds of the modality-specific areas, such as the prestriate cortex, as persisting remainders of the islands of predominantly specific sensory reference that developed in the second stage; he suggests that parts of the association cortex even further removed from the modality-specific areas are related to the general cortex of the first stage. The comparative studies thus suggest a radical shift in our view of the relation between the "primary sensory" and "association" areas of the cortex. Instead of the traditional picture of the specific projection area as the only cortical representation of a given modality, and of the association cortex as only the receiver and integrator of the outflow from the projection area, we see two (or even three) sensory representations in parallel.

How do the new and the old sensory systems differ? Bishop suggests that, as the specific somesthetic centers emerged, new central pathways developed concomitantly. These new pathways differed from those already existing in the increased proportion of large, myelinated fibers they contained. The large dorsal root fibers fed preferentially into the new system. Among those carrying kinesthetic information, it seems likely that this tendency applied especially to fibers from the mechanoreceptors of the joints, since neurons responsive to joint rotation are abundant in the new system, but not elsewhere (Carreras & Andersson, 1963; Mountcastle, 1957; but see also Oscarsson, 1958). Fibers from the muscle spindles and tendon organs are also present in the new system (Albe-Fessard, 1967; Oscarsson, 1966), contrary to earlier indications. The large mechanoreceptive fibers from the skin and subcutaneous tissues likewise tended to be drawn into this system, and these increased their efficiency by developing complex and compact peripheral endings either around the base of hairs or often in hairless skin by enclosure of filamentous networks within capsules of nonnervous tissue (Lele & Weddell, 1959).

Bishop recognizes three phylogenetically old afferent tracts in the spinal cord besides the cerebellar pathway. These three tracts, composed in the main of relatively small fibers (since the larger central fibers of the old system presumably terminated in the cerebellum), are present in premammalian vertebrates. They are distinguished by their central targets: the oldest ends in the medulla, the next in the midbrain tegmentum, and the final one in the thalamus (the intralaminar nuclei, with which should probably be included the midline and reticular nuclei). All of these targets are in the nonspecific, diffuse system (the reticular formation), but as the cortex became more highly developed, links were established to it.

The old tracts also send fibers to thalamic structures other than the intralaminar group. The anterolateral columns (excluding for the moment consideration of the neospinothalamic component) project to regions within all the major thalamic subdivisions, except the anterior group, the lateral geniculate body, and the pars principalis of the medial geniculate body. Thus, a soma input has been found to n. medialis dorsalis (Anderson & Ber 1959; Mehler, Feferman, & Nauta, 1960), to n. ventralis anter and n. ventralis lateralis (Kruger & Albe-Fessard, 1960), and the posterior group, including the pars magnocellularis of the medial geniculate body, n. suprageniculatus, n. posterior, n. lateralis posterior, and possibly n. pulvinaris (Getz, 1952; Poggio & Mountcastle, 1960; Whitlock & Perl, 1961). It should be noted that the thalamic connections of the old somatic afferent system are largely with the so-called "intrinsic" nuclei (Rose & Woolsey. 1949). These nuclei project to the telencephalon, chiefly to the cortical association areas rather than to areas generally designated as sensory in function.

With the advent of mammals, new tracts made their appearance, and these show further development from lower to higher forms. Bishop mentions two of these tracts, the dorsal column and the neospinothalamic tract, and to these should be added the spinocervical tract (the bundle of Morin, 1955). These three tracts and their central projections comprise the new system, which is defined by their common target in the newly evolved "extrinsic" nucleus of the somesthetic apparatus, n. ventralis posterior (also called the ventrobasal complex). The pathways and centers of the new system are collectively referred to as the "lemniscal" system, since together they make up the medial lemniscus in the rostral midbrain. This classification follows that of Albe-Fessard (1967). The main cortical projection of the new system is the postcentral gyrus (SI of Woolsey, 1947), although fibers also run to SII (Macchi, Angeleri, & Guazzi, 1959) and to areas 4 and 5 (Krieg, 1963). Table 6.1 summarizes the principal anatomical properties of the new and old systems.

The anatomical differences between the new and the old systems are accompanied by contrasting physiological properties. Consider first the consequences of the difference in the predominant size of fibers. Size determines conduction velocity; therefore, the new system can transmit information more rapidly than the old. Bishop also points out that the large fibers generate more current at the synapses, a feature that makes for reliability and faithfulness of transmission. The larger fiber's message gets across and is relatively unchanged, that is, the postsynaptic cells may

TABLE 6.1   SOMATIC AFFERENT SYSTEMS:
ANATOMICAL PROPERTIES

	New (Lemniscal)	*Old (Extralemniscal)*
Structures Served	Skin Deep tissues Muscles Tendons Joints	Skin Deep tissues Muscles Tendons Joints
Receptors	Complex endings	Simple endings Complex endings
Central Fibers	Many large (beta)	All sizes
Tracts	Dorsal column Neo-spinothalamic tract Spino-cervical tract	Spino-reticular tracts Old spinothalamic tracts Old spino-cerebellar tract (ventral)[a]
Distribution	Contralateral	Contralateral Bilateral Ipsilateral
Main Targets	Thalamus N. ventralis posterior	Medulla Reticular formation Midbrain Reticular formation Thalamus Intralaminar nuclei Other intrinsic nuclei Cerebellum
Principal Cortical Terminations	Postcentral gyrus (SI)	Association areas

[a] The dorsal spino-cerebellar tract is omitted from this classification since it is new, but extralemniscal.

approximate relays; in contrast, the small fiber's message may be lost or may be integrated with what its fellows are signaling, such that the postsynaptic cells probably behave more like "funnels and filters" (see Wall, 1961).

The cells of the new system reflect with a high degree of specificity the location and nature of the stimulating agent (Mountcastle, 1957; Poggio & Mountcastle, 1960). They tend to have small and stable receptive fields, which are thought to be still further restricted by inhibitory relationships among adjacent cells (Mountcastle & Powell, 1959), although the size of the field varies with the distance from the tip of the limb. The units appear to be sensitive only to mechanical stimuli, that is, those that cause deformation of tissue. Moreover, subgroups can be distinguished according to their responsiveness to a particular kind of deformation—hair movement, cutaneous pressure, pressure on deep tissues, or joint rotation—with little or no evidence of overlap. Thus, the units of the new system are labeled with both the place and type of stimulation. These physiological characteristics are often called "lemniscal" properties, since they are typical of the lemniscal system, although not all units of this system exhibit these properties, and not all extralemniscal units lack them.

The old, or extralemniscal, system shows a wider range of characteristics, as might be expected from the heterogeneity of its anatomical features. Emphasis is usually placed on its differences from the new system, however. Thus, in the dorsal horn of the spinal cord, which contains the cells of origin of the old tracts, many cells have been found that respond to all types of cutaneous stimulation—touch, pressure, temperature changes, itch-producing substances, and crushing injury. Despite the fact that these cells are "common carriers," it seems likely that they have a way of conveying specific information about the stimulating agent. In contrast to the method of labeled transmission lines used in the lemniscal system, these cells respond with different temporal patterns of impulses to different types of stimuli (Wall, 1960; Wall & Cronly-Dillon, 1960). It has also been suggested that temporal patterning may be a factor in specifying location of the stimulus (Adey, Carter, & Porter, 1954; Amassian, 1954; Marshall & Talbot, 1942). Cells that respond to a variety of somesthetic stimuli have also been found at the thalamic level in nuclei connected with the old system, and some of these cells can be activated by sound as well. Many have large and rather labile receptive fields (Poggio & Mountcastle, 1960).

Finally, the systems differ in their spatial relations to the periphery. The new tracts transmit information from only one lateral half of the body to the thalamus and cortex of the contralateral side, whereas the old pathways and centers may receive from either or both body-halves. Thus, in the ventrobasal complex and in the postcentral gyrus or its homologue (centers of the new system), unit receptive fields are almost without exception on the contralateral side of the body; in contrast, the fields of cells in the posterior group (a center of the old system) may be ipsilateral, bilateral, or contralateral (Poggio & Mountcastle, 1960). When the spatial relations to the periphery are considered in greater detail, further differences between the two systems are apparent. The cells of the new system exhibit an orderly arrangement, such that the body is represented in a coherent fashion, forming a map or homunculus, in which the face and distal parts of the limbs are disproportionately represented (Woolsey, Marshall, & Bard, 1942). This arrangement has been amply confirmed by single unit studies. However, these same studies have failed to find an orderly representation in the old system, at least in the posterior group (Poggio & Mountcastle, 1960), although there is evidence for at least a rough topographic arrangement in some extralemniscal structures (e.g., the topographic representation of the ipsilateral side of the body in cortical area SII). Table 6.2 summarizes the principal physiological properties of the new and old systems.

Interaction between the Old and New Systems

Considering the contrasting properties of the two systems, it is easy to see why the lemniscal system came to be identified with epicritic functions and the extralemniscal with protopathic. The

TABLE 6.2   SOMATIC AFFERENT SYSTEMS:
PHYSIOLOGICAL PROPERTIES

	New (Lemniscal)	Old (Extralemniscal)
Adequate Stimuli	Hair movement Cutaneous pressure Deep pressure Muscle stretch Muscle tension Joint rotation	Hair movement Cutaneous pressure Deep pressure Heat exchange Itch-producing substances Injury Muscle stretch Muscle tension Joint rotation
Unit Specialization	Stimulus-specific	Includes common-carrier and hetero-sensory units

Transmission	Rapid, reliable
	
	Faithful across
	  synapses
	Private lines
		Includes slow,
		  vulnerable elements
		Includes interaction
		  effects at synapses
		Includes nonspecific
		  lines with possible
		  differentiation by
		  temporal patterning

Receptive Fields	Small, stable
	
	Contralateral
	  (except face)
		Includes large, labile
		  fields
		Includes ipsilateral
		  and bilateral fields

Organization	Topographic	Includes nontopographic arrangement
Main Body Parts Represented	Hands Feet Face	Less specialization

lemniscal pathways and centers might seem to be ideally suited
to carry out precise discrimination. Having made this assumption,
one is then led to view the extralemniscal system as competent to

serve only crude aspects of sensory function and thus contributing nothing to discrimination. Conversely, if one begins by considering the extralemniscal system, its many endings in the reticular formation might suggest that it is especially suited to serve in arousal and hence in activity directed toward seeking pleasure and avoiding pain. For such affective aspects of behavior, the lemniscal system might seem to contribute nothing.

Such direct translation between neural properties and behavior is hazardous. In this case, the translation suggests that the new and old systems operate quite independently. Against this view is the phylogenetic evidence that the new system was differentiated out of the old system (Erickson, Jane, Waite, & Diamond, 1964), or, in functional terms, that the new system probably developed to facilitate mechanoreception mainly for the apices of the limbs, against the background of a parent system capable of handling the entire range of somesthetic functions for all parts of the body. It is likely that the motor apparatus had a similar phylogenetic history: a new motor system (pyramidal), concerned with facilitating movements of the apices of the limbs, was superimposed on an old motor system (extrapyramidal) that was competent to direct movements of all parts of the body.

Besides these phylogenetic considerations, there is direct evidence against the notion that the old and new sensory systems operate independently. Sites of convergence have been found at virtually all levels from the periphery to the cortex. In the skin and deeper tissues, there is not only complete interdigitation of the branches of large and small fibers, but common sites of peripheral termination. Thus, the encapsulated end-organs are supplied not only by large fibers but by small, accessory fibers as well (Weddell, 1941). With increasing knowledge of the cutaneous nerve plexus, it has also become clear that the "touch spots" are not the result of activity in a single end-organ but rather in a cluster of terminations of several fibers belonging to more than one sensory unit. It seems clear that almost every mechanical stimulus applied to the body surface must excite both the old and the new systems.

Furthermore, within the central nervous system the information carried by the lemniscal and the extralemniscal pathways is not entirely separable. Part of the lemniscal input (deriving from the spino-cervical tract) is provided by collaterals of the extralemniscal fibers running to the cerebellum (Ha & Liu, 1966). On the other hand, lemniscal fibers (those of the dorsal column), after ascending for several segments, give off collaterals which converge in the dorsal horn on cells of origin of extralemniscal tracts (Albe-Fessard, 1967). At the level of the medulla, ascending extralemniscal fibers in the reticular formation are met by a descending pathway from SI, the main cortical projection area of the lemniscal system (Albe-Fessard, 1967).

Convergence between the two systems occurs at higher levels as well, probably in the thalamus and certainly in the cortex. It has long been thought that the intrinsic thalamic nuclei receive inputs from the extrinsic nuclei, and this has been confirmed for the visual system (Altman, 1962; Bishop, 1959). Thus, by analogy, it seems likely that n. ventralis posterior, the extrinsic nucleus of the new somesthetic system, likewise sends fibers to the intrinsic nuclei, which as noted above receive an ascending input from the old, extralemniscal pathways. For the cortex, it has been shown that SI and SII are reciprocally connected to areas in the cerebellum (Hampson, 1949; Henneman, Cooke, & Snider, 1952). Thus, even SI, the purest cortical representation of the lemniscal system, is subject to extralemniscal influences. SII is even more clearly an area of convergence between the two systems, since it receives a lemniscal input from n. ventralis posterior and from SI and an extralemniscal one not only from the cerebellum but also from the posterior group of thalamic nuclei (Rose & Woolsey, 1958). Other cortical sites for which there is evidence of input from both systems include the motor area, the posterior parietal lobule, and the newly discovered somatic representation in the orbital frontal region (Korn, Wendt, & Albe-Fessard, 1966). Even more striking than these instances of areal convergence is the observation that single cells may receive from both systems. For example, a unit in the motor cortex may have an input via the lemniscal system for the contralateral hindleg and an input via the extralemniscal system for the other three legs (Albe-Fessard, 1967).

The close relationships between the old and the new systems from the receptors to the highest neural level make it appear dubious that their final outputs are separable, such that each mediates a qualitatively different form of sensation. Perhaps it could be argued that these interconnections serve not so much to yield an integrated product as to enable the new system to suppress the old, as Head originally suggested for the peripheral nerves. This is merely an unsupported hypothesis, however, proposing a situation that would appear to be biologically wasteful. As Hebb (1949) has pointed out, it is not plausible to assume, for example, that the fibers that might mediate a toothache are constantly suppressed throughout an entire lifetime if the tooth remains sound.

The Old System and Protopathic Sensation

Arguments such as that advanced above call into question the idea that the extensive connections between the new and old systems can be explained away as having only a suppressive function. The evidence suggests instead that they operate in close conjunction with each other. Thus it appears unlikely, on these grounds alone, that the old system is solely responsible for protopathic, or affective, sensation, whereas the new system independently mediates epicritic, or discriminative, sensation. But let us examine each part of this neuropsychological proposition in detail.

The notion that sensations charged with pleasantness or unpleasantness are mediated by a special system originating in the periphery and extending the length of the neuraxis implies that the emotional response is inherent in the *afferent* activity, an implication not at all in accord with modern views of the neural substrate of affective states. It is well known that such states can be dissociated from afferent activity by a variety of means: the affect can be provoked without sensory stimulation and, conversely, sensations that usually provoke affect will under certain conditions fail to do so. It seems preferable, then, to regard the affective aspect of sensation as expressive of a central rather than an afferent state.

Moreover, since sights and sounds, as well as bodily sensations, are potent arousers of emotion, there seems little reason to believe that the somesthetic modality alone has a special system within its neural apparatus devoted to affective experience. It is worth noting that, although there are phylogenetically old systems for vision and audition, no one has suggested that they give rise to protopathic visual or protopathic auditory sensations, that is, affective sensations that are undifferentiated, unlocalized, and capable only of eliciting reflexive withdrawal or approach. To realize how implausible such a suggestion would be, one has only to consider the behavior of animals whose abilities do not depend on the new geniculo-cortical systems, for example, the speed and accuracy of responses directed toward small, moving targets in reptiles and amphibia, and the truly remarkable capacities of birds for visual spatial orientation and for differentiation of auditory patterns. There is even more direct evidence against the notion that a system with properties like those of the new geniculocortical ones is the *sine qua non* of discriminative behavior. Recent experimental findings in the tree shrew (Snyder, Hall, & Diamond, 1966) show that ablation of the entire striate cortex, with consequent total degeneration of the lateral geniculate body, does not prevent this animal from seizing small bits of proffered food and even from retaining or quickly relearning preoperatively acquired visual pattern discriminations.

If one asks why the somesthetic modality should have been singled out as the only sense with a protopathic component, the answer probably lies in the fact that the somatic nerves mediate

pain, which, when it is diffuse, persistent, and intensely disagree-
able (as, for example, in causalgia), represents the protopathic
experience *par excellence*. It is therefore important to consider
what is known about the neural basis of pain and, in particular,
whether the more protopathic kinds of pain can be ascribed to the
old somesthetic system, operating alone.

Following von Frey, pain has conventionally been regarded as
a somatic submodality, having its own peripheral receptors and
fibers, its own spinal tract, and a special target in the thalamus.
This view implies that pain results solely from activation of particular pathways and centers and that when these pathways and
centers are activated, pain and no other sensory experience is the
result. But it has become increasingly clear that this view is
untenable, especially for protopathic pain, since it is observations
on this form which provide some of the most compelling evidence
against it.

The tiny, nonmyelinated peripheral nerve fibers (the C group)
were originally thought to be the only carriers for pain, but even
after it became known that the small, myelinated A-fibers could
mediate pain, the C-fibers were still held to be responsible for the
protopathic form. It was assumed that when, as a result of injury
or disease, an area of tissue was innervated only by C-fibers, the
unmodified activity of these high-threshold, slowly conducting
fibers gave rise to pain with protopathic qualities. But, as Melzack
and Wall (1965) have pointed out in their recent discussion of
pain mechanisms, mild stimulation of areas of skin that are
normally innervated may in some cases trigger agonizing pain,
and the latency of its onset may be far too long to be explained
by conduction in C-fibers. Furthermore, when techniques were
developed for studying C-fibers electrophysiologically (Douglas
& Ritchie, 1957, 1959; Iggo, 1958, 1959), it became apparent that
many of them were responsive to stimuli that could not be regarded as noxious at all, such as warmth, cold, and even light
touch; only a very few had such high thresholds that they might
be considered to function as nociceptors, and these seemed to

represent the extreme of a continuous distribution of receptor-fiber thresholds rather than a special group. In fact, Douglas and Ritchie (1959), studying C-fibers in the saphenous nerve, concluded that most of them are given over to signaling touch and light pressure, and that these nonmyelinated "touch fibers" outnumber the myelinated "touch fibers."

Surgical operations undertaken for the relief of intractable pain have also provided evidence against the view that the protopathic form is mediated exclusively by one of the tracts of the old somesthetic system. The lateral spinothalamic tract is the classic pathway for pain, but it is now recognized that there must be other pathways capable of transmitting impulses that give rise to the experience of pain. If the lateral tract were the only one concerned, then transecting it should universally and permanently eliminate pain, yet this is clearly far from being the case. The conception that protopathic pain is based on simple transmission in a pain-specific system is vitiated by the great variety of operations that have been partially but not completely successful in alleviating pain. It is notable that one of these operations, for which substantial therapeutic value has been claimed in cases with phantom limb pain, is a topical removal of the postcentral gyrus, the main cortical projection area of the new system (Stone, 1950). (This result also argues against the notion that the new system has the function of suppressing the old, since if that were so, the operation should have intensified the pain.)

Despite the failure to identify protopathic pain with a special group of peripheral fibers and a special spinal tract, it has been suggested that there is a pain center in certain extralemniscal nuclei of the thalamus, nuclei assumed to mediate protopathic sensation partly on the basis of the large and labile receptive fields of units in this region and their lack of an overall topographical organization. Poggio and Mountcastle (1960), studying the anesthetized cat, found that 60 per cent of the neurons sampled in the posterior group responded only to noxious stimuli; they proposed that these nuclei and their cortical projection field might therefore be the substrate for conscious pain (presumably the kind of pain that is diffuse rather than the kind which can be precisely localized). The data supporting the proposal that this region is largely pain-specific should be evaluated, however, in the light of Casey's subsequent findings in the unanesthetized monkey (1964, cited by Melzack & Wall, 1965). If the animals were drowsy or asleep, units in the homologous posterior region appeared to be exclusively nociceptive, whereas if the animals were awake, the same units became responsive to low-intensity tactile stimulation.

The evidence is thus unconvincing that protopathic pain can be accounted for in terms of the conception that pain is a primary sense-modality having its own special peripheral and central apparatus within the old somesthetic system. Indeed, such a conception might seem more applicable to the normal, or relatively epicritic, form of pain, with the reservation that the "specific" fibers are probably high-threshold mechanoreceptive or thermoreceptive elements (cf. Burgess & Perl, 1967). But rather than assuming that the protopathic and epicritic forms of pain are based on two entirely different neural mechanisms, it would of course be preferable to have one theory capable of embracing both forms. Such a theory, making use of the concepts of central summation and input control, has recently been proposed by Melzack and Wall (1965). The theory proposes that pain is felt when excitation in central transmitting cells of the dorsal horn of the spinal cord reaches or exceeds a critical level. Whether or not this level is reached depends on interactions of these cells with those of two other systems: the substantia gelatinosa, which acts as a gate control, and the dorsal column and spino-cervical tract (pathways of the new system), which operate to open and close the gate. These new, large-fibered pathways conduct rapidly to the brain and so are able to activate descending efferent fibers in time to regulate the flow of impulses still arriving over more slowly conducting elements. On occasions when the descending message tends to close the gate, activity in the small fibers of the dorsal root is relatively ineffective, but when on the contrary, the message opens the gate sufficiently, then not only small-fiber but even large-fiber activity can contribute toward pain. It is assumed that the character of the descending message is determined by a variety of factors and that many different regions of the brain may be involved. Besides this central influence on the gate, there are also peripheral determinants, with activity in the large fibers tending to close the gate and activity in the small fibers having the opposite effect. The theory thus explains protopathic pain as resulting from any of a number of pathological processes that have in common the effect of producing an abnormally open gate.

If the theory is correct—and its ability to explain many formerly puzzling phenomena in terms of modern neurophysiological concepts recommends it—then pain of both the normal and the pathological varieties is the outcome of particular modes of interaction between the old and new sensory systems, and indeed, between these and other systems as well, since the theory recognizes the important role of nonsensory factors in determining whether pain is felt.

The New System and Epicritic Sensation

These considerations on pain make it seem improbable that protopathic sensation can be assigned to the old system, operating alone. Turning now to the complementary proposition that epicritic sensation is mediated solely by the new system, it appears that this is equally questionable. Although certainly the new system is involved in epicritic functions, intactness of this system is not sufficient to preserve such functions unimpaired.

The involvement of the new system in discriminative sensation can be inferred from its relationship to the periphery. For the skin, such epicritic qualities as high sensitivity, precise localization, and fine acuity are all related to a quantitative factor, the density of peripheral innervation. Thus, the parts of the body that are most densely innervated, such as the hand, the foot, and the area around the mouth, show these epicritic qualities most clearly. It is just these parts, of course, that have a strikingly disproportionate representation in the cortical projection area of the new system, the postcentral gyrus (SI); these body parts are served by the largest number of units and, correspondingly, these units have the smallest receptive fields. Moreover, epicritic qualities pertain especially to a particular type of stimulation—the mechanical, and the new system is specialized in this respect also. Its cells are selectively connected to peripheral receptors activated by displacement of tissues, i.e., hair bending, touch-pressure, and joint movement.

It would thus be straightforward to conclude that the new system is especially related to mechanoreception by certain body parts, such that damage to it could be expected to produce hypesthesia for this type of stimulation of these parts. But to propose that the new system is the mediator of every sort of discriminative sensibility, even including, for example, different degrees of warmth or coolness, and that it serves all such functions for the whole body would be to go considerably beyond the data. Even to assume that its properties make it entirely sufficient for certain kinds of discrimination, say those requiring accurate spatial localization of mechanical stimuli, is an extrapolation that deserves scrutiny.

The new system has one property in particular that has perhaps contributed more than any other to the assumption that it is the substrate of spatial localization. Great importance has been attached to the fact that this system is organized topographically, thus forming the cortical homunculus, or brain map. The view is widely held that we know the spatial position of a stimulated point by virtue of the spatial relationships among the parts of this orderly arrangement of nerve fibers, that is, by which cells *within this map* are excited. But, since stimulation of a particular point on the body surface is coded by a unique configuration of cortical cells, one may ask what is contributed by the map-like arrangement *per se*. Some may answer that the value of the map is self-evident—that it provides the spatial framework or coordinate system within which points are located. But this answer would seem to be based on the tacit assumption that the body map in the brain is the neural counterpart of the body map as given by introspection. When this assumption is made explicit, it is clear that it is untenable, given the major flaws in the brain map compared to the veridicality of the introspective map. For example, the brain map is grossly distorted, such that a given distance on the skin has no constant equivalent on the scale of the cortical map. Even more serious are the disarrangements in representation. Thus, the chin and thumb lie next to each other, and the occiput next to the outer aspect of the arm, which in turn is separated from the inner aspect by the side of the head, the neck, and the shoulder (Woolsey, Marshall, & Bard, 1942). A different way of asking the question "What does the map contribute?" is 'What do the flaws in the map take away?" As far as is known, there are no perceptual distortions or errors in localization that mirror the peculiar features of this map, and, indeed, it is hard to say what perceptual errors should be predicted. It seems clear that our ability to touch or otherwise indicate accurately a point stimulated must be related to a *veridical* spatial framework, but that this is not provided by the brain map.

One might propose of course that the order the map shows within restricted regions is important. This might be the case especially when the relation among stimulated points is critical, as in pattern perception. An experiment by Gibson (1962) provides a test of this possibility. If a two-dimensional pattern, such as a cooky cutter, is pressed on the palm, recognition is poor, but if while pressing the pattern, the experimenter rotates it clockwise and counterclockwise, recognition is considerably aided. Since a procedure that plays havoc with any simple, stable pattern of excitation in the brain map improves, rather than disrupts, the perception of a stimulus pattern, it is difficult to suppose that such perception can be explained by an isomorphic neural representation. Furthermore, Gibson's observations on the great variety of active exploratory movements made by subjects in discriminating three-dimensional forms by palpation indicate that the form must be reconstructed from a complex sequence of partial impressions, derived from tracing, rubbing, pressing, hand adjustments, and so forth, activities that must evoke correspondingly complex and changing patterns of excitation in the brain. Arguments against isomorphism as the basis for pattern perception in vision are likewise compelling (Hebb, 1949).

This evidence, although indirect, suggests the map-like arrangement of the new system is not sufficient to account either for the localizations of points on the body surface or for more complex aspects of epicritic sensation. More direct evidence is available, however. If the new system were sufficient, then the classical measures of epicritic sensation, such as tactile thresholds, point localization, and two-point discrimination, should not be affected by damage outside this system. Yet in a study carried out on war veterans with penetrating brain injuries (Semmes, Weinstein, Ghent, & Teuber, 1960), it was found that damage that did not seem to encroach on the postcentral gyrus or even on areas adjacent to it did affect these classical measures of cutaneous sensitivity. Although the incidence of defect was not as great as that following postcentral damage, it was nonetheless substantial. In contrast, sense of passive joint movement was rarely affected except by damage in or near the postcentral region. These findings suggest that cutaneous sensation of a highly discriminative quality is dependent on the integrity of both the new and the old systems, whereas joint sensation is more selectively dependent on the new system.

Results supporting the distinction between cutaneous and joint sensibilities have also been obtained with monkeys: roughness discrimination thresholds (a measure of cutaneous sense) are vulnerable to contralateral cortical lesions outside the projection area of the new system, while size discrimination thresholds (presumably a measure of joint position sense) are unaffected by such lesions (Semmes, Mishkin & Cole, 1968). Such a distinction is likewise favored by electrophysiological evidence showing that units responsive to tactile stimuli are found in both the lemniscal and extralemniscal centers, although units responsive to gentle rotation of joints appear to be exclusively lemniscal.

Perhaps the most telling evidence against the notion that epicritic sensation is mediated solely by the new system was a finding in the brain-injured veterans of deficits ipsilateral to the lesion (Semmes et al., 1960). These deficits were detected mainly on the test of point localization. Since this study, other investigators have also reported ipsilateral sensory deficits in brain-injured patients on tests of cutaneous epicritic function (Corkin, Milner, & Rasmussen, 1964; Vaughan & Costa, 1962). Further, ipsilateral impairments in roughness thresholds and in learning difficult form discriminations have now been found in monkeys with histologically verified unilateral removals (Semmes & Mishkin, 1965b). If the generally accepted view is correct that the new system projects only to the contralateral hemisphere, the foregoing results seem to provide conclusive evidence that the old system must be concerned in epicritic sensation.

The evidence treated so far has dealt with contributions to epicritic sensation made by the hemisphere ipsilateral to a given body part and by areas distant from the postcentral gyrus in the hemisphere contralateral. Contributions from still a third area primarily related to the old system must be considered also, this one adjacent to the postcentral gyrus. The now classical ablation experiments of Ruch and his colleagues (Ruch & Fulton, 1935; Ruch, Fulton, & German, 1938) showed that at least some kinds of discriminative sensibility are impaired not only by lesions of the postcentral gyrus but equally by posterior parietal removals. These investigators found that ablation of either area in monkeys and chimpanzees produced an initial deficit on roughness and weight discrimination thresholds which seemed to be fully recoverable. Only a combination of the two lesions, i.e., complete parietal lobectomy, led to a severe and lasting impairment, yet this was incomplete.

The surprising degree of recovery after the postcentral ablation indicates that, despite the special characteristics of this area which suggest that it might be the substrate of discriminative sensation, areas with different characteristics are able to sustain certain discriminations at a high level. Moreover, the finding that the posterior parietal lesion could produce or augment an impairment suggests that areas to which the old system projects do not merely provide a margin of safety but normally participate in discrimination.

Sensation and Gnosis

The inference concerning the posterior parietal region needs to be examined from another point of view. Traditionally, a distinction is made between elementary sensation, on the one hand, and perception or gnosis, on the other. Thus, proponents of the classical view in neurology might contend that deficits in somesthesis after posterior parietal lesions do not represent a true loss in discriminative sensation but rather a failure of somesthetic associative processes. There are now quite a number of experiments demonstrating deficits on a variety of somesthetic discrimination tasks after posterior parietal lesions in monkeys (Bates & Ettlinger, 1960; Ettlinger & Wegener, 1958; Pribram & Barry, 1956; Wilson, 1957; Wilson, Stamm, & Pribram, 1960). The theoretical orientation of these studies is very different from that of Ruch, that is, their aim is not to discover what parts of the cortex are concerned in sensation but to show that lesions of the "somesthetic association area" produce modality-specific deficits of a higher order. These studies start from the implicit assumption that the substrate of sensation is known to be confined to n. ventralis posterior and its main cortical projection field, the postcentral gyrus; consequently, when it can be shown histologically that this nucleus is intact, it is concluded that the deficits are not ascribable to sensory loss. But the initial premise, which equates sensation with the new sensory system, would seem on the basis of the opposing evidence described in the previous section to be unwarranted. As Fulton and Ruch concluded from their results,

The experiments are difficult to interpret by the traditional concept of a postcentral region which receives all sensory impulses and transmits them to the posterior parietal association area. . . . Both subregions appear capable of independent function which implies that the posterior parietal lobule receives an independent projection (Fulton, 1943, pp. 362–363).

As noted above, the old system sends fibers to n. lateralis posterior (Getz, 1952), which is known to project to the posterior parietal region; fibers also terminate in other nuclei of the posterior group, which may at least in part project to this region. It seems likely, then, that the old system provides the "independent projection" that makes the posterior parietal lobule capable of "independent function" in roughness and weight discrimination.

One might still maintain of course that the posterior parietal region contributes to other, more complex abilities by virtue of its cortico-cortical input from the postcentral gyrus. The paramount example of such an ability would be stereognosis, which has been regarded as the highest expresssion of epicritic function. In assessing the probable nature of the posterior parietal contribution, however, it should not be overlooked that this region receives more than somatosensory inputs. As mentioned above, the old system (which projects in part to this region) is not, or not entirely, modality-specific. Some of the units in the posterior group have been found to respond to auditory stimuli or to both somatosensory and auditory inputs (Poggio & Mountcastle, 1960). Furthermore, the posterior parietal region has connections with the visual system, deriving probably from n. pulvinaris (Chow, 1950), and certainly from the striate and prestriate cortex (Krieg, 1963; Kuypers, Szwarcbart, Mishkin, & Rosvold,

1965). Evidence on stereognostic capacities in the brain-injured veterans referred to earlier makes it appear likely that it is this heterogeneity of inputs, rather than the specific input from the postcentral gyrus, that makes the posterior parietal region important for stereognosis. This suggestion stems from the finding that performance on tactual form and pattern discriminations in these subjects was significantly related to an ability that was not modality-specific (Semmes, 1965).

Briefly, the study was as follows. A variety of object-quality discrimination tasks—roughness, texture, size, 3-dimensional form, and 2-dimensional pattern—was administered to the subjects with brain injuries and to a normal control group. As expected, subjects with sensory defect (assessed by the tests of sensation mentioned earlier) were impaired on all these tasks. But it soon became apparent that sensory defect was not the only cause for poor performance, since the group of brain-injured subjects *without* sensory defects were significantly inferior to the normal controls on the form and pattern tasks, although not on the others. This finding might be taken as support for the classical view that astereognosis is a higher order somesthetic impairment, since the deficits in discrimination were dissociable from sensory loss. But, alternatively, it seemed worthwhile to investigate the possibility that deficits might be accounted for by the disturbance of an essential capacity other than somesthesis. Of the several variables investigated, one proved to be relevant, and this was a measure of spatial orientation. Thus, poor performance on a locomotor task employing path-diagrams, *perceived visually,* was significantly associated with poor scores on the tactual form and pattern tasks, but not at all associated with scores on the roughness, texture, or size tasks.

It had been shown earlier that spatial disability, as measured by this test of orientation, is not modality-specific, i.e., not restricted to information received through a particular sensory channel (Semmes, Weinstein, Ghent, & Teuber, 1955). Other investigators, using different spatial tests and studying different kinds of brain damage, have come to a similar conclusion (Ettlinger, Warrington, & Zangwill, 1957; Luria, 1963). The finding of a relation between somesthetic form and pattern perception and a factor that transcends the somesthetic modality thus challenges the view that stereognosis is based simply on the integration of epicritic sensations, an integration assumed to occur entirely within the somesthetic modality. The finding is in accord with Gibson's view, however, that to detect form, one must appreciate the spatial arrangement of surfaces of the object and that the manual exploratory process is directed toward discovery of this spatial arrangement (Gibson, 1966). These considerations suggest that the impairment in form and pattern perception in the brain-injured cases without sensory defect my be interpretable as a disorientation that manifests itself not only in locomotor space but also in the miniature space encompassed by the hand.

Concluding Comment

The theory that protopathic and epicritic sensation are served by two separate systems of nerves appears to be as untenable for the central afferent pathways as it was shown to be for the peripheral pathways following Head's proposal. It is true that among the great variety of possible sensory experiences, there are extremes that can be labeled protopathic and epicritic, and it is also true that there are a multitude of afferent pathways and centers that can be grouped into phylogenetically old and new systems. But to equate these two extremes of sensation with the two afferent systems is to rely on only one category of evidence, that dealing with the contrasting anatomical and physiological properties of these systems, and to admit only one interpretation of this evidence.

One of the mainstays of the modern theory that the new system alone is responsible for discriminative sensation has been the inference that a system with properties like those of the old one is incapable of mediating this type of sensation. As indicated earlier, investigators point out the old system's close relation to the reticular formation, the lack of specialization of its cells, their large receptive fields, and the near absence in this system of topographical organization. But no matter how plausible this inference has seemed to be, the evidence cited here makes it clear that a mechanism by which the old system could mediate discriminative sensation must nonetheless be found.

Some hints of what one such mechanism might be have already been alluded to (e.g., Wall & Cronly-Dillon, 1960). Whereas the new system probably conveys specific information by the use of transmission lines labeled for place and type of stimulation, the cells of the old system may achieve the same end by responding with different temporal patterns of impulses to stimuli differing in place and type. There is evidence that the auditory modality may likewise employ both methods of coding (e.g., Rose, Brugge, Anderson, & Hind, 1967), and it is possible that here also temporal coding may be phylogenetically the older mechanism. There is also an alternative code that the old somesthetic system would be capable of using to convey specific information. This is one in which stimuli differing in place and type lead to unique spatial patterns of activity developed over an aggregate of neurons. A mechanism of this kind has been proposed for taste quality by Erickson (1963), who suggests that a similar code may be used in vision to signal color and in audition to signal pitch. There is thus no dearth of possible mechanisms by which the old somesthetic system might mediate discriminative sensation.

The argument that the old system must be capable of, and has mechanisms for, serving discrimination implies only that the protopathic-epicritic distinction is not the proper one to apply to the two systems. Even if this distinction were weakened, such that only a difference in refinement of sensation were implied, such an attenuated version, though less objectionable, would have its own disadvantages. For this version carries with it the implication that the old pathway is vestigial and of no use to animals possessing a more advanced one, whereas the evidence from lesion studies indicates that normal discriminative sensation depends on the intactness of the old as well as the new centers. Thus to assume that the two systems differ only in the refinement of sensation they are capable of mediating might miss a more fundamental distinction between them. By analogy, to say that visual sensation mediated by the rods is simply less refined than that mediated by the cones misses the important point that these different types of receptors are specialized for different functions.

The anatomical and physiological differences between the old and the new somatic afferent systems in higher animals strongly suggest that they do differ in their functional roles. If, as the evidence suggests, the old system handled all modes of sensation for all parts of the body, what did the new system add? The new system appears to have developed as a specialized organ within the general somatic apparatus, concentrated on mechanoreception and on serving only a few body parts, those that are most important for exploring the environment. A possibility that follows naturally from this view is that both the new sensory and the new motor systems, with their similar topographic organizations and massive interconnections, evolved as one complex concerned with increasing the precision of sensory control over motor function and of motor control over sensory function. According to this view, the function of topographic organization in these new systems is to aid in sensory-motor matching and hence in exploration and manipulation, that is, active touch. The large, rapidly conducting fibers found predominantly in the new system would seem to fit it particularly well for such a role.

Assuming that the new sensorimotor complex permitted a great increase in the animal's capacity to explore and acquire information from the environment, one might further propose a parallel development of mechanisms for effectively utilizing this information. Both intramodal and intermodal integration would be required, and past as well as present experience would enter in.

If, contrary to the current view that the old systems have remained static or even regressed in functional capacity, one assumes that phylogenetic advances in some aspects of function have also taken place in these less specific parts of the brain, then one might propose for them a role in the interpretation of afferent messages. Such interpretation might depend especially on thalamic and cortical sites of convergence between the specific and the less specific pathways.

Summary

Head's theory that the peripheral somatosensory pathways are divisible, morphologically and functionally, into protopathic and epicritic components has been adapted by some contemporary investigators to the central pathways. The modern version is based largely on the contrasting anatomical and physiological properties of the phylogenetically old (extralemniscal) and new (lemniscal) systems. The theory is evaluated here against several other lines of evidence: the phylogenetic history of the two systems, their interrelationships in mammalian forms, and, more directly, clues to their function from behavioral findings, particularly with regard to pain, discriminative sensation, and gnosis. In each case, the evidence suggests that, contrary to the conception of a protopathic-epicritic dichotomy, both systems are critically involved in both these forms of sensation. It is concluded that the contrasting properties of the two afferent systems need to be reinterpreted, and some tentative hypotheses are proposed.

7

Auditory Agnosia: A Review and Report of Recent Evidence

Luigi A. Vignolo

Impaired recognition of nonverbal sounds and noises as a clinical sign of brain damage in adults has been mentioned since the last century in the neurological literature. To define this condition, clinicians spoke of "psychic deafness" or "mind-deafness" (*Seelentaubheit*), adopting the term coined by Munk (1881) to designate similar deficits he had observed in dogs following

I wish to thank Dr. Donald Shankweiler for his valuable suggestions on the first draft of this chapter, and Professor Egon Weigl for kindly supplying some of the earlier German articles.

bilateral extirpation of the auditory cortex. After Freud's monograph (1891), the term "auditory agnosia" came into use. This expression has sometimes been extended to encompass defective identification of all kinds of auditory material, including speech and music. In this paper, however, it will be employed in its original restrictive sense of *defective recognition of nonverbal sounds and noises*.

The purpose of this chapter is (1) to review some of the evidence regarding auditory agnosia provided by clinical studies of individual patients and (2) to present the results of experimental investigations undertaken to clarify some aspects of auditory agnosia clinical studies had left unresolved.

Clinical Case Reports: Pure Word-Deafness, Amusia, and Auditory Agnosia

A survey of the neurological literature discloses that only in one recent case (Spreen, Benton, & Fincham, 1965) has sound agnosia been described in relatively pure form. As a rule, this symptom was mentioned merely as a concomitant finding in patients with "pure word-deafness" or "sensory amusia" or both. "Pure word-deafness" was defined for the first time by Lichtheim (1885) as a condition in which the ability to understand spoken language, to repeat spoken words, and to write from dictation were lost, while the ability to speak, read, and write spontaneously were preserved. Compared to ordinary Wernicke's aphasia, this form was called "pure" because inner language was intact, there were no paraphasias, and the defect was strictly confined to auditory language input.

The several patients who have been described as suffering from this dissociated type of aphasia (including Lichtheim's) rarely met all the requirements of the theoretical formulation, since paraphasias and disorders of reading and writing were seldom absent. However, they did show particularly severe impairment in all performances implying auditory language reception, so much so that, as Lichtheim observed, they tended to be mistaken for deaf persons, unlike most Wernicke's aphasics, who are sometimes mistaken for confused patients. In order to demonstrate that imperception was limited to speech sounds, the patient's reactions to nonverbal auditory stimuli were reported. In some cases, deafness was excluded merely on the grounds that the patient could hear slight noises, such as the clock ticking or a whispered voice (Kopeczinski & Zilberlast-Zand, 1921; Van Gehuchten & Goris, 1901), or showed normal thresholds for pure tones when examined by Bezold-Edelmann's continuous series of tuning forks (Bonhoeffer, 1915; Henneberg, 1918, 1926; Maillard & Hébrard, 1910; Stertz, 1912). In other cases, one finds descriptions of the patient's reactions to sounds, which implied some sort of recognition. This recognition was sometimes reported to be good. One of Ziehl's patients (1896), in spite of his total inability to understand or repeat words, could tell the sound of the doorbell from that of other bells, identified the doctor's coach from its noise, could tell from the voice who was talking in the next room and recognized musical instruments from their timbre. Henschen's (1918) patient did not grasp speech sounds and yet could recognize a person from his step and the attendants from the quality—soft or coarse, masculine or feminine—of their voices. Klein and Harper's patient (1956), experienced speech sounds "as an undifferentiated continuous humming noise without any rhythm," had no difficulty with noises and tunes, and even recognized the regional accents of people familiar to him.

More often, however, recognition of nonverbal noises was as impaired as that of speech sounds, in spite of normal thresholds for pure tones. For example, to Henneberg's (1906) patient, a cock crowing sounded once like a crow croaking, another time like a donkey or a horse. She could tell that the jingle of a bunch of keys was something tinny, but could not say what it was. Similarly, Quensel's (1908) patient could not recognize the noise made by rattling a purse partially filled with coins; when he was asked to identify the noise made by a watch, a tuning fork, a bunch of keys, and a match by choosing the corresponding objects out of a series arranged in front of him, he kept pointing to the watch.

Most patients with word-deafness were also unable to identify melodies, a condition usually referred to as "sensory amusia." The best descriptions of this defect are found in case reports of patients who were professional musicians (Feuchtwanger, 1930; Souques & Baruk, 1930); these happened to show a concomitant Wernicke's aphasia. However, sensory amusia was occasionally reported to appear independently of aphasia (Quensel & Pfeifer, 1923) or to linger on as the main residual symptom after a transient language disorder (Edgren, 1895). Some of these patients represent further examples of auditory agnosia, since the defect often involved nonmusical sounds and noises in addition to melodies.

Testing Methods

In the synopsis of case reports one often reads the rather uniform conclusion that the patient had a mild, marked, or severe "psychic deafness" or auditory agnosia, but the inspection of the actual records shows that the evidence behind these labels varied widely from one case to the next.[1] Some evidence was derived from the observation of the patient's spontaneous reaction to environmental noises and sounds. However, it was soon realized that under the conditions of everyday life the patient's behavior was characterized by a dramatic and puzzling variability, apparently due to fluctuations of auditory attention. More consistent proof of defective auditory recognition was obtained by means of informal, nonsystematized clinical tests, in which the patient was asked to identify different kinds of auditory stimuli. These

---

1. In some short reports, one finds the bare statement that the patient did not recognize sounds, given as conclusive clinical judgment and unsubstantiated by any accompanying evidence.

were of course restricted to sounds or noises that could be easily
reproduced in the patient's environment, Only after the 1950's
did the use of tape-recordings allow a wider selection of sounds.
The most commonly used auditory stimuli were: (1) Common
noises such as coughing, whistling, clapping hands, knocking on
the door, turning a key in the lock, crackling a sheet of paper,
rattling a matchbox, lighting a match, jingling a bunch of keys,
running water, etc. (2) Sounds of musical instruments. A toy
trumpet, a toy drum, a bell, sometimes a piano were all that was
available in most instances. The elaborate testing situation
arranged for a patient of Kast (1900), who was asked to identify
the sound of a bombardon, a trumpet, a clarinet, and a violin
played by a musician hidden behind a screen, was not a standard
one. (3) Noises of animals such as the barking of a dog, the crowing of a cock, etc. Before the introduction of the tape-recorder
these sounds had to be imitated on the spot by the examiner, who
sometimes used onomatopoeic words.

In each particular case, both the choice of stimuli and the
criteria that decided whether the patient had identified them,
varied widely and were seldom determined in advance. The
examiner was usually satisfied with any reasonably convincing
sign that correct recognition had taken place, so that one finds
that the patient sometimes tried to imitate the sound, sometimes
pointed or nodded towards its source, and mostly tried to name
or describe either the sound or its source. This last modality
of response is one of the commonest and is also the least satisfactory of all, because there are instances in which one wonders
whether the inability to produce the right name for a sound was
really due to auditory imperception or, rather, to anomia or para-
phasia.

Theoretical Interpretations

The ancillary position of auditory agnosia with respect to word-
deafness and amusia, together with the diversity and poverty of

testing procedures may perhaps account for the scarcity of studies devoted to analyzing this symptom. While its absence in cases of word-deafness was underlined by clinical investigators because it emphasized the purity of the language disorder, the possible meaning of its presence was seldom discussed. The main neurological works on aphasia and related disorders devoted exceedingly little space to auditory agnosia compared to its visual counterpart, psychic blindness, or visual agnosia.

In his 1914 *Traité*, Dejerine stated flatly that "true auditory agnosia has neither a clinical autonomy nor a definite pathogenesis." Marie (1926), who dismissed pure word-deafness as "a myth," did not even discuss auditory agnosia. Goldstein (1926) merely said that all or most patients with word-deafness "also have difficulty in grasping [*Erfassen*] noises and melodies," but did not analyze these defects as he had done with visual agnosia. His 1948 book did not add significantly to this statement. Head (1926) briefly mentioned auditory agnosia as one aspect of impaired "symbolic formulation," and said that patients with this disorder are unable to recognize the *meaning* of the sound heard. This interesting statement, however, must be considered as purely speculative, because this author did not bring any clinical evidence in support of it, while—as we shall see—the published cases up to his time of writing did not warrant such an opinion. Weisenburg and McBride's (1935) review of the question is very sketchy. They did include an interesting sound-recognition test in their battery (the subject had to recognize objects from the noise they made when dropped onto a wooden table), but apparently gave it to only one patient of their series, an "expressive-receptive" aphasic, whose performance was virtually normal and raised no comments. Henschen had, of course, devoted a large part of his 1918 monograph on the acoustic sphere to auditory agnosia, in which he discussed all cases with autopsies published up to that time, but his attention was focused mainly on the anatomical correlates of this symptom (see p. 183) rather than on its behavioral analysis.

A cue to the analysis of sound recognition disorders came, however, from Kleist (1928). This author emphasized that the inability to perceive isolated sounds or noises (*perceptive Geräuschtaubheit*) or to grasp sequences of them (*Geräuschfolgetaubheit*) should be distinguished from the inability to understand the *meaning* of noises (*Geräuschsinntaubheit*), where the patient is unable to associate the well-perceived sound with what it stands for (e.g., barking with dog). The first two types of disorder may be considered perceptual-discriminative in nature, since they both reflect an impairment in discriminating the acoustic structure of the stimulus, while the third type may be defined as associative-semantic, because it consists in the inability to associate the acoustic pattern with its meaning.

It appears that other authors, dealing with different types of receptive disorders due to brain damage, have been aware of this basic distinction. Lichtheim (1885) distinguished pure word-deafness, in which the pattern of speech sounds is ill perceived, from transcortical sensory aphasia, in which speech sounds are perceived and repeated well, while word meaning is not understood. Knoblauch (1888) somewhat pedantically applied Lichtheim's diagram to amusia. Discussing visual agnosia, Lissauer (1890) tried to separate the defective *apperception* of sensory impressions from the faulty *association* of the integrated percept with memory images. The nature of such associative defect in agnosia was discussed by Liepmann (1908b). He pointed out that earlier authors, following Meynert and Wernicke, had ascribed higher-level recognition disorders to a defect in concept formation (*Asymbolie, Alogie*) due, in turn, to disruption of the associations between different sensory modalities. In partial disagreement with this view, he stressed that intramodal association defects ("disjunctive or ideational agnosias") play as important a role as the intermodal ones ("dissolution agnosias").

The Perceptual-Discriminative Character of Clinical Auditory Agnosia

Kleist admitted that his *Geräuschsinntaubheit* was purely the product of theoretical speculation, unsubstantiated by clinical evidence. And indeed, if one tries to evaluate the published case reports of sound agnosia in the light of the distinction between perceptual-discriminative and associative-semantic disorders, one finds that in virtually all of them the defect is one of perceptual discrimination rather than one of association. Very rarely, if ever, does one find in case reports hints suggesting the presence of an associative disorder, in addition to the perceptual one. Such might be, for example, the behavior of Henneberg's (1906) patient when she associated the crowing of a cock with a donkey or a horse, i.e., with concepts belonging to the semantic sphere ("animals") of the correct one, thereby suggesting a loosening of the ties linking the perceived sound with its meaning. In the field of amusia, the co-existence of disorders of both levels was explicitly pointed out only by Walthard (1927), who maintained that some errors made by his patient (inability to grasp certain intervals between two notes of the scale) were discriminative in nature, while others revealed an inability to integrate the perceived melodies with their "meaning."

Usually, however, the trouble seemed to consist essentially of a difficulty in grasping the acoustic structure of the auditory message, be it speech, music, or noise. Several observations warrant this conclusion. In the patient's own comments, the emphasis on the acoustic difficulties of speech perception is obvious. Patients say: "It is as if I were listening to you talking in the next room" (Quensel, 1908); "as if I were listening to the speaker from the back row of a crowded lecture room" (Henneberg, 1918); "I can't put the sounds together" (Bonvicini, 1905). Music and speech may sound alike (Mahoudeau, Lemoyne, Dubrisay, & Caraes, 1956; Wohlfart, Lindgren, & Jernelius,

1952), music may be perceived as a nonmusical and unpleasant noise, such as banging on tin cans (Quensel & Pfeifer, 1923), "a brassy noise" (Brazier, 1892), etc. Speech may sound like wind in the trees (Kast, 1900), and, conversely, street noises may be mistaken for speech (Ziegler, 1952). Often several different noises (keys, bell, drum, etc.) were uniformly defined by a vague stereotyped term, as if they awoke only an acoustically undifferentiated impression, e.g., as "rattles" or "squeaks" (Reinhold, 1948), "something ringing" (Schultze, 1965), "something like a grasshopper's sound" (Laignel-Lavastine & Alajounine, 1921). Whenever errors were more specific, they showed misapprehensions which were acoustic in nature; the noise of an elevator in motion was mistaken for the vibration of a tuning fork (Wohlfart *et al.*, 1952), the cry of a cat for someone singing (Barrett, 1910), the tinkling of a glass for the jingling of keys (Schuster & Taterka, 1926). Some features of the defect, such as the selective impairment of high- (Liepmann, 1898) or low-pitched (Quensel & Pfeifer, 1923) noises or of more musical as opposed to less musical noises (Klein, 1927) also afford a perceptual-discriminative explanation rather than an associative one.

Admittedly not all typical features of auditory agnosia can be accounted for by defective sound discrimination. A system that stands for itself is "auditory inattention," which has been found to varying degrees in most patients (Adler, 1891; Kogerer, 1924; Laignel-Lavastine & Alajouanine, 1921; Lichtheim, 1885; Pick, 1892; Quensel, 1908; and others). This varied from impaired reaction to unexpected noises, as in Liepmann's (1898) patient (who ran the risk of being run over by streetcars because he paid no attention to the sound of the horn) to abnormal distractibility during conversation or even during testing sessions (Klein, 1927). Hemphill and Stengel (1940) made an accurate description of inattention of the first type in a patient who also showed "asymbolia for pain" and suggested that both symptoms may reflect the inability to recognize outer signals as *warnings* of danger. In this line, Reinhold (1948) stated that inattention is due to loss of the *meaning* of sounds. However, case descriptions do not support these views, but rather confirm the observations made by Hemphill and Stengel themselves, that "what is lacking . . . is the reflex turning towards the person speaking or the origin of the noise." Whether this is due to an auditory-motor disconnection (Kleist, 1928) or to loss of central inhibition and selection of auditory inputs due to the cortical lesion (Ombredane, 1944), the disorder appears to block radically or divert the entire process of perception and can hardly be considered as having a purely semantic basis.

Auditory Agnosia and Deafness

So evident was the perceptual component in the published cases of word-deafness and auditory agnosia that some authors (notably Freund, 1895) advanced the hypothesis that these symptoms may be due simply to partial deafness of either peripheral or central origin. If by partial deafness one means (as they did) a genuine loss of threshold acuity for certain tones of the scale, this view is no longer tenable, since accurate examinations with Bezold-Edelmann's tuning forks (Bonvicini, 1905) and, later, pure tone audiometry (Mahoudeau *et al.*, 1956; Mahoudeau, Lemoyne, Foncin, & Dubrisay, 1958; Wohlfart *et al.*, 1952; Ziegler, 1952) have established beyond doubt that word-deafness and auditory agnosia may exist in patients without significant hearing loss. Partial deafness due to cochlear damage was indeed found in some cases (Dejerine & Sérieux, 1898; Freund, 1895; Quensel & Pfeifer, 1923) that, however, also had hemispheric lesions and whose recognition disorders were no more severe than those found in patients with intact cochleae (Liepmann & Storch, 1902). As for central deafness, i.e., loss of threshold acuity due to CNS lesions, its role in auditory agnosia is questionable because its existence is itself uncertain. Audiograms have been found to be virtually normal in patients with focal brain stem lesions (Jerger, 1964) and with unilateral temporal damage (Alajouanine,

Aubry, & Pialoux, 1955; Morel, 1935). Only bilateral cortical lesions have been said to entail total hearing loss, provided that they destroy both Heschl gyri. Henschen (1918) judged that nine cases with autopsy (out of the available literature up to his time of writing) met these requirements, and a few other similar cases have been reported since (Bramwell, 1927; Clark & Russell, 1938; Misch, 1928).

The following should be noted, however: (1) In most of these cases, hearing was inadequately examined, the diagnosis being based on the clinical impression that the patient behaved "like a deaf person" (Marchand, 1904; Mills, 1891; Wernicke & Friedländer, 1883). This impression may be due to auditory inattention, which has been considered a typical sign of bilateral temporal involvement (Bischoff, 1899), and which in fact was sometimes emphatically reported (e.g., Anton, 1899; Berger, 1911; Mott, 1907). The observation of Klein (1927) shows how easily severe auditory inattention may be mistaken for total deafness. (2) In some patients, examined in the acute stage of the illness (Bramwell, 1927; Misch, 1928), deafness may have been a transient effect of diaschisis. (3) Negative cases have been reported showing minimal hearing loss on audiometry, though the autopsy disclosed bilateral temporal lesions destroying or disconnecting both Heschl gyri (Mahoudeau et al., 1958; Wohlfart et al., 1952). (4) It has been shown that bilateral lesions of the auditory cortex in primates do not impair the perception of pure tones (see Neff, 1961). The foregoing considerations tend to question the reality of cortical deafness even in patients with bilateral lesions.

While the attempt to explain auditory agnosia as the consequence of gaps in the tonal scale is not convincing, the possibility remains that this symptom is related to subtler hearing disorders, such as those that have been found to affect the ear contralateral to the lesion in brain-damaged patients examined with more refined audiological techniques. Delayed perception (sometimes leading to diplacusis) and distorted appreciation of sound qualities (often leading to unpleasant sensations) have been described in patients with thalamic lesions (Arnold, 1946a, 1946b), and similar defects, in addition to auditory allesthesia, have been found in a left temporal patient (Arnold, 1943). Following unilateral cortical lesions, defective auditory memory and auditory-motor coordination (Schubert & Panse, 1953), marked instability of perception of serial acoustic stimuli (Richter, 1957), and impaired recognition of distorted or masked speech (Bocca, Calearo, Cassinari, & Migliavacca, 1955; Jerger, 1964) have also been reported. In some cases, these defects have been held responsible for the accompanying sensory amusia (Arnold, 1946a, 1946b), and pure word-deafness (Richter, 1957). Although none of these patients showed the clinical picture of auditory agnosia, the possible relationship of this symptom with less conspicuous hearing defects such as those described above deserve further investigation.

Anatomical Findings

The problem of the relationships between auditory agnosia and central deafness leads us to discuss the anatomical findings in patients with defective auditory recognition. The evaluation of these findings is difficult, because reports vary greatly in accuracy and reliability and also because the evidence often must be extricated from a welter of contrasting interpretations, in which the clinicopathological correlations concerning auditory agnosia are intermingled with those concerning word-deafness and amusia.[2] If, however, one restricts one's attention primarily to the

2. These clinico-pathological data joined those derived from myelogenetic studies in fueling heated controversies about the auditory cortical representations in man. Some of the main issues at stake were the location of the auditory center in Heschl's convolutions as opposed to the entire posterior part of T_1 and T_2 (Flechsig vs. Wernicke), the possibility of point-to-point cochlear representation within Heschl's convolution (Pfeifer vs. Bornstein) and Henschen's plea for separate representation for noises (T_3), words (T_1 and T_2), and music (temporal pole). Detailed accounts of these debates are found in Bonvicini (1929), Henschen (1918), and Pfeifer (1936).

hemispheric side of the lesion associated with auditory agnosia, a few simple points can be made. Most cases showed bilateral cortical and/or subcortical lesions of the temporal lobes, involving the posterior part of T_1. At least a sizable part of either the right or the left Heschl convolution was spared in all cases except those described by Mahoudeau et al., (1958) and Wohlfart et al., (1952).

Cases in which a strictly unilateral lesion was found are much rarer. In two cases the lesion was limited to the left temporal lobe and was strictly subcortical (Liepmann & Storch, 1902; Schuster & Taterka, 1926). A lesion limited to the right temporal lobe was found in only one case, the very clear-cut case of auditory agnosia without aphasia described by Spreen, Benton, and Fincham (1965). However, in a patient of Pötzl's (1939, 1943), whose autopsy revealed a bilateral lesion, the clinical course of the illness showed that the older, right hemisphere lesion had been solely responsible for the auditory symptoms. Another right hemisphere lesion was suspected on the basis of clinical findings only (without autopsy) in a case of Nielsen and Sult's (1939). Quensel and Pfeifer's (1923) patient had sustained a right temporal trauma and did not show any neurological evidence of damage to the left hemisphere. However, these authors assumed that the trauma had also caused a "contre coup" lesion in the left temporal lobe.[3]

The unilaterality of lesions in some of these patients was challenged by Strohmayer (1900) who, on the basis of his own experience with one case of word-deafness, claimed that damage in the opposite hemisphere cannot be ruled out unless an accurate microscopic examination of brain sections has been made. One might in turn reply, with Marie (1926), that cortical degeneration so slight as to be detected only on microscopy is not a sufficient

---

3. There are two additional cases of word-deafness due to a left cortico-subcortical lesion (Henneberg, 1926; Van Gehuchten & Goris, 1901) and three cases of sensory amusia due to damage presumably limited to the right hemisphere (Jellinek, 1956; Pittrich, 1956; Würtzen, 1903); however, auditory agnosia in these patients was either absent or not assessed.

sign of pathology and recall that the transitory word-deafness of Veraguth's (1900) patient, whose autopsy revealed such a bilateral microscopic damage, disappeared suddenly after a nose-bleed and was later judged to be hysterical in nature (Henneberg, 1918). At any rate, careful histological studies were carried out in two unilateral cases (Liepmann and Storch, 1902; Schuster & Taterka, 1926) and failed to show any contralateral lesion.

Summary and Discussion

The main points disclosed by this review may be summarized. In almost all published cases, agnosia for nonverbal sounds and noises was a secondary finding in patients who had been considered worthy of thorough investigation of the auditory functions because they presented some other auditory symptom—notably pure word-deafness or sensory amusia or both—to a paradigmatic degree. The procedures and criteria for assessing this disorder were very variable and often inadequate. Whenever the published records were sufficiently detailed to warrant a qualitative analysis of the recognition disorder, this appeared to be perceptual-discriminative rather than semantic-associative in nature. However, auditory agnosia was found to be independent of hearing loss, in the sense of diminished threshold acuity. Inattention was often present. For a number of cases, autopsy findings were eventually available. Most of these turned out to have bilateral damage involving the posterior third of the temporal lobes. Strictly unilateral lesions were found in three cases: they included the left hemisphere in two cases and the right hemisphere in one.

In spite of the wealth of data gathered on this topic, the study of individual cases still offers but a very approximate and sketchy picture of auditory agnosia, due to three main reasons: biased sampling (virtually only patients with presumed word-deafness or amusia were studied, and they cannot be considered representative of the entire brain-damaged population), heterogeneous testing conditions, and incomplete anatomical data. As a consequence, several questions, knowledge of which is crucial to understanding the meaning of auditory agnosia in the context of other neuropsychological defects, are still a matter for controversy. Two of them seem particularly important and will be discussed here. They are the relationships of auditory agnosia with aphasia and with the hemispheric side of the lesion.

The first question is centered around the relationship between verbal and nonverbal auditory comprehension. All we know from the individual cases reported by the clinicians is that the subtle acoustic discrimination of noises is often impaired in pure word-deafness. This is not surprising, if one considers that the distinctive feature of this form of aphasia seems to be precisely the inability to identify the sounds of speech, which entails a selective impairment not only of auditory comprehension but also of those language modalities, such as repetition and writing to dictation, that depend upon accurate perception of speech sounds.

In these cases of auditory agnosia with pure word-deafness, it would be reasonable to assume that both receptive disorders, verbal and nonverbal, reflect the disruption of a common mechanism, i.e., defective discrimination of complex acoustic patterns. However, to what extent is this hypothesis applicable to the relationship between recognition of noises and language comprehension of all the other forms of aphasia?

To quote an extreme example, there is a type of aphasia, the so-called "transcortical sensory" aphasia, in which the comprehension disorders do not seem to depend on faulty discrimination of the speech sounds but rather on the inability to associate the well-perceived words with their meaning. These patients can repeat (hence acoustically perceive) well the very same words and sentences they do not understand. Although a few cases of this type have been described, their ability to recognize sounds or noises has not been reported, probably because it did not represent such a pressing diagnostic problem here as in word-deafness. In 1962 I had the opportunity of examining auditory recognition in an aphasic of this type. This was a patient with severe fluent aphasia characterized by verbal jargon, good repetition, and poor comprehension. His ability to repeat words and sentences and to imitate the sounds (e.g., whistling) performed by the examiner testified that sound discrimination was preserved. In spite of this, he did poorly when asked to identify tape-recorded familiar sounds by choosing the corresponding picture out of a series of pictures put in front of him: on hearing the barking of a dog, he once looked puzzled and then pointed alternatively to the horse, rabbit, and calf; on hearing a flute, he pointed to the piano; miaowing he associated with a dog. These mistakes suggested an inability to attach each sound with its precise meaning—a type of agnosia that reminded one of Kleist's (1928) sound-meaning deafness (*Geräuschsinntaubheit*). Interestingly, these mistakes were similar to those that occurred if words were given instead of sounds; the patient pointed to a toad when asked to show a lizard, to a train when asked "bus." Here too one could assume that the same or a very similar mechanism underlay both verbal and nonverbal defects, But whereas an acoustic-discriminative defect seemed to underlie auditory agnosia associated with pure word-deafness, a semantic-associative one seemed to underlie auditory agnosia associated with transcortical sensory aphasia.

Cases like this one stress the need to investigate sound agnosia systematically in different types of aphasia. However, the comparison between the extreme forms such as word-deafness or transcortical sensory aphasia, while theoretically promising, meets with practical difficulties, because such forms are quite rare.[4] Therefore, it seems advisable to adopt another line of

4. Out of 200 aphasics examined at our aphasia unit by means of a comprehensive battery, we found only one patient who could be classified as word-deaf because of his poor auditory verbal reception, as compared to perfect reading (however, he had paraphasic speech); and four "transcortical sensory" aphasics, defined as patients with fluent speech, repetition scores above the group median, and comprehension scores below group median (Boller & Vignolo, 1966). Unfortunately, they were all seen before the beginning of systematic research on auditory agnosia.

research, i.e., to study the relationships between auditory recognition of verbal and nonverbal material in an unselected sample of aphasics.

As to the relationships of sound agnosia with the hemispheric side of the lesion, the published case reports of auditory agnosia following unilateral brain damage are too few to clarify the role of lesions of either hemisphere in the production of this symptom. Surveying the cases of sensory amusia, Köhl and Tschabischer (1952) noted a certain difference in the quality of the disorder according to the damaged hemisphere: they stated that, by and large, a lesion of the right hemisphere was often associated with a "bad ear" (*Falschohr*), while a lesion of the left hemisphere was more often associated with defective understanding of melodies and sometimes with impaired recognition of rhythms. Recently, the problem of hemispheric asymmetry in sound recognition has been the object of important experimental work initiated by the Montreal group. Milner (1962) gave some subtests of the Seashore Measure of Musical Talents to patients with focal temporal epilepsy before and after lobectomy and found that performance on the subtests requiring comparisons of tonal patterns or judgments of tone quality was affected by right temporal lobectomy, but not by left temporal lobectomy.

Working with normal subjects, Kimura (1964) presented different unfamiliar melodies (woodwind passages of chamber music) to each ear simultaneously through earphones, and found that melodies arriving at the left ear (i.e., predominantly to the right hemisphere) were recognized significantly more often than those arriving at the right ear. Shankweiler (1966b) used Kimura's test in neurosurgical patients and showed that right temporal lobectomy selectively impaired the recognition of unfamiliar melodies. In another study (1966a) he found that the reproduction of familiar tunes presented through a loudspeaker also was significantly more impaired by right than by left temporal lobectomy.

All these findings suggest that the right temporal lobe is

predominant in the perception of complex nonverbal auditory patterns[5]. However, it is still not clear which stimulus character- istics are crucial in determining this hemispheric asymmetry, nor if it extends to all nonverbal auditory material, including the meaningful noises commonly used in clinical examinations. These uncertainties caution that "nonverbal" auditory recogni- tion is not a unitary concept, but may cover different operations, according to the stimulus material and to the type of task. In analyzing this concept, the distinction between a perceptual- discriminative level and an associative-semantic level, suggested by the classification of Kleist (1928), may prove useful. It appears obvious, for example, that to recognize a complex and non- familiar passage of music among a group of similar melodies is a difficult operation from the perceptual point of view but does not involve semantic identification at all; while to recognize a type of animal from its noises is a far easier task from the purely perceptual standpoint, but it additionally requires the integrity of a semantic decoding mechanism, whereby the perceived noise is associated with a definite source or event. It is possible that these different levels of nonverbal auditory recognition are affected differently by the hemispheric side of the lesion. The answer to this must come from the study of unselected samples of patients with unilateral lesions of the right and left hemispheres, carried out by means of tests pinpointing as selectively as possible each of the two levels.

Experimental Studies

In the following sections, I will present the results of two recent studies carried out with Dr. Hans Spinnler and with Dr. Piero

5. This contrasts with the fate of verbal auditory material, such as digits, letters, and nonsense syllables (Kimura, 1961a, 1967), that are processed primarily by the left hemisphere.

Faglioni in order to investigate the relationship of auditory agnosia with aphasia and with the hemispheric side of the lesion.

Materials and Methods

The methodological approach, the type of patients studied, and the collateral examinations employed were the same in both studies. Auditory recognition was investigated by means of quantitative tests. Tape-recorded sounds and noises were presented through a loudspeaker put on the table at about 75 cm. in front of the patient. Testing sessions took place in a quiet but not soundproofed room. The tests were given to normal control and brain-damaged subjects with unilateral hemispheric lesions. Control subjects were patients who had been referred to the clinic for diseases that did not involve the CNS above the thoracic spinal level. The brain-damaged sample represented a relatively varied population, in that it included patients admitted to the wards, examined as outpatients, or treated in the aphasia or physical rehabilitation units. Etiology was mainly vascular (about 75%) and there were about as many recent lesions (less than three months from onset) as long-standing ones. Patients were excluded from the study only if they: (1) considered themselves left-handed or ambidextrous or were reported to be such by their relatives; (2) had a clinical picture or past history pointing to involvement of both cerebral hemispheres; (3) could not be given the test because of physical or mental disability (e.g., confined to bed, impaired consciousness, etc.). No other criterion of selection was applied. The diagnosis of the affected hemisphere relied upon the findings of the neurological examination (paralysis, anesthesia, hemianopia, etc.) and was confirmed by neuroradiological and EEG findings in most cases. The diagnosis of aphasia in left brain-damaged patients was made by means of a standard language examination, currently used in the aphasia unit of our clinic. All left brain-damaged patients who scored below the normal cut-off on at least one Oral Language subtest (description, visual naming, repetition, and comprehension of words and sentences) were considered "aphasic." Aphasic patients were further classified into six broad aphasic syndromes, according to the type of speech production and overall score obtained on the oral expression and comprehension subtests. The definition of the syndromes is given in Table 7.1.

The brain-damaged groups were balanced with respect to age, educational level, etiology, and length of illness in all comparisons. No preliminary audiometric test was administered. However, none of the patients had been clinically deaf before the onset of the illness nor complained of hypoacusis at the time of testing. Moreover, since the groups were balanced with respect to age, there is no reason to believe that hypoacusis specifically affected one experimental group more than any other.

Experiment 1

In this study (Spinnler & Vignolo, 1966) a sound recognition test was given to 35 controls and to 95 patients with unilateral hemispheric damage (51 aphasics, 16 nonaphasic left brain-damaged patients, and 28 right brain-damaged patients).

The test consisted of ten meaningful sounds or noises: (1) the song of a canary; (2) gunshots; (3) the crying of a baby; (4) storm wind; (5) the grunting of a pig; (6) ambulance siren; (7) the braying of a donkey; (8) the rumble of a train; (9) the roaring of an airplane; (10) the yapping of a little dog. The subject was asked to listen to the sound played by the tape-recorder and to indicate which of four pictures shown to him represented the natural source of the sound he has just heard. In order to try to secure information about the quality of the recognition disorder, the test was arranged in such a way that the pictures corresponding to a given sound (i.e., the song of a canary) represented respectively (1) the correct natural source of the sound (e.g., a singing canary); (2) the natural source of a sound *acoustically* very similar to the presented sound (e.g., a man whistling); (3) a sound-producing event or object belonging to

TABLE 7.1 DEFINITION OF APHASIC SYNDROMES

Syndrome	Type of Speech Production	Oral Expression Score (mx Score = 4)	Auditory Comprehension Score (mx Score = 4)
Global aphasia	*Laborious articulation:* Speechlessness with recurring utterances; or "syndrome of phonetic disintegration"	0	0–2
Broca's aphasia severe	*Laborious articulation:* Speechlessness with recurring utterances; or "syndrome of phonetic disintegration"; or agrammatism	0–1	3–4
Broca's aphasia mild	*Slight but obvious articulatory disorders:* Phonemic paraphasias with anomia; agrammatism; disprosody	2–4	3–4
Wernicke's aphasia severe	*Fluent speech, without articulatory disorders:* Verbal and phonemic paraphasias, neologisms and/or anomia; or phonemic or verbal jargon	0–1	0–2
Wernicke's aphasia moderate	*Fluent speech, without articulatory disorders:* Verbal and phonemic paraphasias and anomia or marked anomia	0–2	3–4
Wernicke's aphasia, mild	*Fluent speech, without articulatory disorders:* Very few paraphasias and anomia	3–4	3–4

the same *semantic* category of the natural source of the presented sound, but producing a sound completely different from the presented one from an *acoustic* standpoint (e.g., a cock crowing); (4) a sound-producing event, animal, or object that has no relationship with the presented sound from either the acoustic or the semantic aspect (e.g., a train in motion). Thus, three types of errors were possible; *acoustic* errors, when the patient pointed to picture 2; *semantic* errors when he pointed to picture 3; *odd* errors, when he pointed to picture 4.

We adopted the above mentioned distinction between a *perceptual-discriminative sound agnosia*—i.e., an inability to discriminate precisely the sound pattern—and an *associative sound agnosia*—i.e., an inability to associate the perceived sound pattern with its meaning. We assumed that acoustic errors reflected a discriminative disorder and semantic errors reflected an associative disorder, while odd errors had no distinct connotation in this respect.

Before beginning to test, an additional item (the neighing of a horse) was given to the subject as an example. The ten items were then presented in two subsequent rounds, in the same order. Since each response was scored as correct (1 point) or wrong (0 points), the maximum score was 20. The type of error was also recorded.

Scores obtained by the four experimental groups on the test are shown in Table 7.2. A performance was defined as *abnormal*, if it obtained a score inferior to that of all but the worst control patient (cutoff point about 97%) i.e., sixteen. Thirteen aphasic patients scored below the cutoff point, while only two right brain-damaged patients and none of the nonaphasic left brain-damaged patients fell below it. Thus, a poor performance on the test was found only in the aphasic group, while both right and left nonaphasic patients behaved virtually like normal controls.

The incidence of sound recognition defects in the various aphasic syndromes is shown in Table 7.3, which discloses that such defects were very frequently associated with one particular

TABLE 7.2   NUMBER OF PATIENTS OBTAINING A GIVEN
SCORE ON THE SOUND RECOGNITION TEST

SRT score	Control Patients (N = 35)	Right Brain-damaged Patients (N = 28)	Left Brain-damaged patients Nonaphasic (N = 16)	Aphasic (N = 51)
20	16	11	4	13
19	5	6	5	4
18	7	5	5	5
17	3	2		7
16	3	2	2	9
15		1		1
14	1			3
13		1		2
12				1
11				1
10				2
9				1
8				
7				1
6				1
5				
4				
3				
2				
1				

syndrome, i.e., severe Wernicke's aphasia (seven patients out of nine). This finding suggests that the sound recognition defect is specifically associated with disorders of auditory verbal comprehension. The correlation between the sound recognition scores and the comprehension scores was found to be positive and significant (Spearman's $r_s = .56$, $p < .001$).

The performance of the aphasic group differed from that of the other groups also with respect to type of error. Figure 7.1 shows that in aphasics the mean number of semantic errors increased much more than that of acoustic and odd errors. The difference

TABLE 7.3   Number of Aphasics Obtaining a Given Score on the Sound Recognition Test

SRT score	Global (N = 5)	Broca severe (N = 17)	Broca mild (N = 3)	Wernicke severe (N = 9)	Wernicke moderate (N = 13)	Wernicke mild (N = 3)
20		5	1	1	5	1
19	1	1		1	1	
18		3	1			1
17	1	3			2	1
16	2	3			3	
15			1			
14		1		1	2	
13				1		
12				1		
11				1		
10		1		1		
9				1		
8						
7				1		
6	1					
5						
4						
3						
2						
1						
0						

between semantic errors in aphasic and nonaphasic patients is highly significant (p = .00003 on the Mann-Whitney test) while the difference between acoustic errors falls short of statistical significance (p = .054). The figure also shows that aphasics were the only group that made more semantic than acoustic errors, while the opposite trend was consistently present in each of the remaining groups. Aphasics appeared to include a significantly larger number of patients with predominantly semantic errors than the entire nonaphasic brain-damaged sample (Chi² = 4.051 with 1 D.F.; p = .05). Among aphasics there were nine patients in whom one type of error occurred at least five times more frequently than any other type and could therefore be considered as being "markedly predominant." The "markedly predominant" error was semantic in eight patients and acoustic in one patient only. By contrast, it should be noted that the two right brain-damaged patients and the only normal control whose

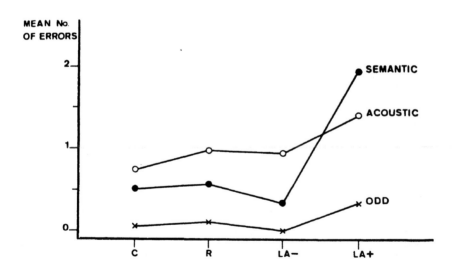

Figure 7.1   *Means of the different types of errors in the four experimental groups.*
C = control patients; R = right brain-damaged patients; LA− = nonaphasic
left brain-damaged patients; LA+ = aphasic patients.

performances scored below cutoff made more acoustic than semantic errors.

In conclusion, this investigation showed that, out of an un-selected sample of patients with unilateral hemispheric damage, defective recognition of meaningful sounds and noises (as tested by us) occurred frequently only in those who showed aphasia and was significantly correlated with the auditory language compre-hension defect. The qualitative analysis of responses showed that aphasia was associated more with semantic than with acoustic errors. This suggested that the aphasics' failure to recognize meaningful sounds was due mainly to the inability to associate the perceived sound with its correct meaning, rather than to a perceptual-discriminative defect. By contrast, the fact that the two right brain-damaged patients who scored below cutoff on the test made more acoustic than semantic errors appeared to be in line with the results reported by Milner (1962) and Shankweiler (1966a, 1966b), indicating that right brain-damaged patients perform defectively on tasks requiring acoustic discrimination. We then advanced the hypothesis that the sound recognition disorders found in aphasia as a consequence of left hemisphere damage are qualitatively different from those following right hemisphere lesions, in the sense that the former are associative rather than discriminative in nature, while the latter are dis-criminative rather than associative. In order to test this hypothesis however, we needed a better test of sound discrimination than the one used in this study. In fact, the recognition of the noises that make up this test is much more a matter of identifying them as meaningful wholes, rather than a task involving the ability to carry out subtle discriminations in the acoustic field. We therefore undertook Experiment 2.

Experiment 2

In this study two tests were used, of which one (the Meaningful Sounds Identification Test) was intended to test the ability to identify the exact *meaning* of sounds, while the other (The Mean-ingless Sounds Discrimination Test) was intended to test the ability to discriminate accurately the *acoustic pattern* of sounds. The tests have been given to 45 controls, 25 patients with lesions of the right hemisphere and 45 patients with lesions of the left hemisphere, 40 of whom were aphasic.

Meaningful Sounds Identification Test—This test was similar to the one used in the preceding study, except that out of the four pictorial alternatives, one was correct, two were "semantic" and one was "odd": there was no "acoustic" alternative. The patient was given two examples (siren, sheep), each of which was repeated twice. Patients who failed on the examples (on second presentation) were not given the test. The test consisted of twenty items; (1) church bell ringing; (2) cow mooing; (3) horse neighing; (4) trumpet; (5) cat miaowing; (6) train rumbling; (7) people praying in church; (8) machine-gun rattling; (9) bus moving off; (10) ambulance siren; (11) canary singing; (12) lion roaring; (13) wind whistling; (14) clock ticking; (15) airplane in flight; (16) baby crying; (17) pigs grunting; (18) violin; (19) motorscooter; (20) donkey braying.

Meaningless Sounds Discrimination Test—The patient was told that he was going to hear two sounds or noises, one after the other. He was asked to listen to them carefully and say whether they were the same or different. He was then given six items (pairs of noises) as examples. Patients who failed on more than two of them were not given the test. The test proper consisted of twenty items. The meaningless sounds were produced empirically by superimposing two or more noises chosen out of sound tracks for radio programs (e.g., a crackling sound on a buzzing background.) No attempt was made to analyze acoustically the complex patterns resulting from these manipulations. They varied widely in structure, changes in amplitude and pitch being sometimes gradual, sometimes abrupt. They lasted from 6 to 10 seconds, duration being held constant for the numbers of each pair. The interval between the first and second noise of any pair was 2 seconds.

Correct responses given within 10 seconds were given 1 point, wrong or delayed (over 10 seconds) responses were given 0 points.

The brain-damaged patients were also given Raven's PM for children and a simple reaction time test (considered as a measure of overall severity of the cerebral lesion). No significant difference was found between the two groups with respect to these variables (mean Raven's PM score: right brain-damaged = 16.5; left = 16.1 points; mean reaction times: right = 184.4, left = 181.3 msec.).

The mean scores obtained by the three experimental groups on the two sound recognition tests are shown in Table 7.4. Both

TABLE 7.4   MEAN SCORES OBTAINED BY THE EXPERIMENTAL
GROUPS ON THE TWO SOUND RECOGNITION TESTS

	Control Patients (N = 45)	Right Brain-damaged Patients (N = 25)	Left Brain-damaged Patients (N = 45)
Meaningful Sounds Identification Test	17.9	17.8	14.5
Meaningless Sounds Discrimination Test	16.2	12.7	16.3

hemispheric groups performed at a normal level on one test, and showed significant failure on the other test. However, the test that was poorly performed varied according to the hemispheric side of the lesion: failure on the meaningful sounds test was specific to left brain-damaged patients (p < .001), while failure on the meaningless sounds test was specific to right brain-damaged patients (p < .001).

In order to single out patients with auditory recognition defects a quantitative definition of abnormally poor performance was developed by taking as standards of reference the mean (M) and the standard deviation (SD) of the scores obtained by the control sample. On each test, a performance was judged to be abnormally poor if the corresponding score was lower than M − 2SD of the control sample. If this abnormally low score was comprised between M − 2SD and M − 3SD, it was considered as reflecting a moderate defect of auditory recognition; if it was lower than M − 3SD, it was considered as reflecting a severe defect. A similar criterion was applied to evaluate the difference between the performance on the two tests in any given patient. A difference between the two test scores exceeding M ± 2SD of the intertest differences found in control patients was considered as reflecting an abnormal discrepancy between the two tests. The discrepancy was defined as *moderate* if the intertest difference was comprised between M ± 2SD and M ± 3SD; *marked* if the intertest difference exceeded M ± 3SD. The normative statistics on which these definitions were based are reported in Table 7.5. The number of

TABLE 7.5   MEANS (M), STANDARD DEVIATIONS (SD), AND CONFIDENCE LIMITS FOR SCORES OF EACH AUDITORY RECOGNITION TEST AND FOR INTERTEST DIFFERENCE SCORES IN THE CONTROL GROUP

Test	M	SD	M − 2SD	M − 3SD
Meaningful Sounds	17.9	1.4	15.1	13.7
Meaningless Sounds	16.2	2	12.2	10.2
	M	SD	M ± 2SD	M ± 3SD
Intertest difference	− 1.6[a]	2.1	+ 2.6 − 5.8	+ 4.7 − 7.9

[a] The negative sign indicates that the Meaningless Sounds Test score is lower than the Meaningful Sounds Test score.

brain-damaged patients who proved to have a defect of auditory recognition on each test is shown in Table 7.6. From these findings, the double dissociation between right and left brain-damaged

TABLE 7.6 DISTRIBUTION OF RIGHT AND LEFT BRAIN-DAMAGED
PATIENTS ACCORDING TO PRESENCE AND DEGREE OF DEFECT ON THE TWO SOUND RECOGNITION TESTS

Defect	Meaningful Sounds Test		Defect	Meaningless Sounds Test	
	Right B.D. (N = 25)	Left B.D. (N = 45)		Right B.D. (N = 25)	Left B.D. (N = 45)
None	21	18	None	13	44
Moderate	4	11	Moderate	7	1
Severe	—	16	Severe	5	—

patients with respect to the two auditory recognition tasks emerges
even more dramatically than from the comparison of the mean
group scores, shown in Table 7.4. Defective recognition of meaningful sounds was found in 27 out of 45 (60%) patients with lesions
of the left hemisphere, as opposed to only 4 out of 25 (16%)
patients with lesions of the right hemisphere. By contrast, defective discrimination of meaningless sounds occurred in 12 out of
25 (48%) right hemisphere-damaged and only 1 out of 45 (2.2%)
left hemisphere-damaged patients. More important still, none of
the right brain-damaged patients was severely impaired on the
meaningful sounds test, and none of the left brain-damaged
patients was severely impaired on the meaningless sounds test.

Table 7.7 shows the distribution of the left brain-damaged
patients according to presence and type of aphasia and degree of
defect on the Meaningful Sound Identification Test. The defect
is limited to patients with aphasia and appears to be specifically
associated with severe Wernicke's aphasia. This confirms the
findings of the preceding study and indicates that the low mean
score of the left brain-damaged group on this test is due to the
poor performance of aphasics.

A further confirmation that the sound recognition defect was
qualitatively different in the two hemispheric groups was provided by the distribution of patients showing abnormal discrepancies between the two test scores. As Table 7.8 shows, the
meaningless sounds scores were significantly lower than the
meaningful sounds scores in 48 per cent (12 out of 25) of the
right brain-damaged group, and in only 2.2 per cent (one patient
only out of 45) of the left brain-damaged group, while the reverse
situation, i.e., meaningful worse than meaningless, was found only
in left brain-damaged patients.

Finally, by putting together the findings of Tables 7.6 and 7.7,
we singled out the patients showing a specific defect on one test
only, i.e., either an exclusively perceptual-discriminative defect
or an exclusively semantic-association defect. A patient was
defined as having such a selective defect if (1) his performance

TABLE 7.7 Distribution of Left Brain-damaged Patients According to Presence and Type of Aphasia and Degree of Defect on the Meaningful Sounds Identification Test

| Degree of defect | Aphasic Patients (N = 40) | | | | | | Nonaphasic Patients (N = 5) |
| | Global (N = 6) | Broca | | Wernicke | | | |
		Severe (N = 6)	Mild (N = 0)	Severe (N = 13)	Moderate (N = 10)	Mild (N = 5)	
None	2	3	—	1	3	4	5
Moderate	1	1	—	3	5	1	—
Severe	3	2	—	9	2	—	—

TABLE 7.8 DISTRIBUTION OF RIGHT AND LEFT BRAIN-DAMAGED PATIENTS ACCORDING TO PRESENCE AND SEVERITY OF ABNORMAL INTERTEST DISCREPANCY

Hemisphere-damaged Group	Abnormal Intertest Discrepancy				
	Meaningful Sounds worse		No discrepancy	Meaningless Sounds worse	
	$(M + 2SD)$	$(M + 2SD)$	$(M \pm 2SD)$	$(M - 2SD)$	$(M - 2SD)$
Right (N = 25)	—	—	13	4	8
Left (N = 45)	9	10	25	—	1

was defective on one test and not on the other, and (2) he showed abnormal discrepancy between the two test scores. Using these rather strict criteria, seven patients turned out to have an exclusively perceptual-discriminative defect; all of them had lesions in the right hemisphere. By contrast, there were nineteen patients with an exclusively semantic-associative defect: all of them had lesions in the left hemisphere and aphasia. In the entire brain-damaged sample, there were only two patients who were defective on both tests and who did not show an abnormal intertest discrepancy: one had a lesion in the right hemisphere, and one in the left hemisphere and aphasia.

Discussion

Auditory Agnosia and Aphasia

Both studies indicate that aphasics as a group specifically failed when they had to identify the meaning of sounds and noises, while their ability to grasp the acoustic pattern of sounds and noises was comparatively preserved. In Experiment 1 aphasics showed a significant increase of semantic but not of acoustic errors, so that they were the only experimental group in which the former type of error was predominant over the latter. In Experiment 2, they specifically failed on the test requiring the semantic identification of sounds, while they performed the acoustic discrimination test like the controls. When the defect on each test was quantitatively defined with reference to the control group, the performance of 27 aphasics out of 40 (67.5%) was found to be defective on the semantic identification task, while the acoustic discrimination task was performed within normal limits by all but one aphasic patient.

This "semantic" type of auditory agnosia reminds one of the disorder that Kleist theoretically defined in 1928 as *sound-meaning deafness.* The fact that no such type of auditory agnosia had been found up to his time of writing (nor, to our knowledge, until now), while it came out so frequently in our study, may be explained as a consequence of the different samples studied. Clinicians traditionally examined patients with a rare aphasic syndrome, pure word-deafness, in which agnosia is primarily discriminative in nature, while we have examined an unselected sample of aphasics, in which no patient with word-deafness happened to be included. In this sample, which is more representative of the entire aphasic population than the one studied by the clinicians, the semantic defect proved to be far more important.

The nature of this disorder may be discussed. Its predominance in the forms of aphasia (Wernicke's and global) with poorer comprehension and its high correlation with the language comprehension scores in the entire aphasic group suggests that the same mechanisms may be at work in the verbal as well as in the nonverbal defect. This view finds confirmation in earlier studies indicating that an unselected group of aphasics make more semantic than discriminative errors also on tasks of auditory language comprehension (De Renzi & Vignolo, 1962; Schuell & Jenkins, 1961). The results of recent investigations, however, provide hints that the underlying disorder may even transcend the auditory sensory modality and be cognitive rather than perceptual in nature. The presence of a specific intellectual impairment in aphasia—which has been variously hypothesized by Marie (1926), Head (1926), Goldstein (1948), and Bay (1962)— has been supported by experimental findings showing that aphasics perform consistently worse than other brain-damaged patients on several nonverbal mental tasks, such as finding hidden figures (Russo & Vignolo, 1967; Teuber & Weinstein, 1956), sorting different items to criterion (De Renzi, Faglioni, Savoiardo, & Vignolo, 1966), and matching drawings of objects with their appropriate colors (De Renzi & Spinnler, 1967) or real objects with the movements needed to use them appropriately (De Renzi, Pieczuro, & Vignolo, 1968). It may well be that the inability to match a meaningful sound with the corresponding picture is merely another expression of the same type of disorder. This could then be conceived of as an associative defect involving one or several sensory modalities and consisting in the inability to put together different aspects of the same concept. The analogy between this disorder and the asymboly in the sense of Meynert and Wernicke (Liepmann, 1908b) is apparent and deserves further study.

Auditory Agnosia and the Hemispheric Side of the Lesion

The findings of Experiment 2 support the hypothesis advanced at the close of Experiment 1. They show, in fact, that auditory agnosia may be found also after lesions of the right hemisphere but that in this case, the disorder is qualitatively different from the one that appears after lesions of the left hemisphere. In striking contrast to the left brain-damaged patients, whose impairment was essentially one of semantic identification of the perceived sound, the right brain-damaged patients as a group failed specifically on the tasks requiring subtle discrimination of acoustic patterns, while they performed the semantic identification task like normal controls. This defect of the right brain-damaged patients had not been brought out in Experiment 1 because the test employed in that study was not a very refined test of sound discrimination. However, it appeared dramatically when the patients were given the meaningless sounds test, which made much greater demands on the ability to carry out subtle differentiations between acoustically similar patterns.

These findings totally agree with those of Kimura (1964, 1967), Milner (1962), and Shankweiler (1966a, 1966b), mentioned in preceding paragraphs, and tend to support the view that the integrity of the right hemisphere is crucial for carrying out accurate discriminations in the acoustic field. In this connection, it is interesting to recall that a similar "perceptual" role has been attributed to the right hemisphere also for other sensory modalities, such as vision (see De Renzi, 1967, for a review of recent experimental evidence).

Conclusion

Our results indicate at least two types of agnosia for nonverbal sounds and noises associated with unilateral hemispheric damage: a perceptual-discriminative agnosia, mainly due to lesions of the right hemisphere, and an associative-semantic one, mainly due to lesions of the left hemisphere and closely linked with aphasia. In agreement with other experimental evidence in normal and brain-damaged subjects, this finding supports the notion of a cerebral asymmetry in auditory recognition: it appears that subtle perceptual discrimination of sounds is subserved mostly by the right hemisphere, while their semantic decoding takes place chiefly in the left hemisphere.

The distinction between a discriminative and a semantic level of auditory recognition, however crude, has proven to be a useful key to understanding auditory agnosia, and it could perhaps be fruitfully applied also to recognition disorders in other sensory modalities. However, it does not account for other important dimensions of auditory recognition, such as attention, memory, and the temporal sequencing of incoming stimuli, recently stressed by Hécaen. An objective evaluation of disorders of these other aspects and of their behavioral and anatomical correlates is the task for future research in the field of auditory agnosia.

References

Ackerly, W., Lhamon, W., & Fitts, W. T. 1955. Phantom breast. *J. nerv. ment. Dis.*, 121: 177–178.

Adey, W. R., Carter, I. D., & Porter, R. 1954. Temporal dispersion in cortical response. *J. Neurophysiol.*, 17: 167–182.

Adler, H. 1891. Beitrag zur Kenntis der selteneren Formen der sensorischen Aphasie. *Neurol. Centralbl.*, 10: 294.

Akelaitis, A. J. 1944. Study of gnosis, praxis and language following section of corpus callosum and anterior commissure. *J. Neurosurg.*, 1: 94–102.

Alajouanine, Th., Aubry, M., & Pialoux, P. 1955. Note préliminaire sur l'atteinte auditive dans l'aphasie. In Th. Alajouanine, *et al.* (Ed.), *Les grandes activités du lobe temporal*. Paris: Masson.

Albe-Fessard, D. 1967. Organization of somatic central projection. In W. D. Neff (Ed.), *Contributions to sensory physiology*. New York: Academic Press. Vol. 2.

Altman, J. 1962. Some fiber projections to the superior colliculus in the cat. *J. comp. Neurol.*, 119: 77–95.

Amassian, V. E. 1954. Studies on organization of somesthetic association area, including a single unit analysis. *J. Neurophysiol.*, 17: 39–58.

Anderson, F. D., & Berry, C. M. 1959. Degeneration studies of long ascending fiber systems in the cat brain stem. *J. comp. Neurol.*, 111: 195–229.

Anton, G. 1899. Über die Selbstwahrnehmung der Herderkrankungen des Gehirns durch den Kranken bei Rindenblindheit und Rindentaubheit. *Arch. Psychiat. Nervenkrankh.*, 32: 85–127.

Arnold, G. 1943. Cortikale Hörstörung bei Leitungsaphasie. *Monatsschr. Ohrenheilk.*, 77: 409–421.

Arnold, G. 1946a. Thalamische Hörstörung mit Paramusie nach Fleckfieber. *Monatsschr. Ohrenheilk.*, 79/80: 11–27.

Arnold, G. 1946b. Zentrale Hörstörung mit Paramusie bei einer Geschwulst in der Gegend des linkes Thalamus. *Monatsschr. Ohrenheilk.*, 79/80: 359–365.

Arrigoni, G., & De Renzi, E. 1964. Constructional apraxia and hemispheric locus of lesion. *Cortex*, 1: 170–197.

Bailey, A. A., & Moersch, F. P. 1941. Phantom limb. *Canad. Med. Assoc. J.*, 45: 37–42.

Balassa, L. 1923. Zur Psychologie der Seelentaubheit. *D. Ztschr. Nervenhlk.*, 77: 143–155.

Barrett, A. M. 1910. A case of pure word-deafness with autopsy. *J. nerv. ment. Dis.*, 37: 73–92.

Barton, M. J., Goodglass, H., & Shai, A. 1965. Differential recognition of tachistoscopically presented English and Hebrew words in the right and left visual fields. *Percept. mot. Skills.*, 21: 431.

Bates, J. A. V., & Ettlinger, G. 1960. Posterior biparietal ablations in the monkey. *Arch. Neurol.* (Chicago), 3: 177–192.

Bay, E. 1962. Aphasia and non-verbal disorders of language. *Brain*, 85: 411–426.

Bay, E. 1967. The classification of disorders of speech. *Cortex*, 3: 26–31.

Benson, D. F. 1967. Fluency in aphasia: correlation with radioactive scan localization. *Cortex*, 3: 373–394.

Benton, A. L. 1959. *Right-left discrimination and finger localization: development and pathology.* New York: Hoeber-Harper.

Benton, A. L. 1962. The Visual Retention Test as a constructional praxis task. *Conf. neurol.* (Basel), 22: 141–155.

Benton, A. L. 1965. The problem of cerebral dominance. *Canad. Psychol.*, 6: 332–348.

Benton, A. L. 1967a. Constructional apraxia and the minor hemisphere. *Conf. neurol.*, (Basel), 29: 1–16.

Benton, A. L. 1967b. Problems of test construction in the field of aphasia. *Cortex*, 3: 32–58.

Benton, A. L., & Fogel, M. L. 1962. Three-dimensional constructional praxis: a clinical test. *Arch. Neurol.* (Chicago), 7: 347–354.

Benton, A. L., Meyers, R., & Polder, G. J. 1965. Some aspects of handedness. *Psychiat. Neurol.* (Basel), 144: 321–337.

Benton, A. L., Sutton, S., Kennedy, J. A., & Brokaw, J. H. 1962. The crossmodal retardation in reaction time of patients with cerebral disease. *J. nerv. ment. Dis.*, 135: 413–418.

Berger, H. 1911. Ein Beitrag zur Lokalisation der korticalen Hörzentren des Menschen. *Monatsschr. Psychiat. Neurol.*, 29: 439–449.

Bischoff, E. 1899. Beitrag zur Lehre von der sensorischen Aphasie nebst Bemerkungen über die Symptomatik doppelseitiger Schläfenlappenerkrankungen. *Arch. Psychiat. Nervenkrankh.*, 32: 730–767.

Bishop, G. H. 1959. The relation between the nerve fiber size and sensory modality: phylogenetic implications of the afferent innervation of cortex. *J. nerv. ment. Dis.*, 128: 89–114.

Black, P., & Myers, R. E. 1964. Visual function of the forebrain commissures in the chimpanzee. *Science*, 146: 799–800.

Black, P., & Myers, R. E. 1965. A neurological investigation of eye-hand control in the chimpanzee. In G. Ettlinger (Ed.), *Functions of the corpus callosum*. London: Churchill.

Blackburn, H. L., & Benton, A. L. 1955. Simple and choice reaction time in cerebral disease. *Conf. neurol.* (Basel), 15: 327–336.

Bocca, E., Calearo, C., Cassinari, V., & Migliavacca, F. 1955. Testing "cortical" hearing in temporal lobe tumors. *Acta Oto-laryngol.*, 45: 289–304.

Boeri, R., & Negri, S. 1954. I fenomeni sensitivi d'amputazione nell' età infanto-giovanile. *Riv. Sperimentale Freniat.*, 78: 721–733.

Boller, F., & Vignolo, L. A. 1966. Il significato dei disturbi della ripetizione nell' afasia di Wernicke. *Sistema Nervoso*, 18: 383–396.

Bonhoeffer, K. 1914. Klinischer und anatomischer Befund zur Lehre von der Apraxie und der "motorischen Sprachbahn," *Monatsschr. Psychiat. Neurol.*, 35: 113–128.

Bonhoeffer, K. 1915. Doppelseitige symmetrische Schläfen und Parietallappenherde als Ursache vollständiger dauernder Worttaubheit bei erhaltener Tonskala, verbunden mit taktiler und optischer Agnosie. *Monatsschr. Psychiat. Neurol.*, 37: 17–38.

Bonvicini, G. 1905. Über subcorticale sensorische Aphasie. *Jahrb. Psychiat. Neurol.*, 26: 126–229.

Bonvicini, G. 1929. Die Störungen der Lautsprache bei Temporallappenläsionen. In G. Alexander & O. Marburg (Eds.), *Handbuch der Neurologie des Ohres*. Berlin: Urban & Schwarzenberg.

Bors, E. 1951. Phantom limbs of patients with spinal cord injury. *Arch. Neurol. Psychiat.* (Chicago), 66: 610–631.

Bossom, J., & Hamilton, C. R. 1963. Interocular transfer of prism altered coordinations in split-brain monkeys. *J. comp. physiol. Psychol.,* 56: 769–774.

Brain, R. 1965. *Speech disorders.* London: Butterworth.

Braine, L. G. 1968. Asymmetries of pattern perception observed in Israelis. *Neuropsycholgia,* 6: 73–88.

Bramwell, E. 1927. A case of cortical deafness. *Brain,* 50: 579–580.

Branch, C., Milner, B., & Rasmussen, T. 1964. Intercarotid sodium amytal for the lateralization of cerebral speech dominance. *J. Neurosurg.,* 21: 399–405.

Brazier, M. 1892. Du trouble des facultés musicales dans l'aphasie. Étude sur les représentations mentales des sons et des symboles musicaux. *Rev. Phil.,* 34: 337–368.

Bremer, F. 1958. Physiology of the corpus callosum. *Proc. Assoc. Res. nerv. ment. Dis.,* 36: 424–448.

Bremer, F. 1966. Étude électrophysiologique d'un transfert inter-hémispherique callosal. *Arch. Ital. Biol.,* 104: 1–29.

Bremer, F., Brihaye, J., & Andre-Baliseaux, G. 1956. Physiologie et pathologie du corps calleaux. *Arch. Suisses Neurol. Psychiat.,* 78: 31–87.

Bressler, B., Cohen, S. I., & Magnussen, F. 1955. Bilateral breast phantom and breast phantom pain: case report. *J. nerv. ment. Dis.,* 122: 315–320.

Broadbent, D. E. 1954. The role of auditory localization in attention and memory span. *J. exp. Psychol.,* 47: 191–196.

Broca, P. 1861. Perte de la parole. *Bull Soc. Anthropol.,* 2: 235–238.

Broca, P. 1865. Sur la faculté du langage articulé. *Bull. Soc. Anthropol.,* 6: 493–494.

Brookshire, K. H., & Warren, J. M. 1962. The generality and consistency of handedness in monkeys. *Animal Behav.,* 10: 222–227.

Burgess, P. R., & Perl, E. R. 1967. Myelinated afferent fibers responding specifically to noxious stimulation of skin. *J. Physiol.,* 190: 451–562.

Butler, C. R. 1966. Cortical lesions and interhemispheric communication in monkeys (macaca mulatta). *Nature,* 209: 59–61.

Bykov, K. 1924–1925. Versuche an Hunden mit durchschneiden des Corpus Callosum. *Zentralbl. Neurol. Psychiat.,* 39: 199.

Cannon, W. B., & Rosenblueth, A. 1949. *The supersensitivity of denervated structures,* New York: Macmillan.

Carreras, M., & Andersson, S. A. 1963. Functional properties of neurons of the anterior ectosylvian gyrus of the cat. *J. Neurophysiol.,* 26: 100–126.

Casey, K. L. 1964. A search for nociceptive elements in the thalamus of the squirrel monkey. Paper read at the American Physiological Society, Providence, R.I.

Charcot, J. M. 1888. Physiologie et pathologie du moignon. Leçon du 18 Juillet. In *Leçons du Mardi*. Paris: Delahaye et Lecrosmier.

Chow, K. L. 1950. A retrograde cell degeneration study of the cortical projection field of the pulvinar in the monkey. *J. comp. Neurol.*, 93: 313–340.

Clark, W. E. L., & Russell, W. R. 1938. Cortical deafness without aphasia. *Brain*, 61: 375–383.

Corkin, S., Milner, B., & Rasmussen, T. 1964. Effects of different cortical excisions on sensory thresholds in man. *Trans. Amer. Neurol. Assoc.*, 89: 112–116.

Costa, L. D. 1962. Visual reaction time of patients with cerebral disease as a function of length and constancy of preparatory interval. *Percept. mot. skills*, 14: 391–397.

Critchley, M. 1953. *The parietal lobes*, London: Arnold.

Critchley, M. 1955. Quelques observations relatives à la notion de la conscience du moi corporel. *Encéphale*, 44: 501–531.

Critchley, M. 1962. Speech and speech loss in relation to the duality of the brain. In V. Mountcastle (Ed.), *Interhemispheric relations and cerebral dominance*. Baltimore: Johns Hopkins Press.

Crone-Münzebrock, A. 1951. Zur Kenntnis des Phantomerlebnisses nach Penis amputationen. *Ztschr. Urol.*, 44: 819–822.

Cronholm, B. 1951. Phantom limbs in amputees. *Acta psychiat. neurol.* (Kbn.), Suppl. no. 72.

Curry, F. K. W., 1967. A comparison of left-handed and right-handed subjects on verbal and non-verbal dichotic listening tasks. *Cortex*, 3: 343–352.

Dejerine, J. 1914. *Sémiologie des affection du système nerveux*. Paris: Masson.

Dejerine, J., & André-Thomas 1912. Contribution a l'étude de l'aphasie chez les gauchers. *Rev. Neurol.*, 24: 214–226.

Dejerine, J., & Sérieux, P. 1898. Un cas de surdité verbale pure terminée par aphasie sensorielle suivi d'autopsie. *Rev. Psychiat.*, 8: 1074–1077.

De Renzi, E. 1967. Deficit gnosici, prassici, mnestici e intelletti nelle lesioni emisferiche unilaterali. In *Atti XVI Congresso Nazionale di Neurologia*. Roma: Pensiero Scientificio.

De Renzi, E., & Faglioni, P. 1963. L'autotopagnosia. *Arch. di Psicol. Neurol. Psichiat.*, 24: 1–34.

De Renzi, E., Faglioni, P., Savoiardo, M., & Vignolo, L. A. 1966. The influence of aphasia and of the hemispheric side of the cerebral lesion on abstract thinking. *Cortex*, 2: 399–420.

De Renzi, E., Pieczuro, A., & Vignolo, L. A. 1968. Ideational apraxia: a quantitative study. *Neurospychologia*, 6: 41–52.

De Renzi, E., & Spinnler, H. 1966. Visual recognition in patients with unilateral cerebral disease. *J. nerv. ment. Dis.*, 142: 515–525.

De Renzi, E., & Spinnler, H. 1967. Impaired performance on color tasks in patients with hemispheric damage. *Cortex*, 3: 194–216.

De Renzi, E., & Vignolo, L. A. 1962. Fattori verbali ed extraverbali della comprensione negli afasici. Atti XIV Congresso Nazionale di Neurologia.

Diamond, I. T. 1967. The sensory neocortex. In W. D. Neff (Ed.), *Contributions to sensory physiology*. New York: Academic Press. Vol. 2.

Douglas, W. W., & Ritchie, J. M. 1957. Non-medullated fibers in the saphenous nerve which signal touch. *J. Physiol.*, 139: 385–399.

Douglas, W. W., & Ritchie, J. M. 1959. The sensory functions of the non-myelinated afferent nerve fibers from the skin. In G. E. W. Wolstenholme & M. O'Connor (Eds.), *Pain and itch; nervous mechanisms*. Boston: Little, Brown.

Downer, J. L. de C. 1959. Changes in visually guided behavior following midsagittal division of optic chiasm and corpus callosum in monkey (macaca mulatta). *Brain*, 82: 251–259.

Downer, J. L. de C. 1961. Changes in visual gnostic functions and emotional behavior following unilateral temporal pole damage in the split-brain monkey. *Nature*, 191: 50–51.

Ebner, F. F., & Myers, R. E. 1962a. Corpus callosum and the interhemispheric transmission of tactual learning. *J. Neurophysiol.*, 25: 380–391.

Ebner, F. F., & Myers, R. E. 1962b. Direct and transcallosal induction of touch memories in the monkey. *Science*, 138: 51–52.

Edgren, I. 1895. Amusie (musikalische Aphasie). *D. Ztschr. Nervenhlk.*, 6: 1–64.

Erickson, R. P. 1963. Sensory neural patterns and gustation. In Y. Zotterman (Ed.), *Olfaction and taste*. New York: Macmillan.

Erickson, R. P., Jane, J. A., Waite, R. & Diamond, I. T. 1964. Single neuron investigation of sensory thalamus in the opossum. *J. Neurophysiol.*, 27: 1026–1047.

Ettlinger, G. 1962. Relationship between test difficulty and the visual impairment in monkeys with ablations of temporal cortex. *Nature*, 196: 911–912.

Ettlinger, G. 1965. In G. Ettlinger (Ed.), *Functions of the corpus callosum*. London: Churchill.

Ettlinger, G., & Elithorn, A. 1962. Transfer between the hands of a mirror-image tactile shape discrimination. *Nature*, 194: 1101–1102.

Ettlinger, G., & Moffett, A. 1964. Lateral preferences in the monkey. *Nature*, 204: 606.

Ettlinger, G., & Morton, H. B. 1963. Callosal section: its effect on performance of a bimanual skill. *Science*, 139: 485–486.

Ettlinger, G., & Morton, H. B. 1966. Tactile discrimination performance in the monkey: transfer of training between the hands after commissural section. *Cortex*, 2: 30–49.

Ettlinger, G., Warrington, E., & Zangwill, O. L. 1957. A further study of visual-spatial agnosia. *Brain*, 80: 335–361.

Ettlinger, G., & Wegener, J. G. 1958. Somaesthetic alternation, discrimination and orientation after frontal and parietal lesions in monkeys. *Quart. J. exp. Psychol.*, 10: 177–186.

Feuchtwanger, E. 1930. *Amusie*. Berlin: Springer.

Flechsig, P. 1901. Developmental (myelogenetic) localization in the cerebral cortex in the human subject. *Lancet*, 2: 1027–1029.

Fogel, M. L. 1964. The intelligence quotient as an index of brain damage. *Amer. J. Orthopsychiat.*, 34: 555–562.

Forgays, D. G. 1952. The development of differential word recognition. *J. exp. Psychol.*, 45: 165–168.

Freeman, L. W., & Heimburger, R. F. 1947. Surgical relief of pain in paraplegic patients. *Arch. Surg.*, 55: 433–440.

Freud, S. 1891. *Zur Auffassung der Aphasien*. Wien: Deuticke.

Freund, C. S. 1895. *Labyrinthtaubheit und Sprachtaubheit*. Wiesbaden: Bergmann.

Fulton, J. F. 1943. *Physiology of the nervous system*. (2d ed.) New York: Oxford University Press.

Gazzaniga, M. S. 1963. Effects of commissurotomy on a preoperatively learned visual discrimination. *Exp. Neurol.*, 8: 14–19.

Gazzaniga, M. S. 1964. Cerebral mechanisms involved in ipsilateral eye-hand use in split-brain monkeys. *Exp. Neurol.*, 10: 148–155.

Gazzaniga, M. S. 1965. Psychological properties of the disconnected hemispheres in man. *Science*, 150: 372.

Gazzaniga, M. S. 1966a. Interhemispheric communication of visual learning. *Neuropsychologia*, 4: 183–189.

Gazzaniga, M. S. 1966b. Interhemispheric cuing systems remaining after section of neocortical commissures in monkeys. *Exp. Neurol.*, 16: 28–35.

Gazzaniga, M. S. 1966c. Visuomotor integration in split-brain monkeys with other cerebral lesions. *Exp. Neurol.*, 16: 289–298.

Gazzaniga, M. S. Bogen, J. E., & Sperry, R. W. 1962. Some functional effects of sectioning the cerebral commissures in man. *Proc. Nat. Acad. Sci.*, 48: 1765–1769.

Gazzaniga, M. S., Bogen, J. E., & Sperry, R. W. 1963. Laterality effects in somesthesis following cerebral commissurotomy in man. *Neuropsychologia*, 1: 209–215.

Gazzaniga, M. S., Bogen, J. E., & Sperry, R. W. 1965. Observations on visual perception after disconnection of the cerebral hemispheres in man. *Brain*, 88: 221–236.

Gazzaniga, M. S., & Sperry, R. W. 1967. Language after section of the cerebral commissures. *Brain*, 90: 131–148.

Geschwind, N. 1964. The paradoxical position of Kurt Goldstein in the history of aphasia. *Cortex*, 1: 214–224.

Geschwind, N. 1965a. Disconnexion syndromes in animals and man. *Brain*, 88: 237–294, 585–644.

Geschwind, N. 1965b. Alexia and colour-naming disturbance. In G. Ettlinger (Ed.), *Functions of the corpus callosum*. London: Churchill.

Geschwind, N. 1966. Carl Wernicke, the Breslau School and the history of aphasia. In E. C. Carterette (Ed.), *Brain Function; Vol. III: Speech, Language, and Communication*. Los Angeles: University of California Press. U.C.L.A. Forum in Medical Sciences no. 4.

Geschwind, N. 1967a. The varieties of naming errors. *Cortex*, 3: 97–112.

Geschwind, N. 1967b. Wernicke's contribution to the study of aphasia. *Cortex*, 3: 449–463.

Geschwind, N., & Kaplan, E. 1962. A human cerebral deconnection syndrome. *Neurology*, 12: 675–685.

Getz, B. 1952. The termination of spinothalamic fibers in the cat as studied by the method of terminal degeneration. *Acta Anatomica* (Basel), 16: 271–290.

Gibson, J. J. 1962. Observations on active touch. *Psychol. Rev.*, 69: 477–491.

Gibson, J. J. 1966. *The senses considered as perceptual systems*. Boston: Houghton Mifflin.

Glickstein, M. 1965. Interhemispheric transfer, macular sparing, and the central visual pathway. In G. Ettlinger (Ed.), *Functions of the corpus callosum*. London: Churchill.

Glickstein, M., Arora, H. A., & Sperry, R. W. 1963. Delayed-response performance following optic tract section, unilateral frontal lesion, and commissurotomy. *J. comp. physiol. Psychol.*, 56: 11–18.

Glickstein, M., & Sperry, R. W. 1960. Intermanual somesthetic transfer in split-brain rhesus monkeys. *J. comp. physiol. Psychol.*, 53: 322–327.

Goldstein, K. 1917. *Die transkortikalen Aphasien*. Jena: Gustav Fischer.

Goldstein, K. 1926. Über Aphasie. *Schweiz. Arch. Neurol. Psychiat.*, 19: 1–38., 292–322.

Goldstein, K. 1948. *Language and language disturbances*. New York: Grune & Stratton.

Goldstein, K., & Scheerer, M. 1941. Abstract and concrete behavior; an experimental study with special tests. *Psychol. Monogr.* 53(2): 1–51.

Guéniot, M. 1861. D'une hallucination du toucher ou hétérotopie subjective des extrémites particulière à certains amputés. *J. Physiol.*, 4: 416–430.

Ha, H., & Liu, C. N. 1966. Organization of the spino-cervico-thalamic system. *J. comp. Neurol.*, 127: 445–470.

Haber, W. B. 1955. Effects of loss of limb on sensory functions. *J. Psychol.*, 40: 115–123.

Hamilton, C. R., & Gazzaniga, M. S. 1964. Lateralization of learning of color and brightness discriminations following brain bisection. *Nature*, 201: 220.

Hampson, J. L. 1949. Relationships between cat cerebral and cerebellar cortices. *J. Neurophysiol.*, 12: 37–50.

Harcum, E. R., & Filion, R. D. F. 1963. Effects of stimulus reversals on lateral dominance in word recognition. *Percept. mot. skills*, 17: 779.

Head, H. 1920. *Studies in neurology*. London: Hodder & Stoughton.

Head, H. 1926. *Aphasia and kindred disorders of speech*. Cambridge: Cambridge University Press.

Head, H., & Holmes, G. 1911. Sensory disturbances from cerebral lesions. *Brain*, 34: 102–254.

Hebb, D. O. 1949. *The organization of behavior: a neuropsychological theory*. New York: John Wiley.

Hécaen, H., & Ajuriaguerra, J. de 1964. *Left-handedness. Manual superiority and cerebral dominance*. New York: Grune & Stratton.

Hécaen, H., Penfield, W., Bertrand, C., & Malmo, R. 1956. The syndrome of apractognosia due to lesions of the minor cerebral hemisphere. *Arch. Neurol. Psychiat.* (Chicago), 75: 400–434.

Hemphill, R. E., & Stengel, E. 1940. A study on pure word-deafness *J. Neurol. Psychiat.*, 3: 251–262.

Henneberg, R. 1906. Über unvollständige reine Worttaubheit. *Monatsschr. Psychiat. Neurol.*, 19: 17–38, 159–179.

Henneberg, R. 1918. Über einen Fall von reiner Worttaubheit. *Neurol. Centralbl.*, 37: 425–427, 539–542.

Henneberg, R. 1926. Hirnbefund bei reiner Worttaubheit. *Zentralbl. Neurol. Psychiat.*, 43: 251–252.

Henneman, E., Cooke, P. M., & Snider, R. S. 1952. Cerebellar projections to the cerebral cortex. *Proc. Assoc. Res. nerv. ment. Dis.*, 30: 317–333.

Henschen, S. E. 1918. Über die Hörsphäre. *J. Neurol. Psychol.* 22, Ergänzungs-Heft, 3: 319–473.

Heron, W. 1957. Perception as a function of retinal locus and attention. *Amer. J. Psychol.*, 70: 38–48.

Herrick, C. J., & Bishop, G. H. 1958. A comparative study of the spinal lemniscus systems. In H. H. Jasper (Ed.), *Reticular formation of the brain.* Boston: Little Brown.

Heusner, A. P. 1950. Phantom genitalia. *Trans. Amer. Neurol. Assoc.*, 75: 129–136.

Hoff, H. 1964, Discussion, International Neuropsychological Symposium, San Gimignano, Italy. September, 1964.

Hoffman, J. 1954. Facial phantom phenomenon. *J. nerv. ment. Dis.*, 122: 143–151.

Iggo, A. 1958. Single C fibers from cutaneous receptors. *J. Physiol.*, 143: 47.

Iggo, A. 1959. A single unit analysis of cutaneous receptors with C afferent fibers. In G. E. W. Wolstenholme & M. O'Connor (Eds.), *Pain and itch; nervous mechanisms.* Boston: Little Brown.

Isserlin, M. 1936. Aphasie. In O. Bumke & O. Foerster (Eds.), *Handbuch der Neurologie.* Berlin: Springer.

James, W. 1887. The consciousness of lost limbs. *Proc. Amer. Soc. Psychical Res.*, 1: 249–258.

Jansen, J., & Brodal, A. 1954. *Aspects of cerebellar anatomy.* Oslo: Johan Grundt.

Jeeves, M. A. 1965. Psychological studies of three cases of congenital absence of the corpus callosum. In G. Ettlinger (Ed.), *The functions of the corpus callosum.* London: Churchill.

Jellinek, A. 1956. Amusia. *Folia phoniat.*, 8: 124–149.

Jerger, J. F. 1964. Auditory tests for disorders of the central auditory mechanisms. In W. S. Fields & B. R. Alford (Eds.), *Neurological aspects of auditory and vestibular disorders.* Springfield, Ill.: Charles C Thomas.

Kallio, K. E., 1949. Phantom limb of forearm stump cleft by kineplastic surgery. *Acta. chir. Scand.*, 99: 121–132.

Kast, A. 1900. Zur Kenntnis der Beziehungen zwischen Schwerhörigkeit und Worttaubheit. *D. Ztschr. Nervenhlk.*, 8: 178–197.

Katz, D. 1920. Psychologische Versuche mit Amputierten. *Ztschr. Psychol. Physiol. Sinnesorgane*, 85: 83–117.

Kimura, D. 1961a. Cerebral dominance and the perception of verbal stimuli. *Canad. J. Psychol.*, 15: 166–171.

Kimura, D. 1961b. Some effects of temporal lobe damage on auditory perception. *Canad. J. Psychol.*, 15: 156–165.

Kimura, D. 1963a. Right temporal lobe damage. *Arch. Neurol.* (Chicago), 8: 264–271.

Kimura, D. 1963b. Speech lateralization in young children as determined by an auditory test. *J. comp. physiol. Psychol.*, 56: 899–902.

Kimura, D. 1964. Left-right differences in the perception of melodies. *Quart. J. exp. Psychol.*, 14: 355–358.

Kimura, D. 1966. Dual functional asymmetry of the brain in visual perception. *Neuropsychologia*, 4: 275–285.

Kimura, D. 1967. Functional asymmetry of the brain in dichotic listening. *Cortex*, 3: 163–178.

Klein, R. 1927. Über reine Worttaubheit mit besonderer Berücksichtigung der Amusie. *Monatsschr. Psychiat. Neurol.*, 64: 354–368.

Klein, R., & Harper, J. 1956. The problem of agnosia in the light of a case of pure word deafness. *J. ment. Sci.*, 102: 112–120.

Kleist, K. 1928. Gehirnpathologische und lokalisatorische Ergebnisse über Hörstörungen, Geräuschtaubheiten und Amusien. *Monatsschr. Psychiat. Neurol.*, 68: 853–860.

Kleist, K. 1934. *Gehirnpathologie.* Leipzig: Johann Ambrosius Barth.

Kleist, K. 1962. *Sensory aphasia and amusia.* New York: Pergamon Press.

Klüver, H., & Bucy, P. C. 1938. The analysis of certain effects of bilateral temporal lobectomy in the rhesus monkey, with special reference to "psychic blindness." *J. Psychol.*, 5: 33–54.

Knoblauch, A. 1888. Über Störungen der musikalischen Leistungsfähigkeit infolge von Gehirnläsionen. *D. Arch. Klin. Med.*, 43: 331–352.

Kogerer, H. 1924. Worttaubheit, Melodientaubheit, Gebärdenagnosie. *Ztschr. Neurol. Psychiat.*, 92: 459–483.

Köhl, G. F., & Tschabitscher, H. 1952. Über einen Fall von Amusie. *Wiener Ztschr. Nervenheilk.*, 6: 219–230.

Kohs, S. C. 1923. *Intelligence Measurement.* New York: Macmillan.

Kopeczinski, S., & Zilberlast-Zand, N. 1921. Un cas de surdité verbale pure. *Rev. Neurol.*, 29: 1338–1344.

Korn, H., Wendt, R., & Albe-Fessard, D. 1966. Somatic projection to the orbital cortex of the cat. *EEG clin. Neurophysiol.*, 21: 209–226.

Krieg, W. J. S. 1963. *Connections of the cerebral cortex.* Evanston, Ill.: Brain Books.

Kruger, L., & Albe-Fessard, D. 1960. Distribution of responses to somatic afferent stimuli in the diencephalon of the cat under chloralose anesthesia. *Exp. Neurol.*, 2: 442–467.

Kuypers, H. G. J. M., Szwarcbart, M., Mishkin, M., & Rosvold, H. E. 1965. Occipitotemporal corticocortical connections in the rhesus monkey. *Exp. Neurol.*, 11: 245–262.

Laignel-Lavastine & Alajouanine, Th. 1921. Un cas d'agnosie auditive. *Rev. Neurol.*, 37: 194–198.

Lawrence, D. G., & Kuypers, H. G. 1965. Pyramidal and non-pyramidal pathways in monkeys. *Science*, 148: 973–975.

Lee-Teng, E., & Sperry, R. W. 1966. Intermanual sterognostic size discrimination in split-brain monkeys. *J. comp. physiol. Psychol.*, 62: 84–89.

Lele, P. P., & Weddell, G. 1959. Sensory nerves of the cornea and cutaneous sensibility. *Exp. Neurol.*, 1: 334–359.

Lemos, A. 1798. Dolorem membri amputati remanentem explicat. Dissertation, Halle.

Lichtheim, L. 1885. On aphasia. *Brain*, 7: 433–485.

Liepmann, H. 1898. Ein Fall von reiner Sprachtaubheit. In *Psychiatrische Abhandlungen*. Breslau: Schletter.

Liepmann, H. 1900. *Das Krankheitsbild der Apraxie ("motorischen Asymbolie")*. Berlin: Karger.

Liepmann, H. 1908a. *Drei Aufsätze aus dem Apraxiegebeit*. Berlin: Karger.

Liepmann, H. 1908b. Über die agnostischen Störungen. *Neurol. Centralbl.*, 27: 609–617, 644–675.

Liepmann, H., & Storch, E. 1902. Der mikroskopische Gehirnebefund bei den Fall Gorstelle. *Monatsschr. Psychiat. Neurol.*, 11: 115–120.

Lissauer, H. 1890. Ein Fall von Seelenblindheit nebst einem Beitrag zur Theorie derselben. *Arch. Psychiat. Nervenkrankh.*, 21: 222–270.

Livingston, K. E. 1945. The phantom limb syndrome: a discussion of the role of major peripheral nerve neuromata. *J. Neurosurg.*, 2: 251–255.

Luria, A. R. 1963. *Restoration of function after brain injury*. New York: Macmillan.

Macchi, G. F., Angeleri, F., & Guazzi, G. 1959. Thalamocortical connections of the first and second somatic sensory areas in the cat. *J. comp. Neurol.*, 111: 387–405.

McFie, J., & Zangwill, O. L. 1960. Visual-constructive disabilities associated with lesions of the left cerebral hemisphere. *Brain*, 83: 243–260.

Mahoudeau, D., Lemoyne, J., Dubrisay, J., & Caraes, J. 1956. Sur un cas d'agnosie auditive. *Rev. Neurol.*, 95: 57.

Mahoudeau, D., Lemoyne, J., Foncin, J. F., & Dubrisay, J. 1958. Considérations sur l'agnosie auditive (à propos d'un cas anatomo-clinique). *Rev. neurol.*, 99: 454–471.

Maillard, G., & Hébrard, S. 1910. Un cas de surdité verbale pure. *Encéphale*, 5(2): 501–503.

Marchand, M. L. 1904. Surdi-mutité par lésion symétrique des lobes temporeaux. *Bull. Soc. Anat. Paris*, 6: 473–475.

Marcie, P., Hécaen, H., Dubois, J., & Angelergues, R. 1965. Les réalisations du langage chez les malades atteints de lésions de l'hemisphere droit. *Neuropsychologia*, 3: 217–245.

Marie, P. 1926. *Travaux et mémoires*. Paris: Masson.

Marshall, W. H., & Talbot, S. A. 1942. Recent evidence for neural mechanisms in vision leading to a general theory of sensory acuity. *Biol. Symposia*, 7: 117–164.

Maspes, P. E. 1948. Le syndrome expérimental chez l'homme de la section du splénium du corps calleux; alexie visuelle pure hémianopsique. *Rev. neurol.*, 80: 100–113.

Mayer-Gross, W. 1929. Ein Fall vom Phantomarm nach Plexuszerreissung. Mit einigen Bemerkungen zum Problem des Phantomgliedes überhaupt. *Nervenzart*, 2: 65–72.

Mehler, W. R., Feferman, M. E., & Nauta, W. J. H. 1960. Ascending axon degeneration following anterolateral cordotomy: an experimental study in the monkey. *Brain*, 83: 718–750.

Meikle, T. 1960. Role of corpus callosum in transfer of visual discriminations in the cat. *Science*, 132: 1496.

Meikle, T. 1964, Failure of interocular transfer of brightness discrimination. *Nature*, 202: 1243–1244.

Meikle, T., & Sechzer, J. A. 1960. Interocular transfer of brightness discrimination in split-brain cats. *Science*, 132: 734–735.

Meikle, T., Sechzer, J. A., & Stellar, E. 1962. Interhemispheric transfer of tactile conditioned responses in corpus callosum-sectioned cats. *J. Neurophysiol.*, 25: 530–543.

Melzack, R., & Wall, R. D. 1965. Pain mechanisms: a new theory. *Science*, 150: 971–979.

Mills, C. K. 1891. On the localization of the auditory center. *Brain*, 14: 465–472.

Milner, B. 1958. Psychological defects produced by temporal lobe excision. *Proc. Assoc. Res. nerv. ment. Dis.*, 36: 244–257.

Milner, B. 1962. Laterality effects in audition. In V. B. Mountcastle (Ed.), *Interhemispheric relations and cerebral dominance*. Baltimore: Johns Hopkins Press.

Misch, W. 1928. Über corticale Taubheit. *Ztschr. Neurol. Psychiat.*, 115: 567–573.

Mishkin, M., & Forgays, D. G. 1952. Word recognition as a function of retinal locus. *J. exp. Psychol.*, 43: 43–48.

Mitchell, S. W. 1871. Phantom limbs. *Lippincott's Magazine*, 8: 563–569.

Mitchell, S. W. 1872. *Injuries of nerves and their consequences.* Philadelphia: Lippincott & Co.

Morel, F. 1935. L'audition dans l'aphasie sensorielle. *Encéphale*, 30: 533–553.

Morin, F. 1955. A new spinal pathway for cutaneous impulses. *Amer. J. Physiol.*, 183: 245–252.

Mott, F. W. 1907. Bilateral lesion of the auditory cortical center: complete deafness and aphasia. *Brit. Med. J.*, 2: 310–315.

Mountcastle, V. B. 1957. Modality and topographic properties of single neurons of cat's somatic sensory cortex. *J. Neurophysiol.*, 20: 408–434.

Mountcastle, V. B., & Powell, T. S. P. 1959. Neural mechanisms subserving cutaneous sensibility, with special reference to the role of afferent inhibition in sensory perception and discrimination. *Bull. Johns Hopkins Hosp.*, 105: 201–232.

Munk, H. 1881. Über die Hörsphären der Grosshirnrinde. Berlin: *Akademie von Wissenschaften.*

Myers, R. E. 1955. Interocular transfer of pattern discrimination in cats following section of crossed optic fibers. *J. comp. physiol.*, 48: 470–473.

Myers, R. E. 1956. Function of corpus callosum in interocular transfer *Brain*, 79: 358–363.

Myers, R. E. 1957. Corpus callosum and interhemispheric communication: enduring memory effects. *Fed. Proc.*, 16: 398.

Myers, R. E. 1961. Corpus callosum and visual gnosis. In J. F. Delafresnaye (Ed.), *Brain mechanisms and learning.* Oxford: Blackwell Scientific Publications.

Myers, R. E. 1965. In G. Ettlinger (Ed.), *Functions of the corpus callosum.* London: Churchill.

Myers, R. E., & Ebner, F. F. 1962. Localization of tactual gnostic functions in corpus callosum. *Neurology*, 12: 303.

Myers, R. E., & Henson, C. O. 1960. Role of corpus callosum in transfer of tactuokinesthetic learning in chimpanzee. *Arch. Neurol.*, 3: 404–409.

Myers, R. E., & Sperry, R. W. 1953. Interocular transfer of a visual form discrimination habit in cats after section of the optic chiasma and corpus callosum. *Anat. Rec.*, 115: 351–352.

Myers, R. E., & Sperry, R. W. 1956. Contralateral mnemonic effects with ipsilateral sensory inflow. *Fed. Proc.*, 15: 436.

Myers, R. E., & Sperry, R. W. 1958. Interhemispheric communication through the corpus callosum. *Arch. Neurol. Psychiat.* (Chicago), 80: 298–303.

Myers, R. E., Sperry, R. W., & McCurdy, N. M. 1962. Neural mechanisms in visual guidance of limb movement. *Arch. Neurol.* (Chicago), 7: 195–202.

Nauta, W. J. H., & Kuypers, H. G. J. M. 1958. Some ascending pathways in the brain stem reticular formation. In H. H. Jasper (Ed.), *Reticular formation of the brain.* Boston: Little Brown.

Neff, W. D. 1961. Neural mechanisms of auditory discrimination. In W. A. Rosenblith (Ed.), *Sensory communication.* New York: Wiley.

Nielsen, J. M. 1939. The unsolved problems in aphasia. *Bull. Los Angeles Neurol. Soc.,* 4: 114–122.

Nielsen, J. M., & Sult, C. W. 1939. Agnosias and the body scheme: five clinical cases. *Bull. Los Angeles Neurol. Soc.,* 4: 69–76.

Ombredane, A. 1944. *Études de psychologie médicale. I: Perception et langage.* Rio de Janeiro: Atlantica Editora.

Orbach, J. 1952. Retinal locus as a factor in the recognition of visually perceived words. *Amer. J. Psychol.,* 68: 555–562.

Orbach, J., & Fantz, R. L. 1958. Differential effects of temporal neocortical resection on overtrained and non-overtrained visual habits in monkeys. *J. comp. physiol. Psychol.,* 51: 126–129.

Orgass, B., & Poeck, K. 1968. Rechts-Links-Störung oder Aphasie? *Dtsch. Z. Nervenheilk.,* 194.

Oscarsson, O. 1958. Further observations on ascending spinal tracts activated from muscle, joint and skin nerves. *Arch. Ital. Biol.,* 96: 199–215.

Oscarsson, O. 1966. The projection of Group I muscle afferents to the cat cerebral cortex. In R. Granit (Ed.), *Muscular afferents and motor control.* New York: Wiley.

Paré, A. 1952. *The apologie and treatise of Ambroise Paré.* Chicago: University of Chicago Press.

Penfield, W., & Rasmussen, T. 1950. *The cerebral cortex of man.* New York: Macmillan.

Penfield, W., & Roberts, L. 1959. *Speech and brain mechanisms.* Princeton, N.J.: Princeton University Press.

Pfeifer, R. A. 1936. Pathologie der Hörstrahlung und der corticalen Hörsphäre. In O. Bumke & O. Foerster (Eds.), *Handbuch der Neurologie,* Berlin: Springer.

Pick, A. 1892. Beiträge zur Lehre von den Störungen der Sprache. *Arch. Psychiat. Nervenkrankh.,* 23: 895–918.

Pick, A. 1908. Über Störungen der Orientierung am eigenen Körper. *Arb. D. Psychiatrischen Universitäts-Klinik in Prag.* Berlin: Karger.

Pick, A. 1915. Zur Pathologie des Bewusstseins vom eigene Körper. Ein Beitrag aus der Kriegsmedizin. *Neurol. Centralbl.,* 34: 257–265.

Piercy, M., Hécaen, H., & Ajuriaguerra, J. de 1960. Constructional apraxia associated with unilateral cerebral lesions—left and right sided cases compared. *Brain*, 83: 225–242.

Piercy, M. F., & Smyth, V. 1962. Right hemisphere dominance for certain non-verbal intellectual skills. *Brain*, 85: 775–790.

Pilleri, G. 1966. The Klüver-Bucy-Syndrome in man. *Psychiat. Neurol.* (Basel), 152: 65–103.

Pittrich, H. 1956. *Sensorisch Amusie mit Paramusie nach rechtsseitiger Temporalverletzung.* Goettingen Institut für den Wissenschaftlichen Film.

Pitres, A. 1897. Étude sur les sensations illusoires des amputés. *Ann. med.-psychol.*, 5: 5–19, 178–192.

Poeck, K. 1963. Zur Psychophysiologie der Phantomerlebnisse. *Nervenarzt*, 34: 241–256.

Poeck, K. 1965. Über die Orientierung am eigenen Körper. *Akt. Fragen Psychiat. Neurol. (Basel)*, 2: 144–167.

Poeck, K., & Orgass, B. 1964. Die Entwicklung des Körperschemas bei Kindern im Alter von 4–10 Jahren. *Neuropsychologia*, 2: 109–130.

Poeck, K., & Orgass, B. 1966. Gerstmann's syndrome and aphasia. *Cortex*, 2: 421–437.

Poeck, K., & Orgass, B. 1967a. Über Störungen der Rechts-Links-Orientierung. *Nervenarzt*, 38: 285–291.

Poeck, K., & Orgass, B. 1967b. The role of aphasia in disturbances of the body schema. Presented to the Academy of Aphasia, Ann Arbor, Mich.

Poeck, K., & Orgass, B. 1969. An experimental investigation of finger agnosia. *Neurology*, 19.

Poggio, G. F., & Mountcastle, V. B. 1960. A study of the functional contributions of the lemniscal and spinothalamic systems to somatic sensibility. Central nervous mechanisms in pain. *Bull. Johns Hopkins Hosp.*, 106: 266–316.

Poppelreuter, W. 1917. *Die psychischen Schädigungen durch Kopfschuss im Kriege 1914–1916.* Leipzig: Voss.

Pötzl, O. 1939. Zur Pathologie der Amusie. *Z. Neurol. Psychiat.*, 165: 187–194.

Pötzl, O. 1943. Bemerkungen zum Problem der korticalen Vorgänge bei der akustischen Wahrnehmung. *Monatsschr. Ohrenheilk.*, 77: 422–430.

Pribram, H. B., & Barry, J. 1956. Further behavioral analysis of parieto-temporo-preoccipital cortex. *J. Neurophysiol.*, 19: 99–106.

Quensel, F. 1908. Über Erscheinungen und Grundlagen der Worttaubheit. *Ztschr. Nervenheilk.*, 35: 25–73.

Quensel, F., & Pfeifer, R. A. 1923. Ein Fall von reiner sensorischer Amusie. *Ztschr. Neurol. Psychiat.*, 81: 311–330.

Reinhold, M. 1948. A case of auditory agnosia. *Brain*, 73: 203–223.

Reitan, R. 1966. Problems and prospects in studying the psychological correlates of brain lesions. *Cortex*, 2: 127–154.

Richter, H. E. 1957. Akustischer Funktionswandel bei Sprachtaubheit. *Arch. Psychiat. Nervenkrankh.*, 196: 99–113.

Riddoch, G. 1917. The reflex functions of the completely divided spinal cord in man, compared with those associated with less severe lesions. *Brain*, 40: 264–402.

Rose, J. E., Brugge, J. F., Anderson, D. J., & Hind, J. E. 1967. Phase-locked response to low-frequency tones in single auditory nerve fibers of the squirrel monkey. *J. Neurophysiol.*, 30: 769–793.

Rose, J. E., & Mountcastle, V. B. 1959. Touch and kinesthesis. In J. Field (Ed.), *Handbook of physiology. Neurophysiology*. Washington, D.C.: American Physiological Society.

Rose, J. E., & Woolsey, C. N. 1949. Organization of the mammalian thalamus and its relationships to the cerebral cortex. *EEG clin. Neurophysiol.*, 1: 391–404.

Rose, J. E., & Woolsey, C. N. 1958. Cortical connections and functional organization of the thalamic auditory system of the cat. In H. F. Harlow & C. N. Woolsey (Eds.), *Biological and biochemical bases of behavior*. Madison: University of Wisconsin Press.

Rosenzweig, M. R. 1951. Representation of the two ears at the auditory cortex. *Amer. J. Physiol.*, 167: 147–158.

Ruch, T. C. & Fulton, J. F. 1935. Cortical localization of somatic sensibility; the effect of precentral, postcentral and posterior parietal lesions upon the performance of monkeys trained to discriminate weights. *Proc. Assoc. Res. nerv. ment. Dis.*, 15: 298–330.

Ruch, T. C., Fulton, J. F., & German, W. J. 1938. Sensory discrimination in monkey, chimpanzee, and man after lesions of the parietal lobe. *Arch. Neurol. Psychiat.* (Chicago), 39: 919–938.

Russell, I. S., & Ochs, S. 1963. Localization of a memory trace in one cortical hemisphere and transfer to the other hemisphere. *Brain*, 86: 37–54.

Russell, W. R., & Espir, M. L. E. 1961. *Traumatic aphasia*. Oxford: Oxford University Press.

Russo, M., & Vignolo, L. A. 1967. Visual figure-ground discrimination in patients with unilateral cerebral disease. *Cortex*, 3: 113–127.

Rutledge, L. T., & Kennedy, T. T. 1960. Extracallosal delayed responses to cortical stimulation in chloralosed cat. *J. Neurophysiol.*, 23: 188–196.

Schubert, K., & Panse, F. 1953. Audiologische Befunde bei sensorischer Aphasie. *Arch. Ohren-Nasen-Kehlkopfheilkunde,* 164: 23–40.

Schuell, H., & Jenkins, J. J. 1961. Reduction of vocabulary in aphasia. *Brain,* 84: 243–261.

Schultze. H. A. F. 1965. Die klinische Analyse kombinierter hirnpathologischer Störungen. *Beitr. Neurochr.,* 9: 1–110.

Schuster, P., & Taterka, H. 1926. Beitrag zur Anatomie und Klinik der reinen Worttaubheit. *Ztschr. Neurol. Psychiat.,* 105: 494–538.

Schwab, O. 1927. Über vorubergehende aphasische Störungen nach Rindenexzision aus dem linken Stirnhirn bei Epileptikern. *D. Zeitschr. Nervenheilk.,* 94: 177–184.

Sechzer, J. A. 1964. Successful interocular transfer of pattern discrimination in split-brain cats with shock-avoidance motivation. *J. comp. physiol. Psychol.,* 58: 76–83.

Semmes, J. 1965. A non-tactual factor in astereognosis. *Neuropsychologia,* 3: 295–315.

Semmes, J., & Mishkin, M. 1965a. A search for the cortical substrate of tactual memories. In G. Ettlinger (Ed.), *Functions of the corpus callosum.* London: Churchill.

Semmes, J., & Mishkin, M. 1965b. Somatosensory loss in monkeys after ipsilateral cortical ablation. *J. Neurophysiol.,* 28: 473–486.

Semmes, J., Mishkin, M., & Cole, M. 1968. Effects of isolating sensorimotor cortex in monkeys. *Cortex,* 4: 301–327.

Semmes, J., Weinstein, S., Ghent, L., & Teuber, H. L. 1955. Spatial orientation in man after cerebral injury: I. Analyses by locus of lesion. *J. Psychol.,* 39: 227–244.

Semmes, J., Weinstein, S., Ghent, L., & Teuber, H. L. 1960. *Somatosensory changes after penetrating brain wounds in man.* Cambridge, Mass.: Harvard University Press.

Shankweiler, D. 1966a. Defects in recognition and reproduction of familiar tunes after unilateral temporal lobectomy. Paper presented to the Eastern Psychological Association, New York.

Shankweiler, D. 1966b. Effects of temporal-lobe damage on perception of dichotically presented melodies. *J. comp. Physiol.,* 62: 115–119.

Shankweiler, D., & Studdert-Kennedy, M. 1967. Identification of consonants and vowels presented to left and right ears. *Quart. J. exp. Psychol.,* 19: 59–63.

Shapiro, G. 1966. Somatosensory thresholds and discrimination in amputation stumps. Paper presented to the Eastern Psychological Association. New York.

Simmel, M. 1956. Phantoms in patients with leprosy and in elderly digital amputees. *Amer. J. Psychol.,* 69: 529–545.

Simmel, M. 1962. Phantom experiences following amputation in childhood. *J. Neurol. Neurosurg. Psychiat.*, 25: 69–78.

Smith, A. 1966. Speech and other functions after left (dominant) hemispherectomy. *J. Neurol. Neurosurg. Psychiat.*, 29: 467–471.

Smith, A., & Burklund, C. W. 1966. Dominant hemispherectomy: preliminary report on neuropsychological sequelae. *Science*, 153: 1280–1282.

Smith, K. U. 1951. Learning and the associative pathways of the human cerebral cortex. *Science*, 114: 117–120.

Snyder, M., Hall, W. C., & Diamond, I. T. 1966. Vision in the tree shrews (Tupia glis) after removal of striate cortex. *Psychonom. Sci.*, 6: 243–244.

Souques, A., & Baruk, H. 1930. Autopsie d'un case d'amusie (avec aphasie) chez un professeur de piano. *Rev. Neurol.*, 1: 545–556.

Sperry, R. W. 1961. Cerebral organization and behavior. *Science*, 133: 1749–1757.

Sperry, R. W. 1964. The great cerebral commissure. *Sci. Amer.*, 174: 2–12.

Sperry, R. W., & Gazzaniga, M. S. 1967. Language following surgical disconnection of the hemispheres. In F. L. Darley (Ed.), *Brain mechanisms underlying speech and language.* New York: Grune & Stratton.

Sperry, R. W., Stamm, J. S., & Miner, N. 1956. Relearning tests for interocular transfer following division of optic chiasma and corpus callosum in cats. *J. comp. physiol. Psychol.*, 49: 529–533.

Spinnler, H., & Vignolo, L. A. 1966. Impaired recognition of familiar sounds in aphasia. *Cortex*, 2: 337–348.

Spreen, O., Benton, A. L., & Fincham, R. W. 1965. Auditory agnosia without aphasia. *Arch. Neurol.*, 13: 84–92.

Stamm, J. S., & Sperry, R. W. 1957. Function of corpus callosum in contralateral transfer of somesthetic discrimination in cats. *J. comp. physiol. Psychol.*, 50: 138–143.

Stauffenberg, W. von. 1914. Über Seelenblindheit. *Arb. hirnanat. Inst. Zürich*, H. 8.

Stertz, G. 1912. Über subkortikale sensorische Aphasie nebst einigen allgemeinen Bemerkungen zur Auffassung aphasischer Symptome. *D. Zeitschr. Nervenheilk.*, 39: 327–365.

Stone, T. T. 1950. Phantom limb pain and central pain. *Arch. Neurol. Psychiat.*, 63: 739–748.

Strauss, H. 1924. Über konstruktive Apraxie. *Monatsschr. Psychiat. Neurol.*, 56: 65–124.

Strohmayer. W. 1900. Zur Kritik der "subcorticalen" sensorischen Aphasie. *D. Zeitschr. Nervenheilk.*, 21: 371–385.

Tatlow, W. F. T., & Oulton, J. L. 1955. Phantom limbs (with observations on brachial plexus block). *Can. Med. Assoc. J.*, 73: 170–177.

Teitelbaum, H. 1964. A comparison of effects of orbitofrontal and hippocampal lesions upon discrimination learning and reversal in the cat. *Exp. Neurol.*, 9: 452–462.

Teuber, H. L., Krieger, H. P., & Bender, M. B. 1949. Reorganization of sensory function in amputation stumps: two-point discrimination. *Fed. Proc.*, 8: 156.

Teuber, H. L., & Weinstein, S. 1956. Ability to discover hidden figures after cerebral lesions. *Arch. Neurol. Psychiat.*, 76: 369–379.

Thompson, R. 1965. Centrencephalic theory and interhemispheric transfer of visual habits. *Psychol. Rev.*, 72: 385–398.

Tissot, R. 1966. *Neuropsychologie de l'aphasie*. Paris: Masson.

Trescher, J. H., & Ford, F. R. 1937. Colloid cyst of the third ventricle. Report of a case: operative removal with section of posterior half of corpus callosum. *Arch. Neurol. Psychiat.*, 37: 959–973.

Trevarthen, C. B. 1962. Double visual learning in split-brain monkeys. *Science*, 136: 258–259.

Trevarthen, C. B. 1965. Functional interactions between the cerebral hemispheres of the split-brain monkey. In G. Ettlinger (Ed.), *Functions of the corpus callosum*. London: Churchill.

Tunturi, A. R. 1946. A study on the pathway from the medial geniculate body to the acoustic cortex in the dog. *Amer. J. Physiol.*, 147: 311–319.

Valentin, G. 1836. Über die subjectiven Gefühle von Personen, welche mit mangelhaften Extremitäten geboren sind. *Rep. Anat. Physiol.*, 1: 328–337.

Valentin, G. 1844. Integritätsgefühle der Amputirten. *Lehrbuch der Physiologie des Menschen*, 2: 606–609.

Van Bogaert, L. 1934. Sur la pathologie de l'image de soi. *Ann. med.-psychol.*, 14: 519–555.

Van Gehuchten, A., & Goris, C. 1901. Un cas de surdité verbale pure par abces du lobe temporal gauche: trépanation, guérison. *Nevraxe*, 3: 65–82.

Vaughan, H. G., Jr., & Costa, L. D. 1962. Performance of patients with lateralized cerebral lesions. *J. nerv. ment. Dis.*, 134: 237–243.

Veraguth, O. 1900. Über einen Fall von transitorischer reiner Worttaubheit. *D. Zeitschr. Nervenheilk.*, 17: 178–198.

Vetter, R. J., & Weinstein, S. 1967. The history of the phantom in congenitally absent limbs. *Neuropsychologia*, 5: 335–338.

Voneida, T. J. 1963. Performance of a visual conditioned response in split-brain cats. *Exp. Neurol.*, 8: 493–504.

Wada, J., & Rasmussen, T. R. 1960. Intracarotid injection of sodium amytal for the lateralization of cerebral speech dominance. *J. Neurosurg.*, 17: 266–282.

Wall, P. D. 1960. Cord cells responding to touch, damage and temperature of skin. *J. Neurophysiol.*, 23: 197–210.

Wall, P. D. 1961. Two transmission systems for skin sensation. In W. A. Rosenblith (Ed.), *Sensory communication.* Cambridge, Mass.: M.I.T. Press.

Wall, P. D., & Cronly-Dillon, J. 1960. Pain, itch, and vibration. *Arch. Neurol.*, 2: 365–375.

Walshe, F. M. R. 1942. The anatomy and physiology of cutaneous sensibility. *Brain*, 65: 48–112.

Walthard, K. M. 1927. Bemerkungen zum Amusie-Problem. *Schwiez. Arch. Neurol. Psychiat.*, 20: 295–315.

Warrington, E. K., & James, M. 1967. Disorders of visual perception in relation to right hemisphere lesions. *Neuropsychologia*, 5: 253–266.

Webster, D. B., & Voneida, T. J. 1964. Learning deficits following hippocampal lesions in split-brain cats. *Exp. Neurol.*, 10: 170–182.

Wechsler, D. 1958. *The measurement and appraisal of adult intelligence.* Baltimore: Williams & Wilkins.

Weddell, G. 1941. The multiple innervation of sensory spots in the skin. *J. Anat.* (London), 75: 441–446.

Wegener, J. G. 1965. A note on auditory discrimination behavior and the corpus callosum. In G. Ettlinger (Ed.), *Functions of the corpus callosum*, London: Churchill.

Weinstein, S. 1963a. Phantoms in paraplegia. In *Proceedings of Eleventh Annual Clinical Spinal Cord Injury Conference.* V. A. Hospital, Washington, D.C.

Weinstein, S. 1963b. The relationship of laterality and cutaneous area to breast-sensitivity in sinistrals and dextrals. *Amer. J. Psychol.*, 76: 475–479.

Weinstein, S. 1968. Intensive and extensive aspects of tactile sensitivity as a function of body-part, sex, and laterality. In D. R. Kenshalo (Ed.), *The skin senses.* Springfield, Ill.: Charles C Thomas.

Weinstein, S., & Sersen, E. A. 1961. Phantoms in cases of congenital absence of limbs. *Neurology*, 11: 905–911.

Weinstein, S., Sersen, E. A., Fisher, L., & Vetter, R. J. 1964. Preferences for bodily parts as a function of sex, age, and socio-economic status. *Amer. J. Psychol.*, 77: 291–294.

Weinstein, S., Sersen, E. A., & Vetter, R. J. 1964. Phantoms and somatic sensation in cases of congenital aplasia. *Cortex,* 1: 276–290.

Weinstein, S., Sersen, E. A., & Vetter, R. J. 1967. Preferences for bodily parts following mastectomy. *Amer. J. Psychol.,* 80: 458–461.

Weinstein, S., Sersen, E. A., & Vetter, R. J. 1968. Phantoms following orchiectomy. *Neuropsychologia,* 6: 61–74.

Weinstein, S., Sersen, E. A., & Vetter, R. J. 1969. Phantoms following mastectomy. (In press).

Weinstein, S., Vetter, R. J., Shapiro, G., & Sersen, E. A. 1969. The phantom limb in patients sustaining cerebral vascular accidents. *Cortex.* (In press).

Weisenburg, T., & McBride, K. E. 1935. *Aphasia, a clinical and psychological study.* New York: Commonwealth Fund.

Welch, K., & Stuteville, P. 1958. Experimental production of unilateral neglect in monkeys. *Brain,* 81: 341–347.

Wernicke, C. 1874. *Der aphasische Symptomencomplex.* Breslau: Max Cohn & Weigert.

Wernicke, C., & Friedlander, C. 1883. Ein Fall von Taubheit in Folge von doppelseitiger Läsionen des Schläfenlappens. *Fortschritte der Medizin,* 1: 177–185.

Whitlock, D. G., & Perl, E. R. 1961. Thalamic projections of spino-thalamic pathways in monkeys. *Exp. Neurol.,* 3: 240–255.

Whitteridge, D. 1965. Area 18 and the vertical meridian of the visual field. In G. Ettlinger (Ed.), *Functions of the corpus callosum.* London: Churchill.

Wilson, M. 1957. Effects of circumscribed cortical lesions upon somesthetic and visual discrimination in the monkey. *J. comp. physiol. Psychol.,* 50: 630–635.

Wilson, M., Stamm, J. A., & Pribram, K. H. 1960. Deficits in roughness discrimination after posterior parietal lesions in monkeys. *J. comp. physiol. Psychol.,* 53: 535–539.

Wohlfart, G., Lindgren, A., & Jernelius, B. 1952. Clinical picture and morbid anatomy in a case of "pure word-deafness." *J. nerv. ment. Dis.,* 116: 818–827.

Woolsey, C. N. 1947. Patterns of sensory representation in the cerebral cortex. *Fed. Proc.,* 6: 437–441.

Woolsey, C. N., Marshall, W. H., & Bard, P. 1942. Representation of cutaneous tactile sensibility in the cerebral cortex of the monkey as indicated by evoked potentials. *Bull. Johns Hopkins Hosp.,* 70: 399–441.

Würtzen, C. H. 1903. Einzelne Formen von Amusie, durch Beispiele beleuchtet. *D. Zeitschr. Nervenheilk.,* 24: 465–473.

Wyke, M., & Ettlinger, G. 1961. Efficiency of recognition in left and right visual fields: its relation to the phenomenon of visual extinction. *Neurology*, 5: 659–665.

Ziegler, D. K. 1952. Word deafness and Wernicke's aphasia. *Arch. Neurol. Psychiat.*, (Chicago) 67: 323–331.

Ziehl, F. 1896. Über einen Fall von Worttaubheit und das Lichtheim'sche Krankheitsbild der subcorticalen sensorischen Aphasie. *D. Zeitschr. Nervenheilk.*, 8: 259–307.

Contributors

Arthur L. Benton
Departments of Psychology and Neurology, University of Iowa

Colin B. Blakemore
Institute of Psychiatry, University of London

George Ettlinger
Institute of Psychiatry, University of London

Norman Geschwind
Department of Neurology, Harvard Medical School

Josephine Semmes
Laboratory of Neuropsychology, National Institute of Mental Health

Klaus Poeck
Neurologische Abteilung, Medizinische Fakultät der Technischen
Hochschule, Aachen

Luigi A. Vignolo
Clinica delle Malattie Nervose e Mentali, Università di Milano

Sidney Weinstein
Laboratory of Neuropsychology, New York Medical College

Name Index

233

Subject Index